COGNITIVE-BEHAVIOURAL SOCIAL WORK IN PRACTICE

To the memory of Albert Kushlick, MD FRCP
Died on 25 August 1997
and
To Mark, Alice and Joe

Cognitive-behavioural Social Work in Practice

Edited by Katy Cigno and Diana Bourn

Aldershot • Brookfield USA • Singapore • Sydney

Published by
Ashgate Publishing Limited
Gower House
Croft Road
Aldershot
Hants GU11 3HR
England

Ashgate Publishing Company
Old Post Road
Brookfield
Vermont 05036
USA

British Library Cataloguing in Publication Data
Cognitive-behavioural social work in practice
1.Social service 2.Cognitive psychology 3.Behaviour therapy
I.Cigno, Katy II.Bourn, Diana
361.3'019

Library of Congress Catalog Card Number: 98-70985

ISBN 1 85742 373 9 (Hbk)
ISBN 1 85742 374 7 (Pbk)

Typeset by Manton Typesetters, 5–7 Eastfield Road, Louth, Lincolnshire,
Printed and bound by Athenaeum Press, Ltd.,
Gateshead, Tyne & Wear.

Contents

List of boxes

List of figures

List of tables

Contributors' details

Diana Bourn is Lecturer in the Child Protection Studies Centre, School of Social Work, University of Leicester and a Social Worker in a Social Services Children and Families Team.

Peter Burke is Senior Lecturer, School of Community and Health Studies, University of Hull.

Katy Cigno is Senior Lecturer in the Department of Social Work, University of Hull and a Practice Teacher with Wakefield Community and Social Services Department.

Dave Dagnan is Consultant Clinical Psychologist, West Cumbria Healthcare NHS Trust.

Clive Hollin is Professor of Criminological Psychology in the Centre for Applied Psychology at the University of Leicester and a Fellow of the British Psychological Society.

Barbara L. Hudson is Lecturer in Applied Social Studies and Fellow of Green College, University of Oxford.

Dorota Iwaniec is Professor and Head of Department of Social Work and Director of the Centre for Child Care Research, The Queen's University of Belfast.

Mansoor A.F. Kazi is Senior Lecturer in Social Work and Applied Social Studies, University of Huddersfield, and Director of the Centre for Evaluation Studies at the same university.

Albert Kushlick was, until his recent and untimely death, Consultant Psychiatrist in Learning Disability, North Downs Community Health Trust and a freelance behavioural consultant.

Safina Mir is a Community Care Social Worker, Bradford Social Services Department.

J.P.J. Oliver is Senior Lecturer, School of Psychiatry and Behavioural Science, University of Manchester, and Regional Coordinator for Mental Health Development, NHSE (North West).

Jonathan Parker is Lecturer in Clinical Social Work, School of Community and Health Studies, University of Hull, and an accredited behavioural and cognitive psychotherapist.

Peter Raynor is Professor of Applied Social Studies, Department of Social Policy and Applied Social Studies, University of Wales, Swansea.

Tammie Ronen is Senior Lecturer, The Bob Shapell School of Social Work, Tel-Aviv University, and President of the Israeli Association of Behaviour Therapy.

Brian Sheldon is Professor of Applied Social Research and Director of the Centre for Evidence-Based Practice, University of Exeter.

Carole Sutton is Principal Lecturer in Psychology, School of Health and Community Studies and Director of the Centre for Parent Education and Training, De Montfort University.

Gillian Tober is Head of Training, Leeds Addiction Unit, Team Leader, Leeds North Community Addictions Team, Honorary Lecturer, University of Leeds, and a member of the Executive Committee for the Study of Addiction.

Peter Trower is Senior Lecturer in Clinical Psychology, University of Birmingham.

Maurice Vanstone is Lecturer in Applied Social Studies, University of Wales, Swansea, and until recently held a joint appointment as Senior Probation Officer in the Mid Glamorgan Probation Service and Lecturer at Swansea.

Foreword

Carole Sutton

A useful image which I use when trying to help students understand how concepts like policy, research and practice can be made sense of and integrated is that of a triangle: the bottom of the triangle is policy, associated with values; the two other sides are research, associated with theory, and practice. These concepts are fundamental to social work, and the image, I find, helps students grasp the interplay between them.

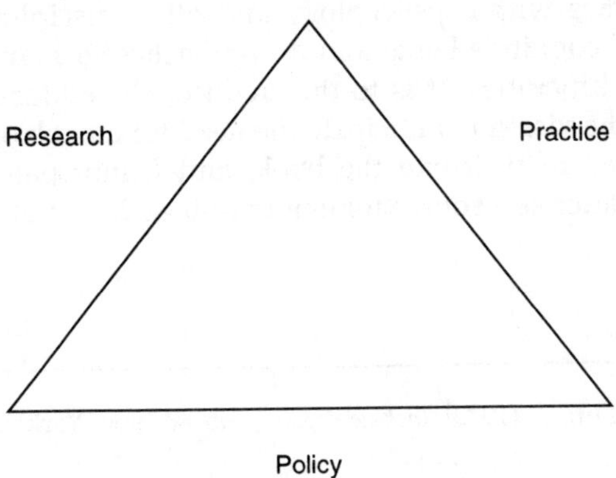

Social work has for decades been influenced by ideologies of human behaviour which do not hold up under the challenges of reality. It has only occasionally been influenced by theoretical ideas which are well grounded in rigorous research, and when it *has* taken such research on board, this has served it well. For example, the time-linked 'task-centred' approach, identified in a well-designed research project by Reid and Epstein in 1972 as more helpful to clients than an open-ended, unstructured approach, is still a reliable tool in most social workers' repertoire. It has clear links to learning theory and cognitive-behavioural practice, and is likely to continue to serve clients and social workers well in the future. We should continue to base our work upon such well-grounded approaches.

It is already becoming apparent that the new Labour government is likely to be just as committed to investigating 'What works' as was its predecessor; social work is being placed under very close scrutiny indeed in respect of its funding and administration. As we hear from the media day by day, policy and practice in the fields of health, education, business and leisure are all being influenced by research reports: reports about diet, health, education, the air we breathe, and the value of animal companions to human well-being. In these circumstances, it behoves us all to look closely at the research underpinnings of social work so that we can demonstrate both accountability and cost-effectiveness.

In my view, the only way the profession can survive is by demonstrating its commitment to evidence-based practice – and by 'evidence' I mean the most rigorous and reliable data which are available. Why should organisations be funded from the public purse if they cannot demonstrate that their theory has been tested and that their results have been closely evaluated according to the highest standards of research?

In these circumstances, the publication of this book is extremely timely. Numerous studies within psychology and other disciplines attest to the effectiveness of cognitive-behavioural approaches in helping people in a wide range of difficulties. It is to the credit of the editors, therefore, that they have had the vision to anticipate the need for a book of this kind.

I am delighted to welcome the book, and I anticipate that it will be eagerly sought after as a source for evidence-based, cost-effective practice.

Reference

Reid, W. and Epstein, L. (1972) *Task-centred Casework*, New York: Columbia University Press.

Acknowledgements

Katy Cigno is grateful for the support of many colleagues during the preparation of this book. Particular thanks are due to Dennis South for his patience and technical assistance.

Diana Bourn is grateful for the support and encouragement given by many colleagues, particularly Clive Hollin and Jocelyn Jones.

Introduction

Katy Cigno and Diana Bourn

There have been far-reaching changes in social work policy and practice in recent years in response to political, social and economic change. Legislative changes and specialisation within the profession brought about substantial shifts. At the same time, policies specifically designed to erode the welfare state throughout the 1980s and early 1990s, involving severe cut backs on local and health authorities, undermined social services and decreased resources. Social workers were criticised in the media and in child abuse inquiries. In the Beckford Inquiry, for example, they were criticised for concentrating too much on the parents and doing too little to protect the child, and in the Cleveland Inquiry they were criticised for over-zealous action in their intervention in families, to the detriment of parents.

In this context, the Behavioural Social Work Group met in 1995 to consider 'Whither Behavioural Social Work?' In the opening address, Brian Sheldon and Geraldine Macdonald, professors at the Universities of Exeter and Bristol respectively, noted that while there was a sense of loss of direction in social work, a number of publications showed the efficacy of behavioural social work. Similarly, trends suggested that practices and principles that behavioural social workers took for granted in organising their work, such as the use of contracts and working on open goals, were increasingly being integrated into mainstream social work. In some cases, though, behavioural principles and language seemed to be incorporated with minimal understanding and supervision. A bad press – both misrepresenting certain malpractices in residential childcare as being 'behavioural' and blaming social workers – had made social workers reluctant to be proactive.

However, behavioural social work, and increasingly cognitive-behavioural practice, have a good record of effectiveness. We therefore need to stake our claim to the practices that are increasingly being incorporated into social work. Colleagues from other disciplines, particularly psychology, have contributed to social work education and the dissemination of social learning theory principles into practice. Accordingly, we are pleased to include a chapter by a psychologist, Clive Hollin, and one by Albert Kushlick (psychiatrist), Dave Dagnan and Peter Trower (psychologists): all have worked alongside social workers. Albert Kushlick, who had been unwell for some time, died suddenly while this book was in preparation. His influence, spanning more than three decades, on caring practices in the field of learning disabilities has been great.

Our aim is to provide a practical guide to cognitive-behavioural theory and practice in a range of settings, illustrated by case studies and case examples. As editors, we have been keen to encourage contributors to develop their own ideas without censorship. Readers will, we hope, approach the text in a similar frame of mind. The case studies include both accounts and analyses of an area of work (that is, a 'case' in the research sense) as well as of a 'case' in the traditional use of the term in social work (see Yin 1994 for a comprehensive discussion of the meaning and uses of the case study).

The book will be useful for social workers embarking on training and practice, as well as for experienced practitioners and colleagues from other disciplines such as nursing and social and community care. Theory and practice are interwoven, with an emphasis upon practice areas. The chapters cover a diverse range of work with children, families and adults in community and residential settings, written by academics and practitioners.

Chapter 1 gives a broad outline of the underlying theory and research for cognitive-behavioural practice, and the recent political and social context of social work. It is thus seminal to the book, avoiding the need for each contributor to describe in detail the theoretical basis for their work. The author discusses the ways in which cognition, emotion and behaviour are inextricably bound together to form experience. He goes on to describe the therapeutic methods and approaches that have arisen from these types of learning. Effectiveness is on the agenda, and behavioural social work has a good record in effectiveness research. The stages in cognitive-behavioural assessment and intervention are described in a step-by-step manner easily accessible to both newcomers and more experienced practitioners.

Chapter 2 highlights the importance of direct work with children. Here, the aim of cognitive-behavioural therapy is to help children learn and develop social and coping skills in order to achieve and maintain change and promote emotional adjustment. Assessment and treatment, using a self-control model, is discussed. Children can be empowered to learn to 'help themselves' in recovering from abuse or neglect. This is illustrated by an example of work undertaken with an 8-year-old girl who had suffered neglect and sexual abuse.

Chapter 3 focuses on behavioural intervention to decrease the risks of child physical abuse and development of child conduct disorder. Patterson's coercion hypothesis, whereby parent and child become caught in a negative reinforcement trap, thus reinforcing each other's aversive, coercive behaviour, is discussed. The child protection context is outlined, and the use of single-case experimental design to evaluate outcomes is demonstrated.

Combined failure-to-thrive is a condition frequently encountered by child protection practitioners in work with children who have been emotionally abused or neglected. Chapter 4 describes the assessment and treatment of combined failure-to-thrive as an example of effective intervention led by a social worker in a multi-disciplinary team, using cognitive-behavioural methods.

Chapter 5 offers a consideration of the advantages and limitations of behavioural methods when working with children with severe learning difficulties. Lefcourt's locus of control is used as a framework to examine the impact on both children and their carers as they try to ensure that the needs of their children are met.

Chapter 6 is a study of behavioural social work in residential childcare. Learning theory can provide direction and enhance the evaluability of strategies used to help children move towards independence. Such approaches are more desirable and effective than reactive or aimless strategies when working with vulnerable children who may have been neglected or abused. As the authors point out, 'pin-down' as a means of behaviour management in children's homes is not valid in terms of behavioural theory and practice, although it was mistakenly ascribed to behavioural methods by some sections of the media. It was in fact the crude application of a kind of regression therapy. The authors consider the advantages as well as the limitations of behavioural approaches in residential care, and whether there are any negative effects on certain young people.

Chapter 7 begins with an overview of cognitive-behavioural approaches to working with young offenders. The chapter goes on to consider what is known about the general effectiveness of working with this client group. The chapter ends with a look at social and policy issues. The author concludes that there are growing grounds for optimism in the field of working with young offenders: there are barriers to be overcome, but there is now a firm base from which to design effective programmes.

Chapter 8 describes an experimental programme applying cognitive-behavioural methods in the supervision of adult male offenders on probation. The programme, known as STOP (Straight Thinking On Probation), is the first systematic attempt to provide and evaluate a cognitive-behavioural programme for persistent offenders in the context of a British probation service.

Chapter 9 is a vivid account of a cognitive therapy training programme, 'The Birthday Exercise', for the carers of people who have learning disabilities and severe challenging behaviour in residential and daycare units. The chapter considers cognitive-behavioural methods within the context of current issues about partnership with service users.

The application of learning theory has enhanced the understanding of addiction behaviours and has helped progress in the development of interventions which are matched with client need rather than driven by ideological dogma. Chapter 10 describes a cognitive counselling style known as motivational interviewing. Based on the principles of self-management and conditioning, it is proving to be effective. The chapter reviews the contribution of learning theory to the understanding of addictions.

Behavioural methods are used by many practitioners in the mental health field. However, little attention has been paid to applying these methods to the important task of managing psychiatric emergencies. This is especially important for social workers, who, along with their colleagues, are required by statute to intervene in crisis situations. The authors of Chapter 11 discuss the use of behavioural approaches in crisis intervention and the mental health call-out.

Chapter 12 describes an example of assessment and intervention with an older woman in residential care whose behaviour, which included self-harm, disruptive actions and diminished social skills, was creating difficulties for herself and other residents. The chapter reviews policy as well as social and group care with older people.

Chapter 13 gives a brief overview of the dimensions and definitions of the abuse of older people. It goes on to look at responses to the management and treatment of elder abuse, and suggests that a behavioural approach can be effective.

Chapter 14 draws together the strands highlighted by the contributors to the book and looks at the implications for social work education and practice. It is our belief that the evidence for the effectiveness and usefulness of cognitive-behavioural approaches can no longer be ignored by practitioners in social service and social care settings.

The kind of work described in this book is an effective and powerful means of intervention. It is, of course, incumbent that the work is firmly grounded in sound ethical principles and practices, such as the Constitutional and Ethical Guidelines drawn up by the Behavioural Social Work Group in 1984 and revised (1993) to include a policy statement on equal opportunities and anti-discriminatory practice. These guidelines emphasise the importance of minimising harm and maximising benefits; of developing anti-oppressive practice by working on clearly stated goals, agreed wherever possible with the client; of the duty of practitioners to base their work on the available evidence from effectiveness research, and to evaluate with care their own work and practice development. In short, ethical practice includes the necessity to ensure competent practice.

Finally, as several writers in this book point out, there is a need to ensure high practice integrity so that the work is effective. We owe it to our clients to deliver work that is ethically sound, reinforces positive behaviour rather than punishing undesirable behaviour, is open about its methods and objectives, and which is undertaken by workers who are skilled and knowledgeable in the practice and theory of cognitive-behavioural work. We hope that our book will go some way towards achieving this goal.

References

Behavioural Social Work Group (1993) *Constitutional and Ethical Guidelines* (these can be obtained from the Secretary, Rosemary Strange, Copper Beeches, 96 Heath Lane, Earl Shilton, Leicester LE9 7PD).

Yin, R.K. (1994) *Case Study Research: Design and Methods*, (2nd edn), Thousand Oaks, CA.: Sage.

1 Research and theory

Brian Sheldon

The political and professional context

Now here was an unlikely, though none the less welcome, ally in the cause to which this book is ultimately dedicated:

> The commitment to evidence-based medicine increasingly pervades modern medical practice. This kind of commitment should be extended to the social services world. (Stephen Dorrell, Secretary of State for Health and Social Services, *Guardian*, 20 February 1997)

Those of us who had been shouting this into what seemed like deaf ears for some considerable time were well advised to pause here, *not* to write the pained letter, but to reach for our long spoons instead. Probably the worst time to try to write a book on research-based approaches in social work was five or six years ago, when the previous administration (lovely phrase) was at its most bullish; the social work profession, on the other hand, was in a state close to learned helplessness as a result of the aggressive application of commercial principles to community care and the peak of the great epidemic of Mad Reorganisation Disease (MRD) which accompanied this. In 1996, a reviewer, describing my book *Cognitive-Behavioural Therapy* (Sheldon 1995) as 'sectarian', advanced the view that then was certainly not the time to discuss *which* methods of helping might prove more effective (perish the thought) since all but the most basic problem-containment procedures were off the agenda, and probably for good. It could, of course, be argued that had we taken opportunities to debate and act upon the positive *and* the negative findings of effectiveness research from the last forty-odd years, then we might not have been in this particular fix in the first place.

The situation, now and for the immediate future, strikes me as somewhat less threatening, for the following reasons.

Fashions come but fashions go, and the 'sieve of history' has large holes. In those local authorities which sought head prefect status from the previous government by eagerly implementing 'internal market' procedures ahead of the 1991 deadline (I remember predicting that, as in the National Health Service, it would all end in tiers), we now see clear signs of reappraisal, particularly in the child care field – which, remember, can easily get one's name in the papers. Co-operation and prevention via 'lighter touch' approaches rather than competition and 'targeting' are now the orders of the day. Indeed, what else could rationally be done in the face of official figures showing an 80 per cent 'false positive' rate from 20,000 child abuse investigations, with only 5 per cent of families receiving any subsequent help? Imagine a medical screening programme producing such results and what the public reaction would be. Perhaps I am being over-optimistic here, but the smell of burnt fingers *is* quite distinctive.

Requests from senior managers for academics in the know to talk about the case for evidence-based social services are now commonplace. Of all the things that should not be a craze, this idea is fast becoming one. For the sake of our clients and for the profession we should probably go with this flow, providing we keep a sense of balance and pragmatism and remind ourselves that Mary Richmond (1917) was addressing these matters on the eve of the Russian Revolution, and that the first controlled experiments into social work effectiveness were conducted in the 1940s (Lehrman 1949).

It is only an impression, but hard-pressed social workers now seem more willing to take students again. Once an eccentric-seeming decision ('What's in it for us?' was a common response to such requests; answer: 'the survival of the profession to which you belong because someone did it for you'), practice teachers are now seeking specialist qualifications, and appear willing to ally themselves with those courses which offer good support and involvement in all parts of the curriculum. Debates about what the *content* of practice should be increasingly appear on the agenda of practice teachers' meetings and curriculum development committees.

A consortium made up of Exeter University, social services departments in the South and the West, and the Department of Health have between them invested £2.5 million in the cause of developing evidence-based social services. My erstwhile colleague, Professor Geraldine Macdonald, has a grant from the Northern Ireland Office to incorporate into the prestigious Cochrane database a systematic review of controlled trials of the effectiveness of social work. Straws in the wind perhaps, but plenty of them, and in a breeze growing stronger by the day. I am afraid that we shall never see 'the end of ideology' (present-day politicians trumpet it, but human beings as a species probably are not up to it), but such initiatives may help to contain some of its more distracting influences on our field.

This little political foray has been necessary for two reasons. First, because law, policy and regulation impinge upon the day-to-day behaviour of social workers more than is the case for any of the other helping professions, leading sometimes to a state close to 'frozen watchfulness' because of the range and variety of risks they are expected to manage. Second, because it is vital for ethical, technical, and again, for political reasons, that we are seen to be developing a *cumulative* knowledge base (getting better and better at what we do, not just getting different) (Sheldon 1978; Macdonald 1996). If you accept this, it means that we should explicitly select approaches to the problems which come our way on the basis of their research track record, rather than simply affiliating to 'schools', following 'par for the course' local conventions, or just 'doing what comes naturally'. In this regard, I teach and make some use of cognitive-behavioural approaches because of the trends in empirical research, not because of any prior ideological commitment.

Adopting such a position means that occasionally one has to change one's mind and professional behaviour in the light of new evidence. I know how uncomfortable this can be, because I have had to do it on several occasions: upon encountering the first reviews of effectiveness research showing that the methods in which I had been trained (psychoanalytical casework) had proven useless under test (Mullen and Dumpsen 1972; Fischer 1973 and 1976); being beguiled by the mysteries of R.D. Laing's theories about the origins of severe mental illness (Laing 1960), but then being unable to square the circle with the steady trends in genetic and other biological research (see Gottesman 1991; Sheldon 1994); most recently, feeling well disposed to the 'cognitive revolution' in psychology and psychotherapy and signing up to 'New Behaviourism', but then having to pick my way through empirical comparisons with 'Old Behaviourism', and feeling as a result only cautiously optimistic (cf. Feske and Chambers 1995).

John Maynard Keynes, when berated by a reporter for altering his position on economic policy, once said: 'When the facts change then I change my mind, pray Sir, what do you do?' 'Facts' are hard to come by in our epistemologically challenged discipline, but this general stance on evidence and practice seems to me exactly right. But why do we find this process of considered adaptation to new findings so difficult? Some possible factors are described below:

Social work requires an emotional commitment to sometimes unpopular causes. It is easy for such 'these truths we hold to be self-evident' values and sentiments to influence the rather more intellectual process of selecting knowledge for use. When this happens, the congeniality of results often takes priority over due consideration of the *means* by which the evidence for them was gathered. A kind of methodological relativism ensues, within which 'all propositions and findings are created equal', which in turn implies that 'all investigators have won, and all must have prizes'.

Social workers lead anxious lives. It is therefore understandable that they sometimes reach for the security blanket of grand, all-explanatory, Protean, irrefutable theories, rather than devoting scarce time to the demanding business of critically evaluating research papers in pursuit of useful trends. Reviews help here, but only if the authors 'show their working out' alongside their answers and if readers are duly critical of what is being pressed upon them. This is something we are getting better at, but with still some way to go (see Macdonald and Sheldon 1992; Macdonald and Roberts 1995).

The most pessimistic results which have a bearing on these issues come from enquiries (conducted, one imagines, with fingers crossed) into the reading habits of social workers. Over the years these have revealed that, but for a minority of eccentrics, social workers do not *have* reading habits (Brown and McCulloch 1975, Fisher 1996). (By the time this book is published, we should have further empirical information on this issue as a result of a large survey conducted by the Centre for Evidence-Based Social Services at the University of Exeter.) This has not been seen as much of a problem because of the distracting idea, previously popular among senior managers, that services can be provided by 'remote control', via (allegedly) improved departmental structures alone. In reality, day-to-day practice requires informed judgements to be made about highly individual combinations of problems, and catalogue-shop fantasies about pre-packaged, standardised services are likely to lead to ineffectiveness in the face of all but the most basic and predictable patterns of need. If evidence-based social services are to become a reality, then improved information facilities, with informed and active librarians on tap, and with ready access to electronic databases, will be increasingly necessary. More importantly, ways will have to be found to reinforce the *a priori* notion of considered action, rather than the short-term, budget or policy-driven, *ad hoc* containment of problems (see Jordan 1996; Hutton 1995).

The problem with the idea of evidence-based practice is that sometimes research findings come to the 'wrong' conclusions. Nowhere is this more the case than with cognitive-behavioural approaches. Reviews of outcomes in clinical psychology, psychiatry, psychotherapy and social work (Bergin and Garfield 1994; BABCP, 1993; Blackburn et al. 1981, Stuart and Bowers 1995; Macdonald and Sheldon 1992) point to the fact that if therapeutic work is needed, then across the range of problems we encounter, combinations of cognitive and behavioural methods are likely to be more effective than anything else. Moreover, these findings contradict the pattern usually found, that the stricter the methodology employed (for example, randomised controlled trials), the less favourable the 'signal to noise' ratio. An influential review of child protection research described the methodologies typically used to evaluate behavioural approaches as 'streets ahead' of the typical means of assessing the impact of other methods (Gough 1993).

What we are up against here is an 'antibody reaction' produced by ignorance, stereotype and the influence of our complicated history. Books such as this may help remedy matters, particularly given its concentration on live case material. However, the urgent need is for those of us who know the relevant research and its implications to combine to shift the post-qualification training agenda away from 'What Works?' soirées to 'This Works' courses – with subsequent arrangements for consultation and supervision built in.

The best predictor of a believably positive outcome in a study of the effectiveness of social services is that the approaches under test have a close 'logical fit' with what is known from good-quality research about the aetiology of the problems in view. We know quite a lot about relapse-prevention in schizophrenia (Falloon 1984; Birchwood and Tarrier 1992; Falloon and Coverdale 1994; Kavanagh 1992), about depression (Blackburn et al. 1981; Hollon et al. 1991; Dobson 1989; Scott 1989), about panic states and phobias (Beamish et al. 1996; Mathews et al. 1981); about the origins of child management difficulties (Kazdin 1994; Sheldon 1995), and about the effects of partnership and family support work in child protection (Fraser et al. 1991; Thoburn et al. 1995). Some of these results are of such rigour and clarity that it is almost obvious what should be done at a therapeutic level. In my view, if anything does, the huge body of empirical research on *learning* falls into this category.

Learning theory and research

Most of what makes us truly human, most of what makes us individuals rather than clones, most of what gives us a discernible personality – made up of roughly characteristic patterns of behaviour, emotion and cognition – is the result of learning. We also get a little help or hindrance from genetic endowment regarding what we learn and how easy or difficult it is. These influences affect such dimensions as temperament and various aspects of intelligence. However, outside these general predispositions and the possession of a few 'hard-wired' drives towards what Dennett (1991) has called 'the four Fs' (flight, fight, food and procreation), our actions and their internal concomitants are largely the products of experience.

Natural selection has, to a unique degree, favoured *Homo sapiens* with immense behavioural flexibility, with memory and with foresight. The advantages of these gifts for an otherwise physically unpromising primate are that we are less caught out by environmental change – either over time or through change of location – and that we can multiply our influence many times over through advanced forms of social co-operation. Archilocus observed in 650 BC: 'The fox knows many little things – the hedgehog one big one.' Fine for *Erinaceous europeanus* over several millennia until, in the late nineteenth century, Herr Benz decided to pursue the production of horseless carriages.

Learning, or environmental programming, enables us to live in the past, the present and the future simultaneously. The lessons of yesterday's environments, still inside us as a result of conditioning, affect today's behaviour, and also influence the direction and valency of our goals and anticipations. There is nothing 'mechanistic' about this idea, for the patterns are immensely rich and complex. However, if we are to understand their origins, we need to start by investigating the simpler mechanisms of learning and remembering. Outside controlled laboratory conditions, these rapidly extend themselves into long, chain-like sequences of stimulus-association and stimulus-response association. Such quantitative extensions lead to *qualitatively* different patterns of behaviour. In other words, human beings come to know very, very many little things. With our large and complex brains (upwards of 13,000,000,000 nerve cells, and interconnections between them which strain mathematical imagination), we are consequently neither the prisoners of physiological reflexes nor of current environmental contingencies. In us, nature has favoured *conditionability* or, if you like, *programmability,* or *learning*: the ability to profit from experience. The most basic form of learning is classical conditioning.

Classical conditioning

Pavlov won his Nobel Prize for his work on the *physiological* processes of digestion (interestingly, the word in italics is often presented in publishers' proofs as 'psychological' – a good example of higher-order classical conditioning at work, since Pavlov is now associated above all with his contributions to psychology). He and his colleagues embarked upon a project to map the range and the effects of conditioned reflexes from a sense of frustration, because no matter how great the care they took to control the circumstances in which they conducted their experiments, certain psychological phenomena always interfered. In other words, the laboratory animals developed associations and anticipations about food, as they do in ordinary domestic life. These effects fascinated Pavlov, who saw them as a challenge to scientific method:

> In our 'psychical' experiments on the salivary glands, at first we honestly endeavoured to explain our results by fancying the subjective condition of the animal. But nothing came of it except unsuccessful controversies and individual, personal, uncoordinated opinion. We had no alternative but to place the investigation on a purely objective basis (Pavlov 1897, p.183).

I am always trepidacious about introducing discussions of animal experiments into social work textbooks because of the Pavlovian reactions this tends to produce but they are necessary to the debate because they make clear the 'psychological grammar' of the learning processes, so that when we come to investigate the more complex behaviour of humans, the framework is already in place. However, there is nothing contained in the following paragraphs which does not also apply to human beings – indeed, sceptics should remember that we share about 98 per cent of our genetic make-up with the chimpanzee. This is not to say that the other 2 per cent is not of paramount interest – just a cautionary, anti-speciesist comment.

Pavlov's procedure (the appropriate images will probably be in your head as a result of classical conditioning) was to collect saliva directly from the cheek gland of a dog held in place by a harness, in a sound-proofed laboratory. Here is the sequence:

1 A tone is sounded (Neutral Stimulus NS), and no salivary response occurs.
2 The tone is sounded, and meat powder is deposited into a dish in front of the animal or directly into its mouth (Unconditional Stimulus: UCS). This produces salivary flow as a matter of innate reflex. This procedure is repeated several times.
3 The tone (conditioned stimulus: CS) is presented without the meat powder (UCS), and salivary flow occurs in response to this stimulus alone – the dog has learned a new response.
4 Stimuli resembling the CS will tend to produce a similar reaction.

Therefore, classical conditioning is a pattern of stimulus-association learning. Stimuli impinge in *clusters*: there are spatial and temporal connections (features of place, circumstances and time) which throughout evolutionary history it has been useful for animals (and humans) to respond to interchangeably, since one – or one class – might predict the likelihood of the other. Thus anything that might reliably signal the possibility of satisfaction of a basic drive, or the avoidance of danger, and so prepare us for what may ensue, conveys an advantage on 'better-safe-than-sorry' principles. In the case of salivation, this operates by ensuring that the elapsed time between first prospect and food-energy being available for use is shortened, as is the feeding episode during which we would once have been vulnerable to predation. In the case of learned fear-reactions, the advantages operate through the fight/flight mechanism of the body: changes in muscle-tone, heart rate, blood pressure and blood-clotting speed, sweating, breathing rate, pupil size, and so forth, all of which prepare us for more effective escape or for combat. (With a little imagination, the reader should be able to work out the precise advantages conveyed by each of these physiological changes – think *brutal*.)

However, while it is useful to remind ourselves of the power of fierce drives and emotions, it is a mistake to forget the powerfully pleasurable feelings which (through the limbic system in the brain) exert a telling influence on our behaviour and thinking. For example, praise from an admired friend or mentor can produce such warm feelings that all our day-to-day doubts and worries are washed away. It has long been known that the brain contains dedicated centres for pleasure as well as for pain (Olds 1956). The biochemistry of all this is not our particular concern but the environmental effects most certainly are, since decision-making – our own and that of our clients – is not the desiccated intellectual process represented in some textbooks on cognition. It is powerfully influenced by emotion, by chains of conditioned predispositions, and by intrusive memories of past successes and failures (see Dennett 1996).

Let us now come down to earth and look at another classic experiment in this field, that of Watson and Rayner (1920). These pioneers were keen to see whether Pavlov's results applied in human cases of unreasonable fear and anxiety, and they also had ideas about the origins of such conditions. 'Little Albert' (so called in parody of Freud's celebrated 'Little Hans' castration anxiety case), a 6-month-old child (who today would be subject to the sterner provisions of the Children Act) was volunteered for this study by his mother. He was placed in a play pen and introduced to a tame white rat (NS) – no reaction beyond curiosity occurred. A gong was then struck loudly (UCS) every time the animal was introduced. Next, the animal (CS) was repeatedly released *without* the accompanying noise, but it still gave rise to fear and avoidance reactions. The child had learned a new fear (a conditioned response: CR), purpose-built in the laboratory. What the rat learned about toddlers and adults is open to speculation.

Two clinically important phenomena were demonstrated in Watson and Rayner's work. The first is *generalisation.* Pavlov noted from his experiments that anything resembling the CS would eventually, in chain-like fashion, come to produce the same CR. 'Little Albert' came proportionately to fear a whole range of similarly furry objects (including Rayner's fur coat) bearing decreasing resemblance to the original CS. We see this phenomenon of stimulus-generalisation in our own cases, where clients have a bad experience in one setting, but adverse responses spread to a wide range of vaguely similar circumstances. This is a notable feature of post-traumatic stress disorder (see Joseph et al. 1995) and of social phobias, leading to increasing withdrawal. The details are more complex, but the basic mechanisms are substantially the same as those encountered in laboratory studies. This is an ethically unsettling experiment, but it was conducted a long time ago, and standards are different now. However, it is a study we can learn from, and it should be remembered that the researchers were simply re-creating circumstances that often occur naturally, otherwise there would be no phobics. Those who remain queasy about it might like to try the following thought experiment.

Imagine that Stanley Milgram's conformity experiments (Milgram 1974) – the most important in social psychology – had never taken place. You have to persuade a modern ethics committee of the value of inviting people to electrocute someone (an actor) just because he failed a word-pairing test. In reality, no electric shock is to be inflicted, but the subjects do not know this. How many would comply up to the 'Danger – Serious Shock, 350V' level just because a man in a grey lab coat said that they 'had no choice' but to continue? (Worryingly high numbers of subjects did in the original experiments, so we found out something more about ourselves and our relationship to perceived authority.) What do you think would be your chances of persuading the imaginary ethics committee to allow you to conduct this experiment today? If you failed, what would be the consequences of this loss of chastening knowledge about the way we are, or at least of the way that we can be in the unhappy circumstances that we often allow to creep up on us? Shortly after Watson and Raynor's experiment, useful clinical applications of their findings appeared in the literature (Cover-Jones 1924). Perhaps demanding experiments are sometimes worth it – I think so.

Let us return to the point about generalisation. Happily, it can produce therapeutic benefits in the opposite direction, as in a recent study (Sheldon and Macdonald 1996) where modest investment by a local authority in sponsored day care for the children of poor parents, most of whom presented with behavioural and developmental problems, was seen to result in a range of improvements under home conditions too. In cases where morale is low, small initial gains can spread to increasingly more demanding circumstances through a feeling of competency being reacquired.

The second important phenomenon demonstrated by Pavlov, and confirmed in many other studies since, is that of *extinction*. In one sequence of trials, the bell (CS) was rung again and again without the accompanying

UCS; the result was a gradual disappearance of salivation on cue. Some kind of 'unlearning' of the conditioned response had taken place. One can see the evolutionary advantage of this ability to de-associate, in that some loose clusterings or even close pairings of signals – either of potential danger or potential satisfaction – would always have been unreliable, so there is no point in continuing to respond to what might be rare, or due to chance combinations.

In summary, classical conditioning is the associative mechanism through which we learn what to fear or to approach, which circumstances reliably predict danger, and which predict opportunities for satisfaction. It works through emotional arousal. Both pleasant and unpleasant emotions are involved, and cognition – expectations and attributions – comes in later. So far, I have represented it as a useful, adaptive ability able to give us an 'edge' on once very hostile or ambivalent environments, as the environmental-programming mechanism which, long ago, allowed us to win out over the ice and the bear, and to predict where food might be found in times of scarcity. However, it also carries costs, particularly in today's more complex and settled environments, where (however tempting sometimes) attacking an adversary, a bank manager say, or running away will seldom prove a socially effective response.

Many of our clients who have emotional problems, unreasonable fears, undue anxieties, who have learned to avoid what would be better confronted and dealt with, have learning histories containing what look to outsiders like 'irrational associations'. Here is a set of such maladaptive connections (all plausibly explainable through the Pavlovian model) which I have encountered in my own practice:

- An 8-year-old physically abused child who, once in care, responded to virtually *any* situation of routine dependence on an adult (particularly a male adult) with fear and aggression.
- A middle-aged, pregnant woman with a pre-existent fear of hospitals (brought on by her mother's blood-curdling accounts of her own gynaecological and obstetric experiences) who fainted in the street and subsequently fought off all would-be helpers (who had called an ambulance) and thereafter regarded *all* outdoor circumstances as threatening and unsafe.
- A young man stuck in a crowded lift for twenty minutes who panicked and thereafter regarded *all* confined spaces as threatening, including his room at work if the door was shut.
- A young man who frequently exposed himself in public places and had learned to associate expressions of disgust and revulsion with sexual pleasure – the more of one, the more of the other.

- A man who, as a child, was ridiculed by a teacher for feeling queasy after a routine vaccination procedure, and for a time developed a somewhat self-fulfilling fear of fainting in any formal, enclosed situation.
- A learning-disabled young person who following a car accident, refused to travel in *any* form of vehicle for any purpose.
- A troubled young woman who learned to associate ritual self-injury with feelings of expiation for (largely imagined) sins, and subsequently with sexual arousal.

Classical association is an insufficient explanation for any of the problems referred to above, however. For it should be noted that once an emotional link has been established, it leads to new patterns of *behaviour*, either to diminish aversive arousal (guilt, anxiety) or to increase pleasurable emotion. Such actions rapidly attract reinforcement through the temporarily positive or relief-inducing consequences which follow. Cognitive factors also play a part in such problems, in the form of unreasonable beliefs and selective perception (see in particular Chapter 9). These are not just clinical phenomena. In everyday life, advertisers know well how to exploit our ability to associate one thing with another. What does 'beanz' mean? How do you sell an, on the face of it, unpromising product, such as meat stock cubes? Answer: link it to images of stable family life where people still eat meals round the table. Conversely, the term 'social worker' has by this same process come to evoke fear and anger through associations with draconian child-snatching practices, or hopeless naivety in the face of obvious danger (other children). This is Pavlovian conditioning, courtesy of the tabloid press, with little direct, only vicarious, exposure (see Chapter 14).

An interesting question is: why do the processes of extinction and habituation (reviewed above) not lead to a natural weakening of troublesome emotional, behavioural and cognitive connections? The answer is that this does happen to a degree via natural exposure. Most of us have had fears and anxieties which we have lost through counteracting experience (the fifth case in the list above – do count carefully – was me, I confess, but I later went on to train as a nurse). The problem is that *some* patterns of acquisition involve either very painful, dramatic pairings of stimuli (for example, the car crash victim in the example given above) or regular repetitions of aversive experience so that connections are re-established again and again. For example, someone with anxieties regarding groups of strangers is unlikely to perform well socially in such situations, and is therefore likely to attract puzzled or critical responses which rekindle the fear. A further reason is *avoidance*. In the example of the claustrophobic person in the list above, little or no natural exposure occurred because he would never go in a lift or enter a confined space, preferring to pant his way up fire exit stairs in tall buildings or to feign sickness if asked to accompany someone on the tube. All of these avoidant responses tend to attract reinforcing consequences in their own right through a process of *negative reinforcement*. They also defer the 'unlearning' of stimulus connections.

There are yet further complications to a simple paired-association model of classical conditioning.

The possibilities for conditioning are endless (as we see from accounts of the more exotic sexual fetishes), yet phobic and anxiety-avoidance reactions tend to form clusters. There are millions of electric sockets in the world, but few electro-phobics; there are thousands of arachnophobics in Britain (Bernard Levin is a prime case), yet spiders here pose no risk – though the situation in Australia or Africa is quite different. The concept of *preparedness* throws some light on such strange patterns (see Seligman 1971; Shanks 1995). We appear to be particularly prone to acquire fears of certain classes of things: heights; enclosed spaces; small, scurrying things; anything large and looming, sudden, noisy or fast. There is no secure evidence here, but the most likely explanation is that over the millennia, natural selection has favoured these reactions. I fell through my roof last year while clearing leaves from the gutterings and learned a few new things about conditioning: the sheer depth of fear of which I was capable as I hung for fifteen minutes, bruised and bloodied, twenty feet over a stairwell, and the power of the instinct for survival, catching myself doing a little triumphal dance after I eventually managed to swing to safety. Such things are in us, but unfortunately they get connected via classical conditioning to remarkably ordinary and objectively non-threatening situations – a fear of travelling on public transport, or in the air (statistically safer than the car trip to the airport); a fear of spiders which generalises to a fear of kitchen cupboards, or even to tomato stalks in the salad; or a fear of the 1 per cent of germs which not even bleach can kill. (I now clean windows on a step-ladder equipped with little stabilisers.)

Some individuals are more conditionable to some circumstances than others. I have met many people suffering phobic reactions or extremes of anxiety, but few who did not have a history of minor episodes of the same sort of thing. Eysenck (1965) demonstrated this difference in the laboratory many years ago. The apparatus was simple: a machine generating a mild shock, plus a galvanic skin response (GSR) recorder (which measures arousal via the sweating reflex). Subjects were pre-assessed on the Introversion/Extraversion scale of the Eysenck Personality Inventory (EPI) and divided into two distinct groups. The pairing of signal and aversive stimulus, then later the presentation of the signal alone, produced significantly higher GSR readings for introverts than extroverts. Therefore, there are some personality configurations on the shoulder of a curve of distribution for these tendencies who are either more 'punishment-sensitive' and easier to condition (probably because of central nervous system differences) than those on the opposite slope, who are harder to condition, relatively punishment-insensitive individuals. In other words, some people are more prone to acquire fear reactions than others, and will require more extensive therapeutic help to aid them to feel safe even in environments which most of us would regard as not very challenging. Biology and environment *interact* to produce such probabilistic differences.

It is increasingly recognised that cognitive factors also play a part in the acquisition of 'unreasonable' fears. Human beings do not simply respond to threatening stimuli; they interpret them. Thus, above and beyond the simpler classically conditioned fears based upon direct experience, there is a range of not entirely rational thoughts about such problems: that if sufferers confront their *bêtes noires* they will die of a heart attack as a result; that such stresses will make them mentally ill, and so forth. Cognitive-behavioural therapists seek to dispel such interpretations via an educational, reality-testing approach which seeks to equip clients with coping mechanisms to tide them over until these fears subside in the face of controlled exposure.

Having given an outline of stimulus-association conditioning and its effects, I now turn to another major theory of learning, this time concerned with *stimulus-response* associations: the influence of consequences on behaviour.

Operant conditioning

The more we learn about child development, the more we are forced to abandon the environmental determinism of the 1960s and acknowledge the active, experimenting contribution of children themselves. Much of child development 'unfolds' from within. Very young babies show signs of a strong urge to explore, to *operate upon* (hence the word 'operant') and to manipulate their environments (see Donaldson 1978). Such activities rapidly attract consequences of a positive, aversive or relief-producing kind. Some of these consequences just happen, such as reaching out and touching something hot; some we deliberately organize, for example withdrawing attention from bad behaviour. Some sequences are 'stamped in', others 'stamped out' (Thorndike 1898: (note the date; these theories are popularly thought to follow those of Freud, but are in fact different products of the same era)). Nothing new here, and once again the contribution of behavioural psychology has taken the form of carefully charting the dynamics of this way of acquiring new responses.

Thus, from the earliest years, by accident and by design, human beings are exposed to sets of *contingencies* ('If you, then ...'), which experiences amount to a sub-Darwinian process of natural (and unnatural) selection of behaviour patterns. The towering contribution is that of the American psychologist B.F. Skinner (1953 and 1971), whose project was to develop an entire psychology without reference to interior goings on. If you now find yourself thinking of rats, do remember that this is a Pavlovian reaction.

Adopting an earlier principle, let us start with Skinner's animal experiments. He gave his name to a glass-sided box equipped with a food dispenser and a release lever or disc which the animal (usually a rat or pigeon – never both) could operate from the inside. All other factors are under the control of the experimenter. Here is a summary of Skinner's procedures:

- A rat which, let us say, has missed its breakfast, is placed in a glass-sided box with a food release lever, and engages in exploratory (operant) behaviour, eventually bumping into the lever and hitting the jackpot. The rat tries this again, and clumsy initial operation quickly gives way to expert tapping. The rat's unlikely behaviour (for a rat) has been *positively reinforced,* so it is repeated; or rather, the other way around: it has learned a new pattern of behaviour. Thus, a positive reinforcer is a stimulus which strengthens, amplifies or increases the rate of a behavioural sequence that it follows.
- Next, imagine a Skinner box with a wire grid for a floor, capable of delivering an irritating and continuous level of shock until an encounter with the lever turns this off for a period. As in the previous case, the rat spends a lot of time operating the respite lever. This process is called *negative reinforcement.* It also leads to an increase in new behaviour, but this time with the object of removing an aversive set of conditions. Thus a negative reinforcer is a stimulus the removal of which strengthens, amplifies or increases the frequency of the behaviour pattern which led to it. Does this sound familiar?
- Next, consider a situation where depressing the lever in the Skinner box leads every time to a loud noise. Prior learned behaviour is decreased, probably extinguished, under these conditions. The animal quickly learns an avoidant reaction. Thus a punishing stimulus decreases or extinguishes a behaviour pattern which it follows; or rather, the other way around.

Why do we need such technical terms to describe what we can recognise as analogues of everyday happenings? Well, another way of making the important point that humans can learn practically *anything* (for example, that trust is usually repaid; that people can change; that aggression pays; that tight, vigilant control equals safety) is to say that almost any set of stimuli can acquire reinforcing or punishing associations through the consequences they bring, or have brought in the past. Some examples serve to illustrate the point: most people would identify physical pain as a punishing stimulus, but through classical and operant association, for some people (masochists) it can become a cue which strengthens sexual arousal to the point where it becomes an end in itself. Most of us in our lives have received praise from someone we despise. It is hard to think of such compliments as 'punishing', though they may satisfy the technical definition and make co-operative behaviour less likely in the future. (Thus the present authors hope *not* to have a favourable review of this book from Monsieur Le Pen, however gushing.)

The process works the other way around too, as this wartime reminiscence by the historian Richard Cobb (regarding his commanding officer) shows:

> He displayed a watchful and petty hostility to all university graduates under his command, and a positive loathing for those who had been to Oxford or Cambridge, as if they had gone there on purpose, in some mysterious foreknowledge that they would be meeting him at some point later in life. From the start, I could not help feeling rather flattered that he should have taken such an active, vigilant dislike to myself; I thought that it did me credit, it was a sort of tribute. There is something very satisfying about being disliked by the right sort of people (Cobb 1997, p.86).

Good advice for social workers, perhaps?

Thus, the only scientific basis on which the valency of stimuli can be decided is through a close study of their *effects* – not on any prior classifications of intent. If you doubt it, try giving your GP a fiver for his trouble next time you visit the surgery (this experiment works best in non-fundholding practices).

This book contains many case examples within which patterns of reinforcement have led to the development of serious problems, and within which a reordering of reinforcement contingencies has had a positive impact upon them (see, for example, Chapters 3 and 12), but here are a few more general examples from my own practice by way of introduction:

- A young boy who had already been excluded from one previous school on grounds of disruptive behaviour had learned that aggression always produced attention, whereas getting on with school work not only produced little or none (the 'sleeping dogs' effect), but also exposed his academic weaknesses.
- A lonely man with a serious drink problem had learned that brushes with the police after altercations in public houses usually resulted in his daughter coming to stay with him until he was 'better'.

- A young, learning-disabled man's experience had taught him that running away from his foster carers typically led to a period in police care (exciting), a car ride home (interesting), and a kindly reunion (comforting) .
- A 12-year-old boy felt that his needs came a poor second to his parents' troubles, but discovered, by accident (operantly), that a random, peer-inspired episode of fire-setting had the effect of jerking his father out of the depressed state he had been in since a serious industrial accident, and produced some concern from his mother. More fires broke out.
- A young woman suffered from schizophrenia. Her parents sought to persuade her out of her paranoid delusions by investigating them in detail and trying to refute them empirically. When not expressing delusional thinking (most of the time), she was left to her own devices by her relieved parents. Delusion-inspired behaviour increased.
- A newly qualified social worker discovered that her standing with management was more dependent on up-to-date records and attendance at meetings than on the quality of her face-to-face work with clients. She reluctantly embraced 'virtual reality social work' and spent more time at her word-processor.

All of the problems in the above cases are arguably the products of reinforcement contingencies. In most of the examples, the parties were unaware, or only partly aware, of the patterns shaping them into short-term adaptive, long-term maladaptive behaviour. However, although these relatively crude forces are usually the most important, there are other factors at work in the acquisition of happiness-threatening patterns of behaviour, with, as usual, attendant therapeutic opportunities.

One of Skinner's most important discoveries was that *schedules of reinforcement* affect the acquisition of new behaviour (see Ferster and Skinner 1957); that the rate and the sequencing of reinforcement strongly influence performance. In Skinner's animal experiments, *continuous reinforcement* ('one for one' patterns of reward) led to the most effective sequences of behaviour acquisition until satiation effects took over. However, regarding efficiency, it was possible to shape behaviour towards an acceptance of lower but still predictable patterns of reinforcement via the introduction of tolerable 'piece-work' rates – say one reinforcer per four presses. In human terms, this is the equivalent of working hard all month for a delayed but predictable pay cheque. However, behaviour under the control of continuous reinforcement is easily extinguished. Apart from a brief 'spurt' to test out the contingencies, responsiveness falls off rapidly if reinforcers are withdrawn.

The natural environment, either of animals or of humans, rarely delivers reinforcement on a continuous schedule. It is far more likely that rewarding breakthroughs will happen occasionally and after considerable labour. Skinner and his colleagues experimented with such *variable ratio* and *intermittent* patterns of reinforcement, following the shaping-up of a behaviour pattern. The best way to envisage what happens is to think of the behaviour of gamblers. All of us fall into this category from time to time. The 'fruit machine of life' delivers unpredictable sweetness to us now and again. We then try to work out exactly what the contingencies were, occasionally resorting to 'superstitious' interpretations – the lucky pen for the exam, the tie I wore last time I got a job. Such patterns of hopeful persistence in the face of delayed gratification are extremely resistant to extinction. This is bad news, given that most troublesome behaviour is shaped-up in this way, but good news for would-be helpers if they build this knowledge into their practice as a means of sustaining gains already made.

The main message of these experimental findings (well replicated in therapeutic outcome studies) is that reinforcement contingencies need to be *very* reliable if they are to hold sway over the problem-reviving power of occasional, unpredictable reinforcement which 'immunises' responses against extinction. An example may help here. Aggressive or other anti-social behaviour in children (remember that this is the commonest cause of a breakdown in foster care arrangements) may be resisted, ignored, talked over or even punished, but unless the contingencies are tightly in place, stray reinforcement effects may revive the behaviour and make it even less influenceable in future. This is one of the main reasons why some behavioural programmes (to say nothing of other less focused therapeutic attempts) fail, and why otherwise well-disposed carers give up on troubled and troublesome children.

This brings us to the point where the operant and classical models of learning come together, through the existence of *conditioned reinforcers.* In animal experiments, anything which reliably precedes or accompanies reinforcement – a light, perhaps – comes in time to acquire symbolic signalling and arousing properties of its own. This is why, in human terms, good essay grades can reinforce studying behaviour, which then leads to the award of a diploma, which itself stands for increased social status and job prospects, which factors have implications for the satisfaction of more basic needs for security and satisfaction.

The main therapeutic techniques derived from this model of learning are as follows:

- Encouraging clients to take note of *discriminative stimuli* (S^ds – reinforced stimuli) the signals which predict future trouble (S^{Δ}_{S} – delta stimuli) or pleasure (Sd^r – reinforcers), or are known to elicit certain patterns of behaviour. Anyone who has tried to give up smoking will be aware of the power of these cues – a cup of coffee, the end of a meal, a drink, etc. But it is also necessary to help clients to identify more complex, external prompts, such as what it is about the behaviour of others that signals that it is time to curl up or withdraw, and what other options might be available? How best to signal to a child behaving aggressively that this behaviour will not prevail? In this regard, many of us will have known otherwise kindly teachers who nevertheless could fix us with a special 'make my day' look, inhibiting further bad behaviour.

- Where a problem results mainly from an *insufficiency* of certain behaviour, it may be possible simply to identify and *positively reinforce* a low-level adaptive response so that it is 'amplified', performed more frequently, and its place in the individual's repertoire strengthened. In other words, we can work to improve the consequences for desirable behaviour. A good starting point is simply to raise the question with oneself: what pays off for this person, in this setting, group, family or organisation? Answers confirmed by observation often differ substantially from official pronouncements and spoken intentions.
- A performance may be *shaped* by the selective reinforcement of approximately similar behaviours, until they become progressively more like the performance desired.
- Where the problem results mainly from an *excess* of unwanted behaviour, it may be possible to identify and positively reinforce a response which is *incompatible* with existing (unwanted) responses: we may be able to encourage an alternative set of activities, which could eventually replace (crowd out) the existing behaviour, or which prevent the individual from gaining reinforcement for the unwanted behaviour.
- Again, in respect of an excess of unwanted behaviour, it may be possible to apply *negative reinforcement*, so that whenever the individual stops this behaviour and performs some desirable alternative, an aversive stimulus is terminated. Here the removal of the aversive stimulus (such as being ignored) is made contingent upon someone refraining from undesirable behaviour and engaging in some more appropriate activity, and this serves to strengthen the alternative response.
- It may be possible to reduce the frequency of undesirable behaviour by *extinction* – just by removing the reinforcement currently available for it. In this way, unwanted behaviour is not encouraged by the positive consequences it brings.
- In certain cases, unwanted behaviour can be eliminated by *punishing* it (discouraging it) whenever it occurs – by ensuring that an aversive

consequence results from its performance. More sophisticated adaptations of this principle are available which attach different levels of strength of opposition to different activities. These are called *response-cost schemes,* and involve the assignment of an agreed 'price' to each different pattern of unwanted behaviour according to its seriousness. Such programmes may be useful where there is a range of different responses which the social worker is anxious to discourage in different degrees: a sort of inverted shaping approach, best used with other schemes to reward adaptive, pro-social behaviour. Remember, though, that many of our clients already inhabit (unpredictably) punishing environments. Response-cost schemes, which are mainly used with children, should aim to make necessary controlling sanctions more predictable, measured, rational and acceptable.

Learned helplessness

It is difficult to know where best to place this discussion, since experimenters in both the classical and operant paradigms have contributed to our understanding of the phenomenon, well known to social workers, of collapse of morale and the inability of individuals to engage their troublesome circumstances even though help to do so is at hand.

To repeat the point: people can learn virtually anything. One of the most damaging things to learn is that one has little or no control over one's circumstances, that one is helpless in the face of unpredictable, external forces. The primary function of the cerebral cortex is to aid adaptation to wayward circumstance; the primary purpose of the long period of socialisation which humans undergo is to equip them to track, to model, to predict, and then to adapt to circumstances. What happens when, either by accident or design, this proves impossible?

This interesting question was first investigated in Pavlov's laboratory by Shenger-Kristovnikova in 1921. She conducted a series of experiments to investigate how animals cope with being conditioned to respond to stimuli which are then made contradictory or ambiguous. Such situations are prevalent in the complex social environments of human beings, so the findings have relevance outside the field of animal behaviour (see Peterson et al. 1993). The experimenters taught animals to anticipate food on the presentation of a circle (which signalled food), but not an ellipse (which signalled an aversive stimulus). Then it was made increasingly difficult for the animal to distinguish between these figures by arranging for the circle to become narrowed at the sides, and for the ellipse to fatten out.

Another variation (Masserman 1943) involved the random substitution of consequences, so that the animal was unable to predict whether food or discomfort would follow a given action. The effects of these studies were that the animals' behaviour first became agitated and very uncharacteristic – hence the term 'experimental neurosis' – but that later, and this is the important point, even when the original and obvious stimulus discriminators were replaced, the animals just remained immobile rather than take an easy and obvious escape route. Evidence from analogue studies with human subjects suggests that there is more than a metaphorical relationship between such experiments and what social workers encounter in their day-to-day practice with clients who, frustratingly for would-be helpers, often seem to prefer the devils they know.

Such formulations will have a ring of truth to anyone familiar with the case histories of some psychiatric patients under treatment for reactive depression, or to anyone familiar with the backgrounds of clients labelled as 'inadequate personalities', or of those said to belong to 'problem families'. For these people, nothing works. Cognitive-behavioural approaches help to combat such states by attempting to re-establish some order and predictability into their circumstances through helping them to understand their experiences and reactions and, in a sympathetic, step-by-step way, teaching the skills necessary for the reassertion of first some, then greater control over seemingly unpredictable environments: 'proactivity therapy', based on small beginnings.

Vicarious learning and modelling

Probably the most distinctive feature of all the variants of behaviour therapy is that they do not rely upon verbal influence alone, but seek to *demonstrate* more adaptive, more skilful and, one hopes, more effective approaches to problems. Many of the difficulties which come our way are due to *learning deficits* – to serious gaps in the behavioural repertoires of individuals such as: how to manage difficult behaviour from a child; how to negotiate about rather than fight over conflicts of interest; how to cope with living again in the community after a period in a psychiatric unit; how to be calmly and rationally assertive when put upon. Solutions to these problems are largely a matter of social skills, which may not have been acquired naturally, or which may have atrophied because of intervening experience. The problem is that the natural behaviour of helpers is verbally to review such problems and their historical origins, and then to hope that new understandings and new plans will by some 'osmotic' process translate into new patterns of behaviour. This, studies of the effectiveness of social work, clinical psychology and psychotherapy have been telling us for many years, is a rather optimistic assumption. No one ever learned to swim, to cook or to bring up a child by attending the therapeutic equivalent of tutorials on these subjects. Demonstration, 'hands-on' experience, feedback and meaningful encouragement are required.

Such advice is not simply based upon an *a priori* preference for certain therapeutic styles. As with most other practices in this field, it is derived from research into the factors known to influence learning. As previously noted, vicarious learning (learning by observation and imitation through watching the behaviour of others) begins in early infancy. Three-week-old babies will readily copy facial grimaces. Mothers have known this for centuries, but experimental psychology only caught up in the 1970s (Harris 1972). Less tellingly, I can confirm it from personal experience. I travel on trains quite a lot, and am often confronted with small babies slung over their mothers' chests, so facing me, wide-eyed, over the back of the seat. If you smile or pull a face, the baby will automatically struggle to copy this, although it is too young to have learned this behaviour. (Try it, but don't get caught, since it causes consternation among fellow passengers.)

Think once again of the evolutionary advantage as well as the contemporary utility that this ability to observe, interpret and learn from the experience of others would have conveyed. It means that we do not always have to suffer ourselves in order to avoid suffering. We do not always have to repeat a long series of trial-and-error experiments, chancing occasionally upon a favourable outcome (or not). We can simply watch how others approach problems, break down the performance mentally into steps, and if it seems likely to work, try it out – either piecemeal or wholesale. If it doesn't, then we can drop it altogether, or just retain the promising bits. But, as always in the field of learning, we must remember that while this capability might lead usefully to, say, the ability to look confident when we are fearful, it is also the process by which we can learn, equally effectively, to intimidate, or to deceive with style. Learning itself is morally neutral. Ethical judgements about it have to be made later.

Having discussed the high and low points of modelling effects, we must now turn to the stages and the mechanisms involved, for it is from these that we can acquire an appreciation of the therapeutic possibilities. Vicarious learning can account for the following patterns of change.

It can give rise to the second-hand acquisition of completely new *sequences* of behaviour. Remember adolescence, when, stalled somewhere between childhood and adulthood, most of us experimented cavalierly with strange new ways of walking, dressing, talking, and so forth, mostly gathered from others or from images in the media. Such behavioural symbols of changing identity are tried on, kept, adapted or discarded according to the internal and external reinforcement they produce. The playgrounds of Britain recently came to resemble martial arts training schools thanks to the modelling influence of 'Power Rangers'. The problem is that sometimes there are no suitable models available (for example, of how to walk away without loss of face), so learning deficits accrue which threaten further development.

Emotional reactions can also be learned vicariously. As children, we learn what to fear by watching others behave fearfully, or how to cope by watching others approach threatening circumstances with *sang froid*.

Thought patterns – more particularly problem-solving styles – can be acquired by watching how others cope with challenges, and then inferring (not always accurately) what processes of mental computation and interpretation led them to a given course of action. 'You played with style boys, real style', a charismatic history teacher at my school used to say (he had probably never lifted a cricket bat in his life), so we walked back to the dressing room, beaten, but by morally inferior forces chasing unseemly, narrow, quantitative measures of success (sometimes known as 'wickets' or 'runs'). He would always go for the morale issue, never the technical. We got worse until we worked this out and started net practice on our own. (In case you are thinking public school 'fat cat' thoughts as a result of classical association, this was a secondary modern: very secondary, and not very modern.)

Here are a couple more case illustrations:

- A man in a fairly serious state of depression had been made redundant three times in two years, and his survival plan was based on observations of others not made redundant. His chosen models had allegedly 'kept their heads down' and survived. Yet on every occasion of loss of employment, the reasons given to him were that he appeared to lack initiative, made only a minimal contribution to the team to which he belonged, and was more concerned with the inconsequential details of his own tasks rather than co-operation with colleagues. The approach used – with some success in that he has been off Prozac for over twelve months and is increasingly well regarded at work – was based on the modelling and rehearsal of a more proactive, assertive approach in situations identified by him as important.
- A young boy, referred for aggressive behaviour towards his mother and to people in public places, had learned this behaviour from his father (a soldier who often faced disciplinary charges for intimidating those under his control). Interestingly, the boy's father admitted that he had learned this behaviour from *his* father, also a soldier. 'He was *really* tough, he wasn't always fair, but he was a *real* man and no mistake.' A cast iron set of sanctions and plentiful rewards for reasonable behaviour helped, but mother had to be shown how to operate this scheme in the home environment.

The above cases raise the proposition that if we can learn anti-social, aggressive or self-defeating patterns of behaviour vicariously, then it might be possible to replace these performances by exposure to new models. We could then arrange reinforcement for any resultant trial behaviours, and hope that they come to attract reinforcement naturally. There is, in fact, a substantial literature on which to draw here (Bandura 1969; Hall et al. 1997). It recommends that whatever the nature of the problem in view, modelling and social skill training programmes should be organised according to the following common stages:

1 Identify specific problems resulting from gaps in the client's behavioural repertoire, and decide what new patterns of behaviour could be developed to fill these.
2 Divide the target responses into their component parts (for example, coming into a room full of people; deciding who to stand next to and what to say; introducing oneself; getting in on the conversation, and so forth).
3 Identify with clients any patterns in their thinking (images and inner speech) which may encourage misinterpretation of the motives of others and/or avoidance responses, such as 'People are looking at me. They can tell I don't belong here.'
4 Demonstrate to clients what a competent performance might look like, rehearsing any problematic parts of the sequence, or going through it slowly and deliberately, emphasising options and decision points.
5 Develop more complex performances by chaining together different sequences.
6 Pay attention to any problems of discrimination: identify any difficulties the client may have in knowing whether a certain piece of behaviour is appropriate for a given setting.
7 Gradually introduce difficulties likely to be found in real life as the client becomes more able to cope with its vicissitudes (for instance, not getting an immediate response when trying to make friends; meeting increased persistence after saying 'no' to something).
8 Supervise practical assignments on which clients report back.

Outcome studies in this field point to modelling as an effective technique, providing it focuses on explicitly defined behavioural deficits. The results from more general-purpose programmes are less good. Indeed we in the helping professions are occasionally guilty of taking a useful approach and extending it willy-nilly to every problem that comes our way. This happened with contingency contracts – a useful device for procuring 'truces' between individuals and families where solutions lie genuinely within the gift of the parties, but useless when used merely as a list of externally imposed requirements such as home-school contracts for persistent truants, when little other help is made available to change motivation. In the juvenile offender field (see Chapter 7), unless the present government has the courage to reverse this policy, we may (in line with previous research) yet witness the spectacle of 'boot camps' turning out large numbers of clearer thinking, physically fitter, more socially skilled burglars.

Cognitive factors

Hamlet: Do you see yonder cloud that's almost in shape of a camel?
Polonius: By the mass and 'tis like a camel indeed.
Hamlet: Methinks it is like a weasel.
Polonius: It is backed like a weasel.
Hamlet: Or like a whale?
Polonius: Very like a whale (*Hamlet*, Act III, Scene II).

In the research literatures of psychotherapy, clinical psychology, and in our own field, two strong trends have been visible for some time: the elements of a focused, fairly intensive, task-centred, quasi-behavioural approach, within which due regard is paid to the problem of translating new understandings into behavioural change, are strongly associated with positive outcomes (Reid and Hanrahan 1981; Macdonald and Sheldon 1992; Bergin and Garfield 1994); problems which have behavioural components (virtually all do), but which are also strongly rooted in *internal* factors such as mood and thought patterns, respond well to approaches which seek to analyse, make clear and test out in reality the perceptions, beliefs and other patterns of negative, self-defeating cognition which lead to disengagement and alienation. Depression and the 'learned helplessness' reactions often present in post-traumatic stress disorders (Gilbert 1992; Solomon et al. 1992) are cases in point, but a range of sub-clinical reactions also stand in the way of the more focused and better-motivated approaches to problem-solving social workers try to encourage, which also benefit substantially from this approach (see Scott 1989). These factors may not be primarily *causal* (Lewinsohn et al. 1981), but they do play a role in the maintenance of problems. In this regard, it is worth remembering that headache is not caused by lack of aspirin in the bloodstream.

As a result of the above trends, textbooks in the behavioural field now regularly refer to a 'cognitive revolution' having taken place. For the following reasons, I find myself in an ambivalent frame of mind about these developments. There *is* some supportive research. It is methodologically respectable, but confined to a few areas where the addition of a formal, cognitive component to the helping process produces marginally better results – and more importantly, longer-lasting gains (see Blackburn et al. 1981 and Hollon et al. 1991; but see also Stuart and Thase 1994). However, these results in no way justify taking our eyes off the tried and trusted factors of behaviour-rehearsal, reinforcement contingencies and controlled exposure, all of which have regularly been shown to be influential in cases such as those contained in this volume (see Feske and Chambers 1995). The danger that we *might* stems perhaps from the reinforcement contingencies that operate upon would-be helpers: less direct means of influence have come, in the professional culture, to signify greater skill or prestige – the 'look no hands' effect identified by B.F. Skinner in 1971. Moreover, behavioural approaches are inconvenient; they take one out of the interview room and into the rain; to the school gates and into the classroom – if that is where problems manifest themselves. They require being there at bedtime if that is typically when dangerous fights between parents and children break out. Furthermore, using these approaches one can fail to achieve one's goals clearly and publicly. Thus, there are many short-term reasons for avoiding them and 'going cognitive'. We have skipped down this primrose path before.

On the positive side, however, behaviour therapists have always had to take account of the way stimuli are filtered, over- or under-responded to and eccentrically interpreted, though until recently they have not always done so systematically. Similarly, most cognitive therapists have always been keen to see whether changes in understanding translate into more positive behaviour patterns, though again, they have not always done so systematically. There is scope then for a pooling of findings and techniques, providing the gold-standard outcome criterion of changed *behavioural* performance, in line with case objectives, is retained. Other, more qualitative outcomes are of course welcome, providing they can be plausibly related to this test of effectiveness and are not simply offered up instead of it. One thing is sure: exclusively to favour one set of measures over the other is silly.

To sum up, there are four sets of influences on behaviour: environmental consequences; emotional associations – background genetic predispositions influencing temperament; and conditionability, and cognitive factors which influence the way in which stimuli are recognised, categorised and interpreted in the first place. These cognitive influences may be further broken down as follows.

Perception

This is an old topic in psychology, but the more we learn about it, the less it comes to resemble any simple camera- or tape-recorder-like process, and the more it is seen as an active, constructive process strongly influenced by cognition. In other words, we see, hear, taste and touch with our *brains* and in accordance with our expectations. These are created by experience, and influence the process of interpretation from the outset. Figure 1.1 gives a visual example of this.

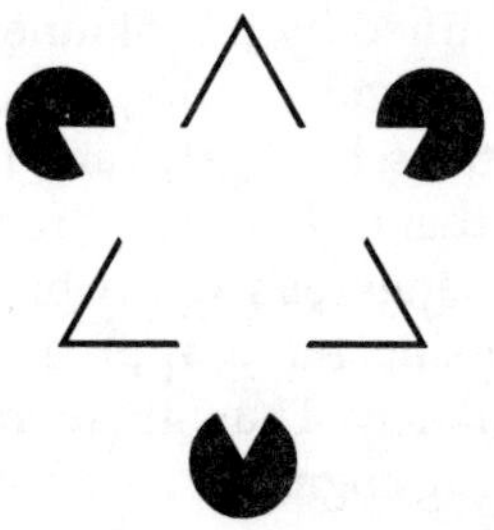

Figure 1.1 Kanizsa Triangle

The interesting thing about this figure is that the bright white triangle at its centre – noticeably whiter than the surrounding ground, and with its suspicion of demarcating lines – has no external existence; it is simply a product of expectation. That is, our brains, which can't focus in on *everything*, quickly register that the most plausible, familiar, worked-last-time explanation for such an unusual configuration is that an inverted white triangle is between us and it. However, this is not just a visual trick. It is perfectly possible to illustrate equivalent phenomena in any of the sensory modalities.

In a series of classic psychological experiments conducted at Cambridge in the 1940s, it was shown that our recall of events is also subject to systematic distortion. Bartlett (1950) presented subjects with a short Inuit folk tale from Canada entitled 'The War of the Ghosts'. This story is (to European eyes) constructed in a haphazard-seeming way, and contains many strange references to the spirit world. The experimenters chose it to produce a test sequence low on cues as to what was, or ought to be, going on. Subjects therefore had very little cultural knowledge through which to make sense of the narrative. Here is a sample:

> And the warriors went up the river to a town on the other side of Kalma. The people came down to the water, and they began to fight, and many were killed.

> But presently the young man heard one of the warriors say: 'Quick let us go home: that Indian has been hit.' Now he thought: 'Oh! They are ghosts.' He did not feel sick, but they said he had been shot (Bartlett 1950, p.47).

Subjects were asked to recall such passages at carefully spaced intervals. As might be expected, the longer the interval, the greater the failure of memory, but also the more *invention* took over. The orderliness of the results across subjects suggests that Bartlett was mapping a human predisposition to subtract from, and to add to, weak or ambiguous stimuli until sense could be made of them. The following quotation summarises the typical results:

> There was a strong tendency to rationalize, common to all subjects. Whenever anything appeared unusual, incomprehensible, or 'queer' it was either omitted or explained. Rather rarely this rationalization was the effect of a conscious effort. More often it was effected unwittingly, the subjects transforming the original without suspecting what they were doing (Bartlett 1950, p.111).

This and similar exercises, easily replicated in the psychology class, have implications for the way social workers make assessments and record data from their cases, but also for the way clients perceive the causes of their problems (see Sheldon 1987). It has been well demonstrated, for example, that people suffering from depression who are played two simultaneous recordings of speech – one positive, the other admonitory – through the separate earpieces of a headset will tend to recall the details of the negative commentary. Controls tend to switch between the two and recall the sequences in roughly equal measure (Eysenck and Keane 1990).

The therapeutic applications which flow from our increased knowledge of the role of selective perception and cognition are all based on the possibility that we may be able to alert clients to a wider range of more positive cues and self-produced commentaries; that we may be able to desensitise them to the negative signals; that they might be encouraged to reality-test the predictive value of negative signals and intrusive thoughts (what will actually happen if they are ignored?), and that we may, by a process of controlled, rational confrontation of pessimistic interpretations, bring about a more accurate, self-encouraging appraisal of assets and of problems.

Attributions

Human beings search actively for *meaning* when confronted by complex stimuli. We seek to attribute causality (sometimes making mistakes) as we try, like amateur scientists, to evaluate potential threats, rewards or sources of relief. Attributive cognitions fall into two main patterns: the external (circumstantial) and the internal (dispositional). The typical direction of causal attribution tends to vary with personality, with experience, with regularly encountered contingencies, and according to emotional state. Thus it appears that some of us are statistically more likely to look to our environments for explanations of our failures, whereas some of us are more likely to blame ourselves. The same can be said of our successes. Generally speaking, women are statistically more likely to look outwards for explanations of success and inwards for explanations of failure. As you might have guessed, the situation is reversed for men (Brown 1986, Chapter 9).

Social workers often encounter individuals whose patterns of self-blaming or self-excusing cognitions seem implausibly unidirectional. Here are a few examples:

- A young woman, worried and preoccupied by memories of persistent sexual abuse in childhood, felt that *she* 'must have done something' to encourage her stepfather.
- A client with a string of different psychiatric diagnoses to her name, living in a hostel, attributed the sound of nearby laughter to cruel jokes being made at her expense, and silence in the house to a wish by her critics that they should not be overheard when discussing her failings.
- A young man with 14 convictions for petty theft constantly complained that if only shopkeepers and householders would take greater precautions, he would not be so cruelly tempted into trouble.
- A man attributed his excessive drinking to family hostility and lack of support, whereas the family were clear that it was his drunkenness which caused their anger and withdrawal.

The point about misattribution is that we all do it. We go beyond the evidence, we 'join up the dots' of our observations and experiences and turn them into a meaningful but not always accurate pattern. We go looking for trouble when the mood takes us. It is these apparently 'reflexive' and over-general predispositions (in either direction) that users of cognitive-behavioural psychology seek to analyse with their clients, and with which we try to get them to experiment.

Catastrophic thinking

The next feature of cognition of interest to us is that of '*awfulising*'. It is easy to see how people with emotional troubles and learning histories filled with bad incidents might be shaped into hyper-vigilance for the first harbingers of trouble, and how, under the influence of anxiety, they might fail to develop proportionate responses. The clue to the existence of catastrophic thinking patterns sometimes lies in the selection of adjectives clients make to describe their circumstances, such as 'awful', 'impossible', 'total'. Here is a favourite example of an interviewer picking his way through a set of similar descriptions and offering a gentle evidential challenge to such self-defeating beliefs:

Therapist: Why do you want to end your life?
Patient: Without Raymond, I am nothing. I can't be happy without Raymond, but I can't save our marriage.
Therapist: What has your marriage been like?
Patient: It has been miserable from the very beginning ... Raymond has always been unfaithful ... I have hardly seen him in the past five years.
Therapist: You say that you can't be happy without Raymond ... Have you found yourself happy when you are with Raymond?
Patient: No, we fight all the time and I feel worse.
Therapist: You say you are nothing without Raymond. Before you met Raymond, did you feel you were nothing?
Patient: No, I felt I was somebody.
Therapist: If you were somebody before you knew Raymond, why do you need him to be somebody now?
Patient: [*puzzled*] Hmmm ... (Beck 1976, pp.289-90).

Vicious circles and emotional tangles are common enough in the lives of our clients, to say nothing of our own. Sometimes they form themselves into closed, self-sustaining, 'cat's cradle' systems of belief, emotions and action. R.D. Laing's rather neglected book *Knots* (1970), more important than his other work in my view, provides many interesting examples:

> She has started to drink
>   as a way to cope
>   that makes her less able to cope
> the more she drinks
> the more frightened she is of becoming a drunkard
> the more drunk
> the less frightened of being drunk (Laing 1970, p.29)

Case histories reveal that the triad of influences – thinking, feeling and behavioural experience – operate in different combinations and strengths. It therefore makes sense for helpers to adapt their approaches according to which of these appears primary. Hypotheses about this are usually developed during the assessment phase, to which we must next turn our attention.

Assessment, monitoring and evaluation

The three aspects of case management contained in the above heading are discussed together in this section to emphasise that social workers need to consider a method for monitoring progress and establishing a basis for evaluation from the outset. Otherwise, with what precisely are we comparing any outcome we achieve except (highly negotiable) memories of the *status quo ante*?

Cognitive-behavioural approaches have a well-deserved reputation for evaluative rigour, but this attribute depends upon attention to certain guidelines. Observance of these means that practitioners are to some extent freed from the role of being mere consumers of the research of others, and can also research their own cases, or indeed their own caseloads (see Kazi and Wilson 1996; Reid 1994). Some features of behavioural assessment and evaluation overlap with more familiar approaches; some are distinctive. Here is an account of the main differences of emphasis.

This form of assessment is concerned with *who* does *what, where, when, how often,* and *with whom.* It is also concerned to identify the *absence* or withholding of behaviours which it would normally be useful and reasonable to perform. It deals with the *consequences,* whether intended or not, which actions have for all the parties involved – those who are said to *have* the problem, and those for whom someone else's behaviour is said to *be* a problem. The emphasis here is on both visible, problematic behaviour, and the absence or the inadequacy of adaptive behaviour where this might reasonably have been expected to reduce negative consequences.

Behavioural assessment is also concerned with internal sensations, such as thinking patterns, doubts, worries, fears, frustrations and depression, but practitioners in this field try to keep the level of inference low, and are rather more likely to make use of standardised assessments to bolster their intuitions (see Fischer and Corcoran 1994). However, it should be noted that internal conditions also give rise to visible behavioural excesses or noteworthy deficits: self-preoccupation and ineffective ritual activity in the case of worrying; motionlessness, fixed expression, lack of social responses and lack of attention to dress and hygiene in the case of depression. People either *do* or *do not do* things as a result of emotional states and adverse patterns of thinking, and before-and-after comparisons of these observable things provide a good check as to whether what clients *say* they feel as a result of help is reliable evidence. Having both kinds of information assists us in reducing the influence of 'demand effects' – clients trying to please or to deceive by verbally living up to expectations (a fact of therapeutic life, I am afraid).

Considerable emphasis is placed on *contemporary* behaviour and the thoughts and feelings which accompany it. The tendency to search for the long-lost causes of problems is, in the absence of major trauma, regarded with some suspicion, for the following reasons:

- because there is no guarantee that they will ever be found
- because the exercise is costly in time and resources
- because when views as to the 'original causes' of problems *can* be elicited, they are not always agreed upon by the protagonists – nor are they necessarily valid
- because dwelling on the history of problems can sometimes serve to intensify bad feeling, and can distract from the necessity of doing something positive in the here and now.

This said, the social worker must balance the above with the need for him or herself and for the client to understand the nature and development of the difficulties in view. One solution is to limit history-taking to brief accounts of the *aetiology* of given problems (the history of specific stages and developments), and to emphasise to clients that trouble is often reactivated every day by what people do or fail to do, and by self-fulfilling expectations. A crucial question here is: what maintains problematic behaviour in force long after the original factors eliciting it have passed into history?

This concern for contemporary events is part of a wider attempt to establish the influential conditions that surround a given problem. Thus we are concerned here with such things as *where* things tend to happen and not to happen; what happens around the client or to him or her just *before* a sequence of the unwanted behaviour occurs; what happens around the client or to him or her *during* the performance of the behaviour; and what happens *after* the performance of the behaviour. Any natural correlation or variance in these factors provides useful extra information. A simple example would be when John wets the bed every night *except* when he sleeps with his brother or *except* when he stays at his grandmother's – therefore he has some control. Examples of ABC (Antecedents, Behaviour, Consequences) charts based on such concerns will be found in later chapters, for example Chapter 13.

At some stage, decisions have to be made with clients about which sequences of behaviour need to be increased in frequency and/or strength and direction, and what sequences can be decreased in these ways. A further question is: what new *skills* would be required in order for the client to behave otherwise?

The need for flexibility is always stressed in chapters on assessment in social work textbooks. While it is a matter of common sense that assessment procedures that are rigid and forced will probably be self-defeating, there is an equal need to make them as clear and specific as possible. Our main concerns here should be to produce clear *formulations* of problems – to try to put together a concise summary of how problems have developed and what might be maintaining them. These accounts do not have to contain 'established truth', just a coherent, 'best available' view that is potentially testable in practice. A good formulation leads to clear *hypotheses* about what might affect the problems under review – it should be the sort of statement that can be easily checked up on. The sentence 'Mr Brown's low level of self-esteem is due to poor ego-development' contains a bad hypothesis since it is circular, and because there is little that could ever happen to disprove it. 'Mary's avoidance of people is likely to reduce if she learns how to start conversations' is better. If Mary receives help with starting conversations, begins to mix with others, and yet does not talk to them much and does not stay long in their company, then the hypothesis as it stands is probably wrong, so we know something more. Hypotheses lead to both *long-term and short-term goals.* These have ideal characteristics similar to those mentioned above. A clear goal is one which provides feedback on progress towards some specific, and at least partially pre-defined, end-state. Thus we need to tell from the objectives that we set with our clients whether our assessment policy is on the right track or not. The objective 'to improve communication in the family' has little real meaning of its own. What will family members do more of, less of, do differently, do in different combinations or in different places as a result of family communication being improved? Obviously, 'circumstances alter cases'. The point is that some pre-described state – representing whatever behavioural, cognitive and emotional factors are held to be involved – should be the target of our interventions.

This focused approach, which accounts substantially for the greater impact of cognitive-behavioural methods, also depends upon a clear sense of *priorities* being established during assessment. An earlier generation of textbooks encouraged social workers to take a very broad view of problems (Pincus and Minahan 1973). Though thought-provoking, these accounts sometimes had the side-effect of dissipating professional influence and diffusing available motivation for change. Priorities may be negotiated according to the following principles:

- that they are required by statute or departmental policy in the face of manifest risks
- that they represent central, broadly influential sets of problems
- that they are in accord with clients' views of what their troubles are
- that in the face of low morale, a fairly easy to achieve goal may influence motivation for further work.

This next stage is unique to the behavioural approach. It consists of securing a pre-intervention count of the number of problem-related items of behaviour (incidents) or of the number of occurrences of behaviour plausibly associated with an attempted resolution, and then comparing these rates with what happens under the influence of professional help. The usual forms of these comparisons are called a *single case design* (Sheldon 1995, Chapter 3; Kazi 1996). See Figure 1.2 for an example.

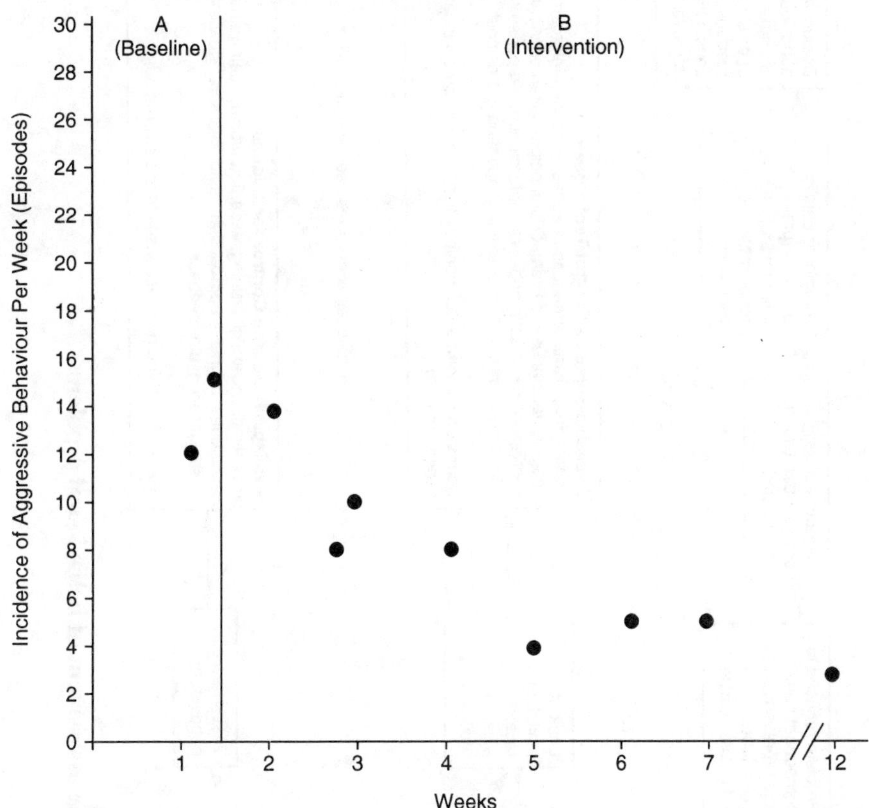

Figure 1.2 A differential reinforcement for other behaviour, plus response-cost scheme to control aggressive behaviour in a 9-year-old boy

Note: Aggressive behaviour was operationally defined as: shouting at mother or passers-by in the street; threatening mother or members of the public; swearing, pushing or throwing objects.

Source: Sheldon (1995)

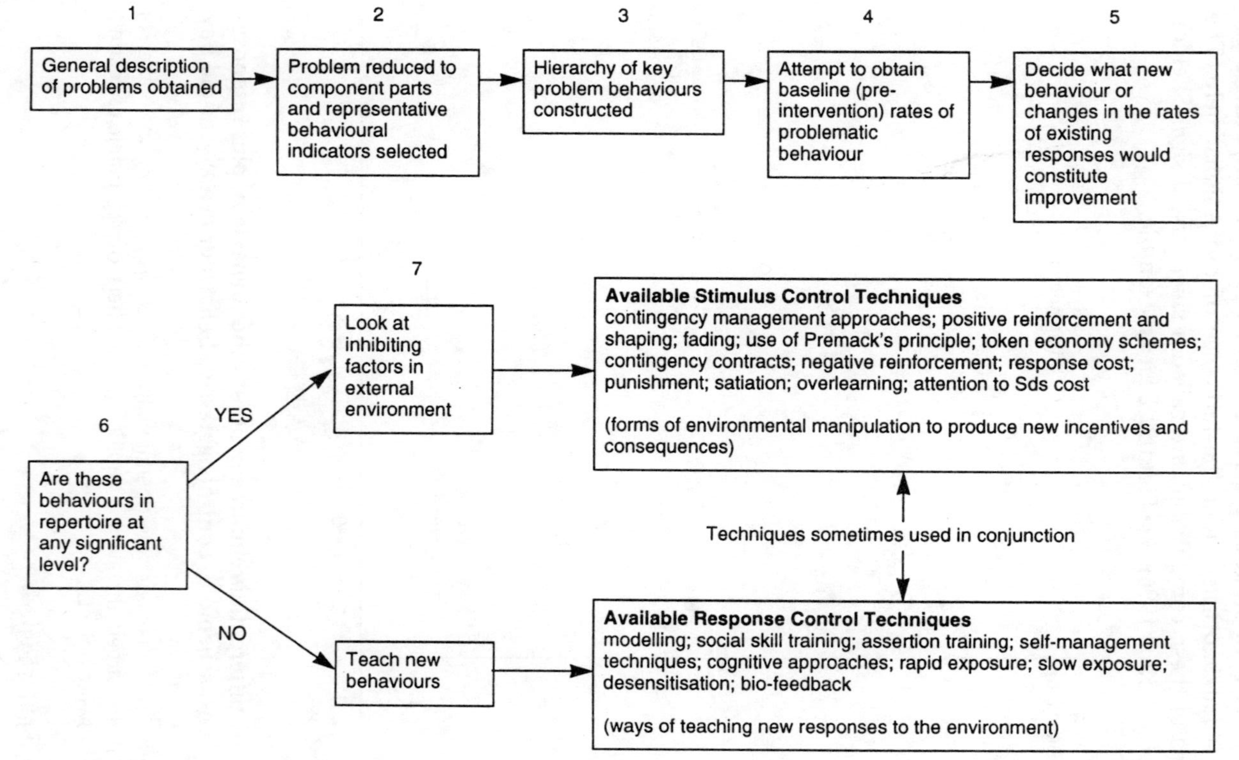

Figure 1.3 Stages in the assessment of behavioural problems

Source: Sheldon (1995)

Figure 1.3 summarises the points made in this introduction. If it looks unduly formulaic, be assured that I know well that cases rarely proceed in so neat a fashion. It is presented as an 'ideal type' flow-chart with which working realities can be compared. If a stage has to be missed, then at least with this chart in mind the fact will not be overlooked, and the issue can always be returned to later as time, urgency, risk and level of co-operation allow.

Conclusions

Well, there aren't any spectacular ones. I have tried to make a case for a greater respect for research evidence in deciding how best to help the clients who come our way or who are forced to deal with us. At present, studies strongly indicate that we should not allow our traditional therapeutic role to be further eroded, nor our concern to prevent rather than merely to contain to be further displaced. However, as regards the psychological underpinnings of these roles, we should, as a matter of urgency, replace the body of theory and research on which we have traditionally relied with a cognitive-behavioural formulation. This book contains numerous examples of what such an approach (alongside our other important functions as advocates and organisers) implies at a practical level.

Acknowledgements

My thanks are hereby extended to Sue Bosley, Secretary in the Centre for Evidence-Based Social Services at the University of Exeter, for her patient help in the preparation of this chapter, and to Professor Geraldine Macdonald of the University of Bristol for her usual, helpful astringency. As editor for this chapter, Katy Cigno has resorted only infrequently to S^{Δ} communications, so my thanks to her too.

References

BABCP (British Association for Behavioural and Cognitive Psychotherapies) (1993) *Behavioural & Cognitive Psychotherapy*, Supplement 1.

Bandura, A. (1969) *Principles of Behavior Modification*, New York: Holt, Rinehart & Winston.

Bandura, A. (1977) *Social Learning Theory*, Englewood Cliffs, NJ: Prentice-Hall.

Bartlett, K. (1950) *Remembering*, Cambridge: Cambridge Psychological Library.
Beamish, P., Lanello, L.L.P.F., Granello, D.H., McSteen, P. et al. (1996) 'Outcome studies in the treatment of panic disorder: A review', *Journal of Counseling and Development* ,Vol. 74, pp.460–7.
Beck, A.T. (1976) *Cognitive Therapy and the Emotional Disorders*, New York: International Universities Press.
Bergin, A.E. and Garfield, S.L. (1994) *Handbook of Psychotherapy and Behavior Change* (4th edn) Chichester: John Wiley.
Birchwood, M. and Tarrier, N. (eds) (1992) *Innovations in the Psychological Management of Schizophrenia: Assessment, Treatment and Services*, Chichester: John Wiley.
Blackburn, I.M., Bishop, S., Glen, I., Whalley, L.J. and Christie, J.E. (1981) 'The efficacy of cognitive therapy in depression', *British Journal of Psychiatry*, 137, pp.181–9.
Brown, M. and McCulloch, I. (1975) *Social Workers' Use of Research*, Clearing House for Social Services Research, University of Birmingham.
Brown, R. (1986) *Social Psychology* (2nd edn) New York: Free Press.
Cobb, R. (1997) *The End of the Line*, London: John Murray.
Cover-Jones, M. (1924) 'A laboratory study of fear: The case of Peter', *Pedagogical Seminary*, 31, pp.308–75.
Dennett, D.C. (1991) *Consciousness Explained*, London: Allen Lane.
Dennett, D.C. (1996) *Kinds of Minds: Towards an Understanding of Consciousness*, London: Wiedenfield and Nicolson.
Dobson, K. (1989) 'A meta-analysis of the efficacy of cognitive therapy for depression', *Journal of Consulting and Clinical Psychology*, 57, pp.414–19.
Donaldson, M. (1978) *Children's Minds*, London: Fontana Press.
Eysenck, H.J. (1965) *Fact and Fiction in Psychology*, Harmondsworth: Penguin.
Eysenck, M. and Keane, M.T. (1990) *Cognitive Psychology*, London: Lawrence Erlbaum Associates.
Falloon, I.R.H. and Coverdale, J.H. (1994) 'Cognitive-behavioural interventions for major mental disorders', *Behavioural Change*, II, pp.213–22.
Falloon, I.R.H., Boyd, J.L. and McGill, C.W. (1984) *Family Care of Schizophrenia*, New York: Guilford Press.
Ferster, C.B. and Skinner, B.F. (1957) *Schedules of Reinforcement*, New York: Appleton-Century Crofts.
Feske, U. and Chambers, D. (1995) 'Cognitive-behavioural versus exposure-only treatment for social phobia: A meta-analysis', *Behaviour Therapy*, 26, pp.695–720.
Fischer, J. (1973) 'Is casework effective? A review', *Social Work*, 1, pp.5–20.
Fischer, J. (1976) *The Effectiveness of Social Casework*, Springfield, IL: Charles C. Thomas.
Fischer, J. and Corcoran, K. (1994) *Measures for Clinical Practice*, Vols I and II, London: Free Press.
Fisher, N. (1996) 'Pilot study on the use of research by child protection workers', University of Sheffield.
Fraser, M.W., Pecora, P.J. and Haapala, D.A. (1991) *Families in Crisis: The Impact of Intensive Family Preservation Services*, New York: Aldine de Gruyter.
Gibbs, L.E. (1991) *Scientific Reasoning for Social Workers: Bridging the Gap between Research and Practice*, New York: Macmillan.
Gilbert, P. (1992) *Depression: The Evolution of Powerlessness*, London: Lawrence Erlbaum Associates.

Gottesman, I.I. (1991) *Schizophrenia Genesis: The Origins of Madness*, New York: Freeman.
Gough, D.A. (1993) *Child abuse interventions: A review of the research literature*, London: HMSO/University of Glasgow Public Health Research Unit.
Hall, J.A., Schlesinger, D.J. and Dinees, J.P. (1997) 'Social skills training in groups with developmentally disabled adults', *Research on Social Work Practice*, 7, pp.187–201.
Harris, P. (1972) in K. Connolly (ed.) *Psychology Survey*, Vol. 2, London: George Allen & Unwin.
Hollon, D., Shelton, R.C. and Loosen, P.T. (1991) 'Cognitive therapy and pharmacotherapy for depression', *Journal of Consulting and Clinical Psychology*, 59, pp. 88–99.
Hutton, W. (1995) *The State We're In*, London: Vintage.
Jordan, W. (1996) 'Social Work and Society' in M. Davies (ed.) *The Blackwell Companion to Social Work*, Oxford: Blackwell.
Joseph, S., Williams, R. and Yule, W. (1995) 'Psycho-social perspectives on post-traumatic stress', *Clinical Psychology Review*, 15, pp.515–44.
Kavanagh, D.J. (1992) 'Recent developments in expressed emotion and schizophrenia,' *British Journal of Psychiatry*, 160, pp.601–20.
Kazdin, A.E. (1994) 'Anti-social behaviour and conduct disorder' in L.W. Craighead, E.W. Craighead, A.E. Kazdin and M.K. Mahoney, *Cognitive and Behavioral Intervention: An Empirical Approach to Mental Health Problems*, Cambridge, MA: Allyn and Bacon.
Kazi, M. and Wilson, J.T. (1996) 'Applying single-case evaluation methodology in a British social work agency', *Research on Social Work Practice*, 6, pp.5–26.
Laing, R.D. (1960) *The Divided Self*, Harmondsworth: Penguin.
Laing, R.D. (1970) *Knots*, Harmondsworth: Penguin.
Lehrman, L.J. (1949) 'Success and failure of treatment of children in child guidance clinics of the Jewish Board of Guardians', *Research Monographs I*, New York: Jewish Board of Guardians.
Lewinsohn, P.M., Steinmetz, J.L., Larson, D.W. and Franklin, J.L. (1981) 'Depression-related cognitions: Antecedent or consequence?', *Journal of Abnormal Psychology*, 90, pp.213–19.
Macdonald, G.M. (1996) 'Evaluating the effectiveness of social intervention', in A. Oakley and H. Roberts (eds) *Evaluating Social Intervention*, Barkingside: SSRU/Barnardos.
Macdonald, G.M. and Sheldon, B. (1992) 'Contemporary studies of the effectiveness of social work', *British Journal of Social Work*, 22, pp.615–43.
Macdonald, G.M. and Roberts, H. (1995) *What Works in the Early Years?*, Barkingside: Barnardos.
Masserman, J.H. (1943) *Behaviour and Neurosis*, Chicago IL: University of Chicago Press.
Mathews, A.M., Gelder, G.G. and Johnson, D.W. (1981) *Agoraphobia: Nature and Treatment*, London: Tavistock.
Milgram, S. (1974) *Obedience to Authority*, London: Tavistock.
Mullen, E.J. and Dumpson, J.R. (eds) (1972) *The Evaluation of Social Intervention*, San Francisco, CA: Jossey-Bass.
Olds, J. (1956) 'Pleasure center in the brain', *Scientific American* 195, pp.105–16.
Pavlov, I.P. (1897) *Lectures on Conditioned Reflexes* (trans. W.H. Gannt, 1928), Moscow: International.

Peterson, C., Maier, S.F. and Seligman, E.P. (1993) *Learned Helplessness: A Theory for the Age of Personal Control*, New York and Oxford: Oxford University Press.

Pincus, A. and Minahan, A. (1973) *Social Work Practice: Model and Method*, Hasca, IL: Peacock.

Reid, W.J. (1994) 'The empirical practice movement', *Social Service Review*, June, pp.65–184.

Reid, W.J. and Hanrahan, P. (1981) 'The effectiveness of social work: Recent evidence' in E.M. Goldberg and N. Connolly (eds) *Evaluative Research in Social Care*, London: Heinemann Educational Books.

Richmond, M. (1917) *Social Diagnosis*, New York: Russell Sage Foundation.

Scott, M. (1989) *A Cognitive-behavioural Approach to Clients' Problems*, London: Tavistock.

Seligman, M.E.P. (1971) 'Phobias and preparedness', *Behaviour Therapy*, 2, pp.1–22.

Seligman, M.E.P. (1975) *Helplessness*, San Francisco, CA: Freeman.

Shanks, D.R. (1995) *The Psychology of Associative Learning*, Problems in the Behavioural Sciences Series, Cambridge: Cambridge University Press.

Sheldon, B. (1978) 'Theory and practice in social work: A re-examination of a tenuous relationship', *British Journal of Social Work*, 8, pp.1–22.

Sheldon, B. (1987) 'The psychology of incompetence', in G. Drewry, B. Martin and B. Sheldon (eds), *After Beckford: Essays on the Theme of Child Abuse*, Egham: Royal Holloway and Bedford New College.

Sheldon, B. (1994) 'Biological and social factors in mental disorders: implications for services', *International Journal of Social Psychiatry*, 40, pp.87–105

Sheldon, B. (1995) *Cognitive-behavioural Therapy: Research, Practice and Philosophy*, London and New York: Routledge.

Sheldon, B. and Macdonald, G.M. (1996) *The Sutton Sponsored Day-care Project* (available from the Centre for Evidence-Based Social Services, University of Exeter).

Shenger-Kristovnikova, N.R. (1921) 'Contributions to the question of differentiation of visual stimuli and the limits of differentiation by the visual analyser of the dog', *Bulletin of the Institute of Science*, Leshaft 3.

Skinner, B.F. (1953) *Science and Human Behaviour*, London: Collier Macmillan.

Skinner, B.F. (1971) *Beyond Freedom and Dignity*, Harmondsworth: Penguin.

Solomon, S.D., Gerrity, E.T. and Muff, A.N. (1992) 'Efficacy of treatments for post-traumatic stress disorder: An empirical review', *Journal of the American Medical Association*, 268, p.6,338.

Stuart, S. and Bowers, W. (1995) 'Cognitive therapy with in-patients: Review and meta-analysis', *Journal of Cognitive Psychotherapy*, 9, pp.85–92.

Stuart, S. and Thase, N. (1994) 'In-patient applications of cognitive-behavioral therapy: A review of recent developments', *Journal of Psychotherapy Practice and Research*, 3, pp.284–99.

Thoburn, J., Lewis, A. and Shemmings, D. (1995) *Paternalism* or *Partnership? Family Involvement in the Child Protection Process*, Studies in Child Protection, London: HMSO.

Thorndike, E.L. (1898) 'Animal intelligence: An experimental study of the associative processes in animals', *Psychological Review*, Monograph 2.

Watson, J.B. and Rayner, R. (1920) 'Conditioned emotional reactions', *Journal of Experimental Psychology*, 3, pp.1–14.

2 Direct clinical work with children

Tammie Ronen

Social workers are involved primarily with the child's environment, and only rarely do they intervene directly with children. This chapter highlights the importance of direct therapy with children, emphasising the unique considerations necessary for this work, and the suitability of the social worker for this mode of intervention. Cognitive-behavioural therapy as a direct intervention with children aims to train children in applying skills in order to achieve and maintain change and to generalise treatment outcomes, thus promoting emotional adjustment; in other words, the aim is to facilitate children learning to help themselves. The efficacy of cognitive-behavioural treatments for children is presented, and a self-control model is proposed for directly assessing and treating children's disorders.

Children encompass more than half of the referrals to educational and social welfare services (Kazdin 1988), whether the child is a victim or outcome of environmental processes, is part of a systemic problem in the family or school, or is the immediate source of the problem (Ronen 1997a and 1997b). Yet social workers are hesitant about treating a child directly, perhaps due to their systemic perspective that accentuates a view of the child as part of the family ecology rather than as a separate entity.

Indeed, the rapid and constant fluctuations characterising infants, children and young people, as well as their dependence on adults, render them vulnerable and sensitive to environmental vicissitudes (Kazdin 1988) and to dangerous circumstances that may adversely affect their physical or emotional development (McMahon and Peters 1985). Furthermore, many of children's achievements during development, such as sex roles, expectancies and language skills, are enhanced and maintained by the environment (Bandura and Walters 1963). However, children's simple observations and imitations of the environment are an inadequate foundation for maturation;

children must also be directly trained in specific skills, and taught to modify thoughts and emotional responses. These learning processes ensue during normal child development, yet when difficulties and disruptions arise, interventions with the environment may not suffice, and children may require direct treatment, especially regarding negative affects or traumatic experiences which have a potentially significant impact on children's personality development (Gillis 1993).

Several assumptions underlie the feasibility, desirability and usefulness of direct treatments for children:

- Social learning is necessary for child development. Many roles and behaviours, such as language acquisition, toileting habits and sex roles, are learned by observation, imitation and modelling (Bandura and Walters 1963). Therefore, many childhood disorders could be corrected through training the significant others in the child's environment, for example modifying the child's disruptions in the classroom by counselling teachers (Hughes 1993), or decreasing conduct disorders, sleep disorders or enuresis by training parents (Kazdin 1991; Ronen 1993). Social workers' major involvement in working to change the child's environment or placing the child in different environments is based on this assumption.
- Social learning, although necessary, is only one aspect of child development with implications for direct treatment: intellectual and affective domains have an equally significant impact. The child's cognitive and emotional development enables children to acquire new skills, identify internal cues, process new information, and link new learning to previous experiences, as well as enhance their ability to identify, understand and express those internal events (Harris and Saarni 1989; see also 'vicarious learning and modelling' in Chapter 1). Cognitions and emotions are private events which belong to the child, and can only be known and identified through personal interviews or first-hand observations of the child.
- The two assumptions above pinpoint the fact that many disorders are not acquired through the environment, but rather are related to a lack of skills, cognitive distortions and emotional disturbances. These should be treated not via the child's environment, but via direct training of the child (Kendall 1993).
- Children, young as they are, are human beings who deserve direct intervention. They can and should be active participants rather than passive receptors in the change process (Ronen 1992).
- It is possible to treat even very young children as long as the therapist is capable of adapting the intervention's language, metaphors, tempo

and techniques to the child's pace as well as to the child's cognitive and developmental variables (Knell 1993; Ronen 1992 and 1995a).

I shall go on to describe direct therapy with children, focusing on cognitive-behavioural practice. A self-control model suited to social workers' skills and creative ingenuity will be presented. The following case exemplifies traditional social work practice in comparison with the need for direct intervention.

The case of 'Lee': Abuse and adoption

Lee (a pseudonym) was 8 years old, and had been adopted for one year when her adoptive parents began attending a parent counselling group under my supervision. Her biological mother had died when Lee was 5, after an extended period of heavy drug abuse. The following two years of living with her biological father were characterised by Lee's sudden mood changes and regressive behaviours such as crying, diurnal bedwetting, hitting her friends and vomiting.

Social services discovered that Lee was being sexually abused by her father. At the time of this revelation, Lee was interviewed by social workers, who facilitated her talking about what had happened to her. Lee was placed in a foster home while her father was charged, and she was helped to testify against him in court. Several months later, Lee's father was sentenced to prison, and she was put up for adoption. Her adoptive parents did not know how to deal with her anger and negativity; they felt helpless when she constantly rebelled and refused to accept their demonstrations of love. They decided to seek help, and came to me for consultation.

Encountering Lee's case, traditional social work might focus on three major interventional approaches:

- working with Lee's biological father in order to decrease abuse and teach him anger control, relaxation and assertiveness skills (Kinney et al. 1991)
- placing Lee in a new environment with the hope that this change would 'do the job' (Wolfe 1988)
- involving the adoptive parents in a parent training programme to enhance parental competence and reduce stress (Berry 1988; Gambrill 1995b; Kelly 1983).

Let us examine each of these approaches in terms of the help they could offer Lee.

There is no doubt that Lee's biological father could benefit from therapy. He has abused his child, lacks social skills, and has aggressive tendencies. His history shows a failure to maintain any one job and support the family. Intervention could help his rehabilitation and change his life in the future, after leaving prison. However, there is no way to erase the damage he has already caused Lee. Therapy, if successful, might enable him to build a new family and reduce situational stress and future risk (Wolf 1988), but it would not solve Lee's distress.

Placing Lee in a new home was necessary. She needed to be safeguarded and protected, and she deserved to be given the basic social and psychological necessities of life, such as food, affection, medical care, education and intellectual and social stimulation (Garbarino 1982; Garbarino et al. 1991) to promote her well-being in the present and the future. There is a good chance that at some time in the future, the warmth and love with which she is surrounded could diminish her anger and frustration, allowing her to develop a full, rich, normal life. However, at present she is too bitter and too damaged to appreciate the new family and resources available to her. Therefore, changing the environment is important, but by itself is insufficient for solving her problems.

Counselling Lee's parents is vital for two main reasons. First, the parents who happily agreed to adopt an older child now feel frustrated and helpless in their inability to change Lee's terrible experiences through love. They need help for themselves now in dealing with those feelings. Second, the parents need to acquire skills for educating Lee consistently, to reinforce her social and positive behaviours on the one hand, and to extinguish her manipulative behaviours on the other. Having the skills to deal with her would help them cope with and change some of Lee's problems. However, they are parents and not therapists, and cannot cope with the emotional damage Lee's biological parents caused her, especially in the light of the fact that her previous experiences are frightening and foreign to them. Thus in all probability the family atmosphere might help 'cure' some aspects of Lee's behaviour, but her negative emotions and traumatic memories would not just disappear without direct intervention.

All three modes of social work intervention are important and can contribute to some facet of change. However, children who have experienced traumatic events combined with feelings of guilt and anger cannot so easily overcome these (Germain 1979). If the social workers involved in Lee's case concentrate on interventions in the environment, who can help Lee learn to live with her past traumas? Who will help her achieve a basic sense of confidence and a feeling of safeness in her new family? Who will teach her to trust and express love? How will she get rid of her guilt feelings, believing that she is the one 'responsible' for her father's prison sentence? Who will help her understand that it is not her fault, she has done nothing of which to be ashamed, and that as a child it was not her responsibility? Who can make sure that her experiences do not develop into negative, rigid thoughts about the world?

Direct intervention with children is often the treatment of choice, the most effective intervention, or in many cases, an integral part of an effective intervention programme. Counselling, supervising and preparing the child's environment – traditional foci of the social worker – cannot substitute for the child's need for individual treatment in order to acquire skills, methods and lifestyles that will facilitate adjustment to that environment. Yet children and family social workers often arrange placement in appropriate settings such as foster homes, day care centres, afternoon clubs and so on, or else work with the child's immediate environment such as parents, teachers or other caretakers. Only rarely do they find themselves engaged in direct clinical intervention or primary prevention with children (Ronen 1994a and 1994b).

I propose that social workers' practice theory, approach and their role in the community make them eminently qualified for direct child intervention, and that cognitive-behavioural therapy is an appropriate, feasible and exciting approach that the social worker can use with children, as long as he or she becomes conversant with some basic tenets and techniques.

Unique considerations in direct treatment of children

The fact that the cognitive-behavioural approach underscores the relationship between the person and the environment and that the child's natural environment is the family means that whenever a child is involved, the family will also be involved in treatment, even if the problem is in school or with peers. Consequently, direct therapy with children exposes the whole family, but especially the child, the parents and the therapist, to complex considerations and processes.

The parents might be intimidated by the treatment process, fearing what might transpire between the therapist and their child, and how it might influence their relationship with the child.

For the child, therapy is perplexing because of motivational factors and discrepancies between the therapist and the parents. Children are usually referred to treatment without their consent or against their own will, on the initiative of significant adults in their environment (Kendall and Braswell 1985), thus complicating the issue of motivation. Many children evidence an external locus of control (see Chapter 5), attributing their problems to the environment, not themselves. They may find the therapeutic encounter insulting, inconvenient and wearisome.

The therapist may present different or even contradictory opinions and attitudes and a different demeanour and educational style from that of the parents. Being exposed to the therapist for one hour weekly in contrast to the parental influence 24 hours a day can be very confusing.

Unlike adult therapy, children's treatment is complicated for the therapist in the sense that it often produces more than one client in the family, each having different goals. Parents may wish for one kind of change while the child desires another, and the therapist needs to manoeuvre between the parents' and the child's own goals (and perhaps the goals of other children present in the family). Individual direct treatment of children also entails a unique interplay of knowledge, skills and creative aptitudes in the therapist.

Skills and knowledge are crucial components in implementing effective techniques to ameliorate specific childhood disorders in settings involving the child, the parents and the environment. Yet the therapist also needs to legitimise the use of his or her own artistic, creative and flexible qualities which provide important means for adapting a complicated, rational cognitive model to even very young children who still think concretely and irrationally. Creative methods can be learned to adapt the intervention's language, metaphors and techniques to the child's day-to-day experiences effectively. Unlike adult therapy, child therapy necessitates the ability to activate the child's motivation, curiosity and interest in order for the child to remain in therapy, comply and co-operate (Ronen 1994a).

Social workers often work with children who are at significant crossroads in their lives. At times of crisis, this may necessitate traumatic changes such as removal from the home or placement in foster care, or during acute phases, placement in institutional care. At these times of upheaval, social workers must act quickly and efficiently; they therefore often feel it impossible to consider helping children work through their difficult feelings via direct therapy. Professionals may themselves feel overwhelmed and frightened by the prospect of delving deeper into the child's turbulent emotions, and may retreat to the relative comfort of bureaucratic tasks and familiar duties. Yet in view of the unique role of social workers in the community, those who use therapeutic techniques such as those described in this chapter can make a genuine contribution to the lives of children in need.

The suitability of the social worker to conduct direct treatment of children

Therapists who treat children must be aware not only of each particular child's needs and the best way to treat that child in the clinical setting, but also of the child's natural environment and its part in causing and maintaining the problem, emphasising the appropriateness of social workers assuming the role of direct therapists for children.

Three main challenges face social workers who wish to become involved in direct therapy with children:

- identifying children at risk
- mobilising the child's motivation and agreement to participate in the therapeutic process
- facilitating the child applying and practising appropriate techniques needed for change.

All three of these challenges suggest the suitability of social workers for direct child treatment.

Most professionals such as psychologists and counsellors treat referred children in their offices. Field social workers, being part of the client's natural environment, emphasise the importance of out-reach methods, and are able to pinpoint not only people who overtly wish to be helped, but also those people who are in need but may not have turned to professionals for assistance, such as children with acting-out problems (for example, disorders concerning obedience, aggression and negativism) before they reach the level of disruptiveness that usually serves as an impetus for referral. Furthermore, social workers in the community may be well placed to identify children with acting-in disorders (depression, anxiety, regression and withdrawal) who are in need of therapy but who do not disturb others (Achenbach 1993; Mash and Terdal 1988). It is difficult to identify internalising children at risk or in need who do not refer themselves, due to the insensitivity of their environment to their problems. These children, who often harm themselves and face a risk to their normal, safe development, could be identified by social workers through direct observation and teacher and counsellor contact, and through direct observations of children in their natural environments, such as the home or school.

In order to foster the child's agreement and motivation for change, there is a need to become familiar with the child's interests, hobbies, language, habits and culture. The social worker is already familiar with the child's natural environment, thus facilitating the process of approaching and communicating with the child (Ronen 1995b). Moreover, in order to help the child apply and practise the necessary techniques, there is a need to mobilise the co-operation of the child, the family and the teacher. Knowing the child's significant others makes it easier for the social worker to reinforce the child, as well as to try to achieve a better and closer relationship which can facilitate the therapeutic alliance, preparing the ground for an effective process of helping the child to change.

In addition to their roles as teachers, educators, mediators, change agents and counsellors, social workers should also adopt the additional role of psychotherapists who conduct direct therapy with children. Being a cognitive-behavioural therapist necessitates dynamic and creative thinking, since no single correct strategy or interventional technique exists for treating the variety of clients encountered in social work (Ronen 1995a). This flexibility characterises the social worker, who faces the constant need to make decisions regarding the adaptation of available techniques to particular client-related factors (such as the individual circumstances and characteristics of the client and his or her specific problem) and therapist-related factors (such as the service setting and the therapist's abilities, knowledge and skills). Direct cognitive-behavioural therapy has most likely gained a prominent position in clinical social work because of its pertinence to social work concepts, objectives, ethics and intervention methods. Social work as a profession is founded on the notion that theoretical knowledge can be translated into skills and practical know-how with clear, concrete and well-defined targets for change (Gambrill 1995a; Schinken 1981).

Cognitive-behavioural therapy for direct intervention with children

Cognitive-behavioural therapy with children derives from traditional behaviour therapy with adults, in conjunction with cognitive components that have been adapted to the unique needs of children. This therapeutic mode is recognised as fitting for social workers due to its focus on action and change and its examination of the child's behaviour, emotions and thinking style in the light of his or her strengths, weaknesses and goals (Ronen 1997a and 1997b). Cognitive-behavioural theoreticians and therapists are guided by several main principles (Kendall and Braswell 1985):

- Cognitive mediational processes are involved in human learning
- Thoughts, feelings and behaviours are causally interrelated

- Cognitive activities such as expectations, self-statements and attributions are important in understanding and predicting psychopathology and psychotherapeutic change
- Cognitions and behaviours are compatible. Cognitive processes can be interpreted into behavioural paradigms, and cognitive techniques can be combined with behavioural procedures
- The task of the cognitive-behavioural therapist is to collaborate with the client to assess distorted or deficient cognitive processes and behaviours, and to design new learning experiences to remediate the dysfunctional or deficient cognitions, behaviours and affective patterns.

Cognitive therapy with children stems directly from behavioural therapy, and is highly rooted in Bandura's (1977) theory about the role of expectancies in learning and the capacity for expectancies to be successfully conditioned in therapy. In addition, cognitive child therapy derives from other theoreticians' conceptualisations about cognitive therapy with adults. Unlike adult cognitive therapy, however, which involves the rational modification of thoughts, the cognitive treatment of children requires more teaching of skills and applying of techniques.

Three broad theoretical assumptions underlie cognitive-behavioural therapy approaches and their adaptation to children:

- A person's thoughts, images, perceptions and other cognitive mediating events are presumed to affect behaviour (Beck et al. 1979). Cognitive-behavioural therapy with children recognises the influences and interdependencies of cognitive, affective, social, developmental, biological and behavioural factors in the aetiology and remediation of emotional and personal problems
- Individuals are active participants in their own learning. Active participation comprises an important step towards mobilising the child's motivation and empowerment. A therapeutic method may need to be adapted so that the child can actively participate and develop new cognitive processes
- It is accepted that the utility of cognitive constructs in efforts towards behaviour change must be demonstrated empirically.

Cognitive-behavioural therapy for children consists of a variety of techniques in which children are taught to use cognitive mediational strategies to guide their behaviour and thus improve their adjustment (Durlak et al. 1991). This therapeutic approach pinpoints cognitive deficits, and helps children to develop needed skills within a treatment model that directly links assessment, intervention and evaluation. Therapy is an ongoing and self-evaluating process of assessment, facilitating a process of self-therapy while accentuating the maintenance and generalisation of learned skills to the child's external environment.

Self-control as a main target in child therapy

Direct treatment of children has four main objectives:

- To decrease behaviours which children present too often and which disturb children as well as their environment (such as disobedience, negativism, impulsiveness, aggressiveness)
- To increase behaviours which children do not present enough (such as social skills, assertiveness, shyness, self-esteem, self-confidence)
- To remove anxieties which cause avoidance disorders (such as social fears, fear of authority, fear of separation)
- To facilitate developmental processes (such as enhancing children's language, self-confidence, flexibility).

These four aims aptly combine into the metaphor of a person trying to tune a radio. First one reviews the alternative stations, selecting the programme best suited to one's mood and personal tastes. The volume then needs to be changed for different kinds of programmes: music necessitates a different volume than does talking or a news report, and some music is preferably played loudly while other melodies sound better played softly. Occasionally, a change in programming or the onset of static requires switching channels or fine tuning. Flexibility and a continual readiness for change are needed as required.

Children are not machines and cannot be manipulated in the same way as a radio, but our objectives in child therapy in general coincide with this metaphor. We aim to enable children to become flexible and able to adapt themselves to changing situations and social demands. In other words, children should become able to develop and maintain the ability to direct themselves and demonstrate self-control.

Self-control is conceived as a person's flexible ability to consider actions, make decisions and select the best means for achieving their goals (Kanfer 1977; Rosenbaum 1993; Thoresen and Mahoney 1974). There is no one way to achieve self-control, neither is there one attitude towards what self-control is or how best to achieve it. At times, being able to control oneself calls for the capacity for redressive self-control: to fight for homeostasis, to bring oneself back to routine behaviour by removing specific disruptions, and to develop the ability to overcome, cope with and change specific behaviours (Rosenbaum 1993). At other times, there is a need for reformative self-control: changing one's lifestyle, dislodging poor habits, planning, using problem-solving skills and delaying immediate temptation (Rosenbaum 1993). Both redressive and reformative self-control require cognitive skills to change automatic behaviours into mediated ones using cognitive techniques such as self-talk, relaxation, delaying temptation, and so on. These two actions (redressive and reformative) are consonant with the first two objectives of child therapy – increasing or decreasing behaviour, or using these two objectives to alter lifestyle – in other words, changing the radio's volume, or looking for the right station.

At other times, being able to control oneself means completely abandoning one's habitual, favourite radio stations and looking for new and unfamiliar programmes: in other words, being able to let go of control, focus on emotions and experience, and accept one's behaviour through experiential self-control (Rosenbaum 1993). This coincides with the third and fourth objectives in child therapy – removing anxiety, and facilitating developmental process. For experiential self-control, cognitive skills should be meaningfully and mindfully put aside, and exposure should be the focus of behaviour, with an emphasis on learning to accept, enhance, feel and live with the problem in order to try to resolve or change it. All of these redressive, reformative and experiential skill components belong to the same frame of reference, which is so important in child-rearing and education: being able to achieve self-control.

Self-control is a process which occurs when, in the relative absence of immediate external constraints, a person engages in a mode of behaviour that had previously been less probable than alternative available modes of behaviour (Thoresen and Mahoney 1974). Self-control can therefore be perceived both as a target in child therapy and as the cause of many forms of problematic behaviour. Children develop self-control skills in interaction with their environment as they grow. Particularly important is the development of speech. Luria (1961) described control of behaviour as shifting from being directed by others' talk to the development of self-talk aloud, and then finally to the capacity for silent self-talk. Mischel (1974) suggested that the evolution of self-control resulted in the ability to inhibit impulsive responses.

The cognitive process of self-control involves several steps:

- The ability to notice a disruption in one's habitual (automatic, unmediated) way of thinking (Bandura 1977)
- The evaluation of the disruption as important for one's well-being (Rosenbaum 1993)
- The expectation that a specific course of action will lead to the desired outcomes

- The belief that there is a possibility for self-change (Bandura 1977).

Returning to the radio metaphor, most self-control training programmes have been directed towards teaching children to lower the volume of the radio and learn to listen quietly (to decrease the frequency of unwanted behaviour, and to think more slowly and calmly). Self-control therapy has been applied, for example, to different acting-out disorders such as impulsiveness and hyperactivity (Kendall and Braswell 1985), aggression (Kazdin 1991) and disobedience and disruptiveness problems (Gross and Drabman 1982). Far fewer attempts have been made to administer self-control interventions to internalised children, such as those suffering from depression (Reynolds and Coats 1986) or fears and anxieties (Barrios and Hartman 1988), despite the great need to help such children expand their range of experiences, allow themselves to feel new emotions and learn to live with these emotions rather than constantly trying to overcome them.

The targets of self-control interventions have included interpersonal thinking, means–ends thinking, planning and anticipating skills, self-instruction, coping with stress, inhibiting responses, self-reinforcement and the use of problem-solving methods (Kazdin 1988). One of the earliest models of self-control was developed by Kanfer (1977) and comprised three components: self-monitoring, self-evaluation and self-reinforcement (Kanfer and Schefft 1988).

Self-control model for direct intervention with children

Based on the belief that children can be equal, active partners in direct therapy, and emphasising children's ability to learn, change and direct their own behaviour, I have developed a self-control model which was first applied in treating enuresis (Ronen and Wozner 1995; Ronen et al. 1992) and was later adapted to different problems and modes of intervention (Ronen 1995b) and to settings including adoption, special education institutions, enuresis and violent behaviour.

The self-control model consists of five phases. Each phase involves three main components: learning, practising and application.

The *learning* component consists of teaching children concepts relating to their misconceptions, the processes involved in the occurrence of their problems, mediated and unmediated thinking, and techniques for changing behaviour.

The *practising* component includes exercises that are performed in the intervention setting, plus home assignments. Practice is directed towards helping the child use different self-control techniques in different areas of his or her life, such as learning to identify his or her thoughts and emotional states, monitoring, recording, evaluating, and using self-talk and self-reinforcement.

The *application* component integrates the newly acquired knowledge with the practised techniques. Throughout the whole process of change, the child is perceived as a scientist whose objective is to learn how he or she behaves and how to acquire knowledge in order to change. By emphasising the child's role as an architect, a focus is placed on children's ability to reconstruct and construe their own behaviour (Mahoney 1991). The role of the therapist is to be the child's supervisor, to suggest ways of practising and learning, and to direct the child in the self-help process. Each of the five phases of the self-control model addresses one main target, and techniques towards achieving it.

Phase 1

The first target consists of changing children's misconceptions. The objective is to teach children that the disturbing problem is a behaviour that can be changed if they learn how. Modification of misconceptions is achieved by redefinition and cognitive structuring. Socratic questions and paradoxical examples are used to help children understand that the problem is not a matter of bad luck or illness, but rather is a function of motivation and willpower.

Phase 2

The second target is rational analysis of the behaviour. Children are taught to understand how the identified problem developed. They learn about the connection between their brain, body and final problematic behaviour. Treatment is accomplished by rational analysis of the process, and by helping children accept responsibility for its occurrence (Meichenbaum 1985). Written materials, pictures of the human body and verbal discussions are used. These first two targets are a necessary part of every behaviour change, but are especially important while focusing on the need to address specific, concrete change (redressive disorders) or habitual behaviours (reformative disorders).

Phase 3

The third phase targets the ability to increase awareness of internal stimuli. It is directed towards developing sensitivity in general, and sensitivity to internal stimuli related to the specific problem in particular. Sensitivity is increased to stimuli in general (for example, 'listening' to one's body, trying to concentrate on where and what one feels), and to the internal cues concerning the specific problem in particular. Relaxation, concentration and self-monitoring help in achieving these targets. The third phase is important in every process of change, focusing as it does on developing awareness, but is of most importance when dealing with experiential disorders, such as avoidance disorders, and with children who are over-controlled and afraid of letting go.

Phase 4

The fourth phase targets the specific techniques for self-control by teaching children how to change automatic modes of behaviour to mediated ones. Children are trained in physical exercises, such as choosing to continue to run despite fatigue, as well as in emotional exercises, such as delaying gratification. The techniques used include self-monitoring, self-evaluation, self-reinforcement, problem-solving and imagination.

Phase 5

The fifth phase targets decreasing the disturbing behaviour, maintaining change and avoiding regression by training in over-learning, enhancing self-confidence and through monitoring, assessment, maintenance and working towards generalisation. This phase does not stand independently, but rather is achieved by using Kanfer's (1977) basic model, including self-monitoring, self-evaluation and self-reinforcement. A special emphasis is placed on learning generalisation skills and self-help methods to prevent the need for future therapy.

Single-case design studies, applying this self-control intervention model to children's problems such as sleep disorders and encopresis (Ronen 1993), have demonstrated promising outcomes. A controlled study was also conducted using this model to treat a sample of 77 children aged 7½–12 years with nocturnal enuresis (Ronen et al. 1992). In the enuresis study, the children were randomly assigned to one of four groups – bell and pad, token economy, self-control intervention, or a control group. The outcome revealed a similar success rate for each of the treatment models. However, for the self-control group only, we found an immediate rate of decline in enuresis, a low drop-out rate throughout the intervention, and a low relapse level in comparison with the bell and pad and token economy groups. The cognitive component clearly contributed to the long-term maintenance of improvement in behaviour.

The case of 'Lee' revisited: A self-control intervention

Treating Lee was a challenge for me as a therapist, especially attempting to understand the diversity and paradoxical trends in her behaviour. On the one hand, Lee was very co-operative and, like most children her age, she enjoyed playing with dolls, loved painting and was very excited in telling me about a new song she heard. These communication modes were conducive to an interesting integration of verbal and non-verbal therapeutic processes. On the other hand, it was difficult listening to her rigid, negative verbalisations about the world, other people and the future. She sounded like an old, hard, harsh woman when she stated 'Women are stupid, but men are mean' or when she commented on pictures we were looking at, for example a picture of a lion and a rabbit: 'The lion will eat the rabbit, nothing will be left. I know that. The rabbit is going to die.' Or when she saw a picture of a man reaching his hand out to a child: 'Why doesn't he run away? This man will hit him.'

The individual, direct cognitive-behavioural treatment with Lee had several aims (Ronen 1996):

- to help Lee overcome the traumatic abuse by her father, and to help her live with it as a past trauma without it actively disturbing her life in the present and in the future
- to prepare Lee for developing a meaningful emotional relationship with her adoptive parents
- to help Lee change her rigid, negative attitudes towards the world and to learn to open up and become familiar with her emotions and accept them.

The treatment of Lee integrated all three types of self-control: *redressive,* in order to overcome the specific difficulties in everyday life such as her anger, crying and fears; *reformative,* to change her lifestyle and relationship with her adoptive parents, and *experiential,* to facilitate greater flexibility, acceptance and to enable her to be open to her internal feelings as well as external experiences. The treatment applied all five of the phases of the self-control model.

Phase 1 of the treatment aimed to change Lee's misconceptions about three different subjects. First, the therapy was directed at Lee's misconceptions about her part in being abused. Lee took the blame upon herself for 'letting her father do it', feeling guilt and shame. The second area was over-generalisation: 'If my father did that, then all fathers do that. All men are mean, I shouldn't trust men.' The third theme was her tendency to avoid positive emotion in order to protect herself from getting hurt: 'I don't want to love them. I don't want to be disappointed. I don't want them to hurt me.' Throughout this phase, she was helped to learn to identify her own cognitions.

This first treatment phase started by trying to help Lee understand that, as a child, the abuse was not her fault or responsibility: children are educated to obey parents, and she did what every other child would have done. She did nothing wrong – her father did. The therapy tried to achieve this goal through doll-playing, with a focus on understanding what the dolls felt; using creative imagination; having the safe 8-year-old Lee talking to and comforting the abused 5-year-old Lee, accepting and forgiving her, and so on. During the first weeks, Lee became angry whenever I tried to change her misconceptions, but gradually, through a process which combined Socratic questions (for example, 'do you think a 5-year-old girl is stronger than her father?' 'do you think 5-year-old children can tell their fathers how to behave?'), painting and playing, she started accepting the idea that, as a child, she had been helpless. Lee even became ready to begin talking about self-forgiveness. She reached the point where she could say: 'But I will not be helpless anymore. I am learning judo.' At this stage, we could start working towards the second phase.

During Phase 2 – rational analysis of the process – we tried to analyse the link between emotions, thoughts and behaviours, and attempted to change her automatic negative thoughts into mediated ones. This process was conducted using pictures to show how the brain commands the body, and using games commanding Lee to do things, then watching how she accomplished them. We tried to understand and explain her negative attitudes towards her adoptive parents, focusing on Lee's acting-out behaviour as an outcome of her fears of loving them and then being disappointed. We practised changing her automatic negative thoughts into mediated ones, for example taking the thought 'I shouldn't get close to them', which elicited rejection and avoidance behaviour, and transforming it to another way of thinking: 'Maybe I can try to be nice to them and see what happens.'

Phase 3 – increasing awareness to internal stimuli – focused on Lee's feelings, which she had been avoiding and ignoring. We tried to identify different kinds of emotions, such as fear, anxiety, stress and anger. At first she was not ready to talk about positive emotions, but gradually she agreed to start exercises on happiness, joy, and so on. We attempted to pinpoint the place in her body where she felt sensations (for example, her stomach when she was afraid), and the kind of sensations (contractions), and then learned that there are internal signs for every feeling. Lee drew a ladder, and pointed to the intensity of the emotion she felt by climbing the ladder. She received homework assignments to record one emotion every day, its location in the body, and its intensity.

Exercising self-control comprised Phase 4. Lee practised tasks such as using positive imagery to overcome her traumatic memories and to construct a new picture of a positive future. Relaxation before going to sleep, self-recording, self-talk and changing automatic thoughts to mediated thoughts constituted this phase of treatment.

During the fifth and final phase of using self-monitoring and self-evaluation to decrease the problem, Lee revealed the first signs of looking at herself more positively, and reinforcing and accepting herself.

Lee has not yet solved her problems. She is still occupied with her past memories, and continues to be rigid about starting a new relationship with her new family. However, she does not see the world as only a place of war and injury, and some smiles and positive emotions have broken through the clouds. The way is still long, and we have much to accomplish. In several weeks' time I plan to start working with Lee's family concerning their interaction, and at least I can say now that Lee is not suffering from post-trauma (Ronen 1996). She has started opening up, and I am optimistic about her future.

Conclusion

Direct cognitive-behavioural therapy with children is a challenging intervention for the social worker. The outcomes demonstrated up to the present are not yet conclusive, but already the possible advantages children could gain from such forms of intervention are evident. Children can learn to become able to solve their own problems, fostering their sense of empowerment; moreover, in the long run, such a treatment paradigm seems to enable children to generate other solutions, generalising the skills learned in order to prevent future problems. Direct treatment of children is an important adjunct to the other roles of social workers who act as mediators, parental consultants and social agents. By adding the role of direct intervention, social workers can help prevent future problems with children, and work towards changing their past traumatic experiences.

Direct intervention raises new questions for consideration, such as determining the best intervention mode for a specific child in the light of his or her age and developmental needs, the presented problem and the environmental conditions. Different children of different ages and socio-economic status need different kinds of interventions. By answering these questions, the efficacy of intervention would be at the centre of treatment, and would facilitate, on the one hand, a direct adaptation of adult techniques to children's needs. On the other hand, it would necessitate the development of flexibility and creativity in communicating with children and in therapeutic modes, to include painting, imagery and psychodrama.

Direct cognitive-behavioural therapy with children aims to help individuals find their own resources, learn to recognise and use their own wisdom, and discover personal methods for self-help. As social work involves working with vulnerable populations, the positive forces and empowerment strongly highlighted by cognitive-behavioural therapy constitute an important interventional goal. Instead of establishing long-term dependent relationships between therapists and clients, social workers endeavour to lead clients towards greater independence, self-trust, and capability for self-change (Ronen 1997a and 1997b).

Until recently, most therapies have been directed towards problems and how to overcome them. Adult therapy nowadays includes techniques for teaching people to be happy, opening up to experiences and letting go of problems (Mahoney 1991). Concentrating forms of intervention on opening up to experiences from an early age may contribute towards the maturation of a generation which may then improve its quality of life, enjoy new experiences and focus on happiness rather than on difficulties and sorrow.

Acknowledgement

The author would like to express her deep appreciation to Dee B. Ankonina for her editorial contribution.

References

Achenbach, T.M. (1985) *Assessment and Taxonomy of Child and Adolescent Psychopathology*, Beverly Hills, CA: Sage.

Achenbach, T.M. (1993) 'Implications of multiaxial empirically based assessment for behavior therapy with children', *Behavior Therapy*, 24, pp.91–116.

Bandura, A. (1977) 'Self efficacy: Toward a unifying theory of behavior change', *Psychological Review*, 84, pp.191–215.

Bandura, A. and Walters, R.H. (1963) *Social Learning and Personality Development*, New York: Holt, Rinehart & Winston.

Barrios, B.A. and Hartman, D.P. (1988) 'Fears and anxieties' in E.J. Mash and L.G. Terdal (eds) *Behavioral Assessment of Childhood Disorders*, New York: Guilford Press.

Beck, A.T., Rush, A.J., Shaw, B.F. and Emery, G. (1979) *Cognitive Therapy of Depression*, New York: Guilford Press.

Berry, M. (1988) 'A review of parent training programs in child welfare', *Social Service Review*, 62, pp.302–23.

Durlak, J.A., Fuhrman, T. and Lampman, C. (1991) 'Effectiveness of cognitive behavior therapy for maladaptive children: A meta analysis', *Psychological Bulletin*, 110, pp.204–14.

Gambrill, E. (1995a) 'Behavioral social work: Past, present and future', *Research on Social Work Practice*, 5, pp.460–84.

Gambrill, E. (1995b) 'Helping shy, socially anxious, and lonely adults: A skill based contextual approach' in W. O'Donohue and L. Krasner (eds) *Handbook of Psychological Skill Training: Clinical Techniques and Applications*, Boston, MA: Allyn & Bacon.

Garbarino, J. (1982) *Children and Families in the Social Environment*, Chicago, IL: Aldine.

Garbarino, J., Kostelny, K. and Dubrow, N. (1991) 'What children can tell us about living in danger', *American Psychologist*, 46, pp.376–83.

Germain, C. (1979) *Social Work Practice: People and Environment*, New York: Free Press.

Gillis, H.M. (1993) 'Individual and small group psychotherapy for children involved in trauma and disaster' in C.F. Saylor (ed.) *Children and Disaster*, New York: Plenum.

Gross, A.M. and Drabman, R.S. (1982) 'Teaching self recording, self evaluation, and self reward to non clinic children and adolescents' in P.K. Karoly and F.H. Kanfer (eds) *Self-management and Behavior Change: From Theory to Practice*, New York: Pergamon Press.

Harris, L. and Saami, C. (1989) 'Children's understanding of emotion: An introduction' in C. Saami and P.L. Harris (eds) *Children's Understanding of Emotion*, New York: Cambridge University Press.

Hughes, J.N. (1993) 'Behavior therapy' in T.R. Kratochwill and R.J. Morris (eds) *Handbook of Psychotherapy with Children and Adolescents*, Boston, MA: Allyn & Bacon.

Kanfer, F.H. (1977) 'The many faces of self control, or behavior modification changes its focus' in R.R. Stuart (ed.) *Behavioral Self-management: Strategies, Techniques and Outcomes*, New York: Brunner/Mazel.

Kanfer, F.H. and Schefft, B.K. (1988) *Guiding the Process of Therapeutic Change*, Champaign, IL: Research Press.

Kazdin, A.E. (1988) *Child Psychotherapy: Development and Identifying Effective Treatments*, New York: Pergamon Press.

Kazdin, A.E. (1991) 'Aggressive behavior and conduct disorder' in T.R. Kratochwill and R.J. Morris (eds) *The Practice of Child Therapy*, New York: Pergamon Press.

Kelly, J.A. (1983) *Treating Abusive Families: Intervention Based on Skills Training Principles*, New York: Plenum.

Kendall, P.C. (1993) 'Cognitive behavioral therapies with youth: Guiding theory, current status, and emerging developments', *Journal of Consulting and Clinical Psychology*, 61, pp.235–47.

Kendall, P.C. and Braswell, L. (1985) *Cognitive Behavior Therapy for Impulsive Children*, New York: Guilford Press.

Kinney, J., Haapala, D. and Booth, C. (1991) *Keeping Families Together: The Homebuilders Model*, New York: Aldine.

Knell, S.M. (1993) *Cognitive Behavioral Play Therapy*, Northvale, NJ: Jason Aronson.

Luria, L.A. (1961) *The Role of Speech in the Regulation of Normal and Abnormal Behavior*, New York: Liveright.

Mahoney, M. (1991) *Human Change Processes: The Scientific Foundation of Psychotherapy*, New York: HarperCollins, USA / Basic Books.

Mash, E.J. and Terdal, L.G. (1988) *Behavioral Assessment of Childhood Disorders*, New York: Guilford Press.

McMahon, R.J. and Peters, R.D. (eds) (1985) *Childhood Disorders: Behavioral Development Approaches*, New York: Brunner / Mazel.

Meichenbaum, D.H. (1985) *Stress Inoculation Training*, New York: Pergamon Press.

Mischel, W. (1974) 'Processes in delayed gratification' in L. Berkowitz (ed.) *Advances in Experimental Social Psychology*, Vol. 7, New York: Academic Press.

Patterson, G.R. (1965) 'An application of conditioning techniques to the control of a hyperactive child' in L.P. Ulmann and L. Krasner (eds) *Case Studies in Behavior Modification*, New York: Holt, Rinehart, & Winston.

Reynolds, W.M. and Coats, K.I. (1986) 'A comparison of cognitive behavioral therapy and relaxation training for the treatment of depression in adolescents', *Journal of Consulting and Clinical Psychology*, 54, pp.653–60.

Ronen, T. (1992) 'Cognitive intervention with young children', *Child Psychiatry and Human Development*, 23, pp.19–30.

Ronen, T. (1993) 'Intervention package for treating encopresis in a six year old boy', *Behavioural Psychotherapy*, 27, pp.127–35.

Ronen, T. (1994a) 'Clinical intervention with children: Challenge for the social worker', *Asia Pacific Journal of Social Work*, 4, pp.7–19.

Ronen, T. (1994b) 'Cognitive behavioural social work with children', *The British Journal of Social Work*, 24, pp.273–85.

Ronen, T. (1995a) 'From what kind of self-control can children benefit?', *The Journal of Cognitive Psychotherapy: An International Quarterly*, 9, pp.45–61.

Ronen, T. (1995b) 'The social worker as an educator for self control', *International Social Work*, 38, pp.387–99.

Ronen, T. (1996) 'Constructivist therapy with traumatised children', *The Journal of Constructivist Psychology*, 9, pp.139–56.

Ronen, T. (1997a) 'Cognitive-behavioural therapy: A dynamic model for change' in M. Davies (ed.) *The Blackwell Companion to Social Work*, Oxford: Blackwell.

Ronen, T. (1997b) *Cognitive Developmental Therapy with Children*, Chichester: John Wiley.

Ronen, T. and Wozner, Y. (1995) 'A self control intervention package for the treatment of primary nocturnal enuresis', *Child and Family Behavior Therapy*, 7, pp.1–20.

Ronen, T., Wozner, Y. and Rahav, G. (1992) 'Cognitive intervention in enuresis', *Child and Family Behavior Therapy*, 14, pp.1–14.

Rosenbaum, M. (1993) 'The three functions of self control behavior: Redressive, reformative and experiential', *Work and Stress*, 7, pp.33–46.

Rossman, B.B.R. (1992) 'School-aged children's perceptions of coping with distress: Strategies for emotion regulation and the moderation of adjustment', *Journal of Child Psychiatry*, 33, pp.1,373–97.

Schinken, S.P. (1981) *Behavioral Methods in Social Welfare*, New York: Aldine.
Thoresen, C.E. and Mahoney, M.J. (1974) *Behavioral Self-control*, New York: Holt, Rinehart & Winston.
Wolfe, D.A. (1988) 'Child abuse and neglect' in E.J. Mash and L.G. Terdal (eds) *Behavioral Assessment of Childhood Disorders*, New York: Guilford Press.

3 Intervention to protect the child

Diana Bourn

'If you don't stop swearing, I'll pour washing-up liquid down your throat' is an angry attempt by a parent to change her 4½-year-old son's defiant response to her request to tidy his toys away. Such a response may presage further incidents of inappropriate punishment or over-chastisement that are not successful in decreasing the child's non-compliance or preventing the development of problems associated with conduct disorder. It is equally clear that such a situation may put the child at risk of harm.

Conduct disorder and non-compliance

Conduct disorders account for between a third and a half of all child and adolescent clinic referrals. Rutter et al. (1975) found there was a prevalence of 8 per cent of children aged 10–11 with a conduct disorder in an Inner London borough, and 4 per cent on the Isle of Wight. The prognosis is poor with no clear, effective treatment (Kazdin 1987), so that conduct problems in childhood and adolescence not only predict continued conduct disorder in adulthood, but also in their offspring (Robins 1981). Paradoxically, professionals tend to underestimate its seriousness for both child and parents (Gelfand et al. 1988).

Non-compliance may be a 'king-pin' or central behaviour in the excesses and deficits present in conduct disorder (Jenson et al. 1987). Increasing child compliance may generalise to the improvement of other problematic behaviours such as aggressiveness, arguing and tantrums. Disobedience and non-compliance are common in childhood; however, developmentally, they should decrease in frequency, intensity and duration by the time the child reaches approximately 5 years of age. Normative studies suggest that for non-disabled children, compliance rates to parental requests range from 60 to 80 per cent, whereas compliance rates for clinic-referred children range from only 30 to 40 per cent (Forehand 1977; Delfini et al. 1976). The child who falls within this range may be well on the way to developing a conduct disorder (Gelfand et al. 1988).

Learning compliance and rule-governed behaviour is a crucial developmental task. The child who continues to regulate his or her behaviour by immediate gains rather than by a set of external rules or values will fail to comply with parent or teacher requests, will be unco-operative with other children, and is likely to fail to develop a range of social, academic and work skills. This in turn leads to a subsequent rejection by peers, parents and adults, with the development of poor self-esteem and social isolation (Herbert 1987). A strategic point for intervention may be when children are aged 4–8 years (Webster-Stratton and Herbert 1995).

There is evidence that, by as early as the second year, children who later go on to develop behaviour problems show particular temperamental characteristics. Thomas et al. (1968) measured temperament in a study of 136 New York children. They classified babies according to clusters of temperamental characteristics: 'difficult', 'easy' and 'slow-to-warm-up' babies. Children with significantly irregular patterns of functioning, who were slow to adapt to new situations, whose emotional responses were often at a high level of intensity and whose usual mood was negative, were the most likely to show later problem behaviours.

The coercion hypothesis

According to Patterson (1976), persistent deviant child behaviour may develop when parent and child become caught in a 'negative reinforcement trap' where each rewards the other's aversive, coercive behaviour. A child can terminate an aversive parental command by compliance, but learns that coercive behaviours such as non-compliance, defiance and tantrums with increasing intensity may also terminate the aversive parental demand. The parent, in turn, may negatively reinforce the child's non-compliance and other deviant behaviours by withdrawing the command and failing to respond punitively to the deviant behaviour, or may respond with coercive behaviours of his or her own, such as yelling. The child may then respond to the parental coercive behaviours by complying, thus reinforcing the parental coercive behaviour, or by intensifying his or her own coercive behaviour. In effect, parent–child interactions that are initiated by a parental command are increasingly characterised by a high rate of coercive parent and child behaviours, and increasingly aversive interactions.

Numerous studies have examined the role of ineffective command-giving by the parents of clinic-referred non-compliant children (Delfini et al. 1976; Green et al. 1979; Patterson 1982). Such parents give too many commands; they give vague, unclear commands; they give commands that cannot be fulfilled, and interrupt the child before there is time to comply, and they use more commands which are given in an angry, threatening, humiliating and nagging manner. The parents of children showing anti-social behaviour are more likely to punish but are unskilled in punishment, so that a range of deviant acts may pass unnoticed and unpunished; then, when they *are* confronted, parents react with anger rather than with a more appropriate response. The occasional beating for one extreme act does not solve the problem, and indeed, the severe beating that may occur may have short-term reinforcing effects for the parent, as the child may temporarily behave.

High rates of aversive events among family members have a number of other negative effects, such as reduced family interaction, increased social isolation, fewer shared recreational activities, and increased negative attributions towards other family members (Gambrill 1983).

The modification of these negative interaction styles may have an impact on reducing child abuse. Studies indicate that 60 per cent of child abuse takes place within the context of a disciplinary confrontation. The prevention and treatment of negatively reinforced coercive patterns of interaction requires the parent to learn to be more consistent in the use of positive reinforcers for desirable behaviours, and to learn to punish coercive child behaviour more appropriately and consistently (Patterson 1982). However, Patterson also suggested that children from families caught in a negative reinforcement trap are not as responsive to praise and reinforcement as are other children, although Roberts (1985) found that non-compliant children *are* responsive to maternal praise, both before and after treatment.

Parent training

'Parent training' refers to procedures in which a parent or parents are trained to interact differently with their child, based on the premise that child misbehaviour is inadvertently learned and sustained in the home by maladaptive parent–child interactions. Training is a collaborative process between parent and worker designed to alter the pattern of interaction between parent and child so that pro-social rather than anti-social behaviour is directly reinforced and maintained within the family. This requires developing parenting behaviours such as establishing consistent rules for the child to follow, providing positive reinforcement for appropriate behaviour, delivering appropriate mild forms of punishment for misbehaviours, and negotiating compromises (Kazdin 1987). 'Booster' sessions may be appropriate as the child's developmental needs change or new difficulties emerge.

Parent training has been evaluated in many outcome studies on children with behaviour problems (see Kazdin 1987). It has been shown to be effective in the treatment of oppositional, aggressive and non-compliant child behaviour (Herbert and Iwaniec 1981; Bunyan 1987; Zeilburger et al. 1968). Parent training has brought the problematic behaviours of treated children to within normative levels of their peers who are functioning adequately (Eyberg and Johnson 1974; Wells et al. 1980), with improvements being maintained over time, up to four-and-a-half years later (Baum and Forehand 1981). Siblings also improve, and maternal psychopathology, particularly depression, decreases systematically after parent training (Kazdin 1985).

Parent training is therefore one of the more promising treatments for conduct disorder, but several limitations have been identified. First, some families may not respond to treatment. Many factors other than specific parent–child interaction influence the effectiveness of treatment and child functioning; poor outcome is associated with marital discord, parental psychopathology (Strain et al. 1981), maternal depression (Griest et al. 1981), low socio-economic status (Wahler and Afton 1980), single-parenthood (Strain et al. 1981), social isolation (Dumas and Wahler 1983), unrealistic parental expectations (Twentyman and Plotkin 1982), negatively skewed attributional systems in parents (Larrance and Twentyman 1983) and negatively skewed parental perceptions (Reid et al. 1987).

Second, parent training makes a number of demands on parents, for example in using educational materials, absorbing underlying principles, systematically observing child behaviour, and implementing procedures at home. For some parents, the demands may be too great. Third, some parents will choose not to participate; perhaps they feel they have reached their limits in trying to help the child (Kazdin 1987). However, additional components can be built into a programme to address identified parental difficulties such as anger or stress management problems, problem-solving deficits or cognitive components, such as negative perceptions and attributions, towards the child or to link the carer into community groups and resources.

Finally, since certain parent behaviours correlate highly with child conduct disorders (Milne 1986), measures of parent behaviours such as parental aversiveness are useful indices of treatment outcome (Dadds et al. 1987).

Child protection

Thorough assessment, careful monitoring and evaluation are important in child protection work. The aim is positive, observable behaviour change in the carer and child or their interaction (Cigno 1995). An intervention may need to address several factors in the child's environment, such as problem parenting behaviours and child behaviour problems, as well as efforts to alleviate family stress and isolation within a multi-agency framework (Gambrill 1983). Outcomes are usually better and the social work task easier when parents are involved in the process of child protection (Department of Health 1995). Behavioural social workers frequently use written agreements to clarify mutual aims and objectives, specify the changes needed, and to agree reciprocal responsibilities and tasks and a review date (Sheldon 1980).

A review of the research literature on child abuse interventions available up to 1992 concluded that developing general parenting and child care skills and increasing awareness about the nature of child abuse and the responsibilities of child protection agencies might improve the effectiveness of interventions when they are needed (Gough 1993).

However, some families may not co-operate. Gough (1993) notes that the structure provided by the threat of official sanctions and control may provide the context that some families need for constructive changes; court-ordered treatment might give the necessary motivation to commence treatment, thus allowing the client to appreciate the need for and benefits of the service. Alternative plans may need to be developed for the child if there is no positive change and there is continuing high risk of significant harm or injury to the child.

The family

The family were white, semi-skilled and working-class, with four children, aged 7, 4½ and twins aged 2½ years. The referral to the Family Centre for a behavioural assessment was made by the key worker, the parents having agreed to a referral for specialist advice in managing their children. The names of the two oldest children had been placed on the Child Protection Register and their mother had been cautioned by the police when they were found to have bruising on their faces and buttocks consistent with having been hit with a strap by their mother in a disciplinary confrontation.

Several family and parent characteristics known to be associated with conduct disorder were present in the family: socio-economic disadvantage, poor supervision and monitoring of the children, and harsh and inconsistent punishment. Fear and violence had been features of the father's childhood, and he was wary of social services intervention. The mother had a large, local, extended family network. Working long hours at home as an 'out-worker' in addition to her home and childcare tasks, she was under considerable stress, compounded by poor housing and a low income.

Scott, aged 4½, was identified by his parents as presenting the most pressing problem behaviours, including destructiveness, fire-setting and 'fascination with matches, electric wires and plugs', lack of care, and defiant, non-compliant, oppositional behaviour. They described him as 'being sent from Mars', and said that he was beyond their control, but he was an endearing, lively, friendly and responsive child, who, his teacher said, was very bright. He had asthma and eczema, which, during my period of involvement, was under control and not an immediate cause for concern. He was otherwise in good health. The parents found the 7½-year-old boy easier to manage, although the school found him difficult at times. The 2½-year-old twins were beginning to display temper tantrums and demanding behaviour.

The assessment

A behavioural assessment is thorough, detailed and precise: it aims to specify and prioritise the problem behaviours, pinpoint the maintaining environmental and psychological factors, and identify targets for change. A variety of objective and subjective assessment methods were used. Behavioural interviews were conducted with the parents to gather information and enlist their co-operation. They were given information about the approach to be taken, offered hope and encouragement, and their role as 'parent-therapist' (Milne 1986) was clarified. A Critical Incident Analysis was undertaken to identify the more immediate contingencies in the incident which had resulted in the names of the two oldest children being placed on the Child Protection Register. Other professionals involved were consulted, and social services files were read.

Direct observation in the home was undertaken by the Family Centre social worker at the same time of day each day on an approximately fortnightly basis over a ten-week period, for preliminary observations and to record the frequency of the mother's command-negative and its consequences. The mother undertook the role of participant-observer. She was trained in the use of a simple coding system to record the frequency of Scott's compliance or non-compliance and defiance to specific and defined requests. She also kept ABC diaries, recording the antecedents (A) and consequences (C) of specific child behaviours (B).

Behavioural rating scales provide a comprehensive survey of typical child problem behaviours, and can be used to identify dimensions or response clusters that are missed in behavioural interviews, or are present in some situations but not in others, or which may co-vary with the problem behaviours (Gross and Wixted 1988). Two rating scales were used for initial screening and as pre- to post-treatment evaluation measures. The Eyberg Child Behaviour Inventory was completed by Scott's mother and by his teacher. This scale is designed to assess the behaviour of children labelled 'conduct-disordered', and has been found to give a predictable measure of pre- to post-treatment changes (Robinson et al. 1980). The inventory yields a total Problem Score with a potential range of 1–36, and a Problem Intensity Score with a potential range of 36–252. The Conners Teacher Rating Scale was also used as a pre- to post-treatment measure and to assess for hyperactivity factors. The scale was designed specifically for the assessment of hyperactivity in children (Conners 1969). It consists of 39 items on a four-point scale, and is sensitive to the changes in behaviour resulting from behaviour modification (Gross and Wixted 1988).

A third questionnaire, the Life Aspects Questionnaire, was used to gauge the mother's ratings of her satisfaction with her marital relationship and other significant life aspects. Since marital discord is correlated with child behaviour problems, negative perceptions of the child and poor treatment outcome, it was necessary to assess for this factor.

Selection and definition of target behaviours

Child non-compliance was identified by the parents as a priority problem behaviour. That this was a problem was confirmed in direct observations by the Family Centre social worker. Furthermore, the mother's frequency recordings revealed that child compliance occurred only 30 per cent of the time, well within the clinical range, and predictive of likely development of conduct disorder. Also, since child non-compliance and defiance had been antecedents to the reported incident of over-chastisement, and since the mother's ABC diaries showed use of threats of inappropriate punishment in attempts to manage child disobedience and defiance, it was considered that increasing child compliance with his mother's instructions would reduce the risks of further incidents of over-chastisement: thus monitoring changes in the frequency of mother's command-negative would give an indication of the level of risk to the child, and would be an index of change independent of the mother's participant-observation recordings of child compliance.

Child compliance was defined as:

- Scott's compliance with his mother's instructions to put his toys away in his drawer after being asked twice at the most, and within one minute of being asked the second time
- Scott's compliance with his mother's instruction to get dressed in the mornings within five minutes of being asked (in clothing which was easy for him to pull on, such as a T-shirt and shorts with elasticated waist, and excluding tying his own shoe-laces).

Command-negative was defined as a command which was characterised by at least one of the following:

- a demand for immediate compliance, for example: 'Pack it in – now!'
- when aversive consequences are implicitly or actually threatened if compliance is not immediate, for example: 'If you don't stop swearing, I'll put pepper on your tongue!'
- or when sarcasm or humiliation is directed towards the child, for example: 'If you don't tidy your room now, you'll put on your pyjamas and go to bed' (at 4.15 p.m.).

Command-negative differs from the reasonable command in which a command is reasonably stated and clearly specifies the behaviour expected.

The functional analysis

A functional analysis aims to describe the functional relationships between the antecedent events, the behaviours, and the consequent events that are maintaining the behaviours.

Antecedents

The context is a family background of socio-economic disadvantage and poor housing – factors that can have a direct impact on childcare and family stress. Scott is an active, restless child, whose mother undertakes most of the childcare. Specifically, there is previous learning by Scott that non-compliance may be ignored: his mother's attempts to modify his non-compliance have failed, and she has 'given up'. There is a deficit of effective child management skills: for example, pro-social behaviour may be overlooked or ignored. Positive reinforcement, when given, may be delayed or given verbally across a noisy room without ensuring the child's attention. Indeed, the child's misbehaviour may receive more attention than his pro-social behaviour. The household fails to reinforce compliance: for example, there is no natural reinforcer for getting dressed in the mornings, since breakfast is either omitted or Scott will refuse to sit down and eat it. Non-compliance does not occur with the child's father or with one of his aunts. Scott's non-compliance is worse at home with his mother during the week, when there are time constraints or she is busy or tired.

The immediate antecedents to child non-compliance and defiance are that the mother gives an instruction which may be vague, unclear, interrupted or repeated many times. In response to initial non-compliance, the mother then gives a command-negative.

Behaviour

Scott fails to comply. This may be shown non-verbally: for example, he refuses either by sitting at the bottom of the stairs instead of going to tidy his toys away, or he may 'twirl around' with his trousers on his head instead of getting dressed when asked.

In response to maternal insistence or command-negative, he becomes increasingly defiant, 'argues it out' or swears at his mother.

Consequences

Scott's non-compliance is negatively reinforced, as he avoids aversive parental demands. Similarly, defiance in response to a command-negative given by his mother is negatively reinforced: he avoids the aversive consequences which his mother is either unable or unwilling to carry out, for example summoning his headmistress when he fails to get dressed as asked in the mornings, or pouring washing-up liquid down his throat when he continues to swear at his mother.

When punishment is given, it may be delayed or not actually aversive, for instance playing in his room after being sent there for long periods as a punishment. Indeed, the problems may be further compounded by his efforts to amuse himself, including behaviour such as pulling the stuffing out of his mattress, or the plaster away from the crumbling walls, and playing with electric plugs and wires.

As this pattern continues, there is decreasing use by his mother of reasonable commands, since these are not reinforced by child compliance. There is increasing use of command-negative, which is reinforced by intermittent child compliance. There is a decrease in the mother's belief in her ability to obtain child compliance, which becomes self-fulfilling as her requests become increasingly unassertive, and non-compliance and defiance increase. She 'gives up', although over-chastisement or inappropriate punishment may be used in last-ditch attempts to moderate aversive child behaviour and control the child.

The intervention

The agreed goals were to increase Scott's compliance with his mother's instructions, reduce his defiance and increase her child management skills. Following the assessment, the results were discussed, and the functional analysis was explained with ABC examples.

The initial focus was on increasing child compliance using a positive reinforcement programme, whereby the child was specifically rewarded with stars on a star chart and with praise and approval for compliance with the two instructions from his mother that had been antecedents to the reported incident of over-chastisement. Contracts were drawn up for the agreed goals which specified the 'rules' for the positive reinforcement programme: how, when and where Scott was to be positively reinforced, materially and socially, for compliance with his mother's instructions. The mother practised this in role-plays in the settings in which the behaviour was expected to occur. She was also asked to reward herself for implementing or trying to implement the programme, for example by praising herself, and her partner, who was involved to some extent in the programme, was asked to give her encouragement and social reinforcement for using the programme.

A parent training programme was started in week three, and consisted of an in-home twelve-week training programme (McMahon and Forehand 1986; Dangel and Polster 1988; Scott 1989). Parent training methods included instruction, discussion, modelling, behaviour rehearsal and feedback, *in vivo* coaching and prompting, with feedback and positive reinforcement being given to the mother following observation visits. Handouts detailing child management skills were given at each session, and the mother undertook to discuss these with her partner. 'Homework' tasks were specified each week to practise the newly-learned skills. Discussion about child development, how behaviour is learned and maintained, household rules, and routines and play was interwoven into training sessions. Advice was sought and given about specific concerns and child management problems, such as how to teach a child about 'stranger danger'.

Some practical assistance was given: the key worker was asked to obtain a bed for the oldest boy (who was also participating in the positive reinforcement programme). Small tokens of reward and encouragement included a bag of donated toys, exercise books for the children to draw in, 'Blu-Tack' to stick their pictures – and the star charts – on the walls, and a notebook and folder for the mother. She was also encouraged to use local community resources such as a community education project and the local library.

Single-case design

The study used a single-case design (see Chapters 1 and 6), specifically a multiple-baseline-across-behaviours design, to monitor changes in child compliance. Following baseline recordings, the positive reinforcement programme was introduced sequentially across the two instances of child compliance to his mother's requests. Changes in the frequency of these responses were then monitored during treatment and follow-up. In addition, an AB design was used to monitor changes in the frequency of mother's command-negative. Baseline recordings of the frequency of the mother's command-negative were obtained in the direct observation, and changes were recorded during implementation of the parent training programme.

Results

As can be seen in Figure 3.1, child compliance with the instruction to tidy his toys away in his drawer increased from 40 per cent at baseline to 100 per cent by week six, after the stickers were introduced. This improvement was maintained at five-week follow-up and at an eleven month follow-up. Scott's compliance with his mother's instructions to get dressed in the mornings increased from 30 per cent at baseline to 100 per cent by week six. This improvement was maintained at five-week and eleven month follow-up.

As can be seen in Figure 3.2, there was a high percentage of mother's command-negative in baseline recordings (mean = 79 per cent). During the intervention, there was a steady decrease in the percentage of intervals in which command-negative was given, with a zero frequency at the five-week and eleven-month follow-ups.

Given the limitations of the AB design, it is not possible to conclude that changes in one area (child compliance) caused change in another (frequency of command-negative), nor that the training in precision request-making affected the frequency of command-negative. The results do, however, show a decrease in the frequency of command-negative as child compliance increased as parent training progressed, suggesting there was some correlation.

The results of the evaluation using the rating scales supported the observational data. Table 3.1 gives the scores from the Eyberg Child Behaviour Inventory completed by the mother and the teacher pre- and post-treatment. As can be seen, the results show a decrease in both the mother's and the teacher's ratings for total problem and intensity scores. Table 3.2 gives the normative data.

As can be seen from Table 3.3, the mother's ratings of her satisfaction in her relationship with Scott increased, as did her understanding of child

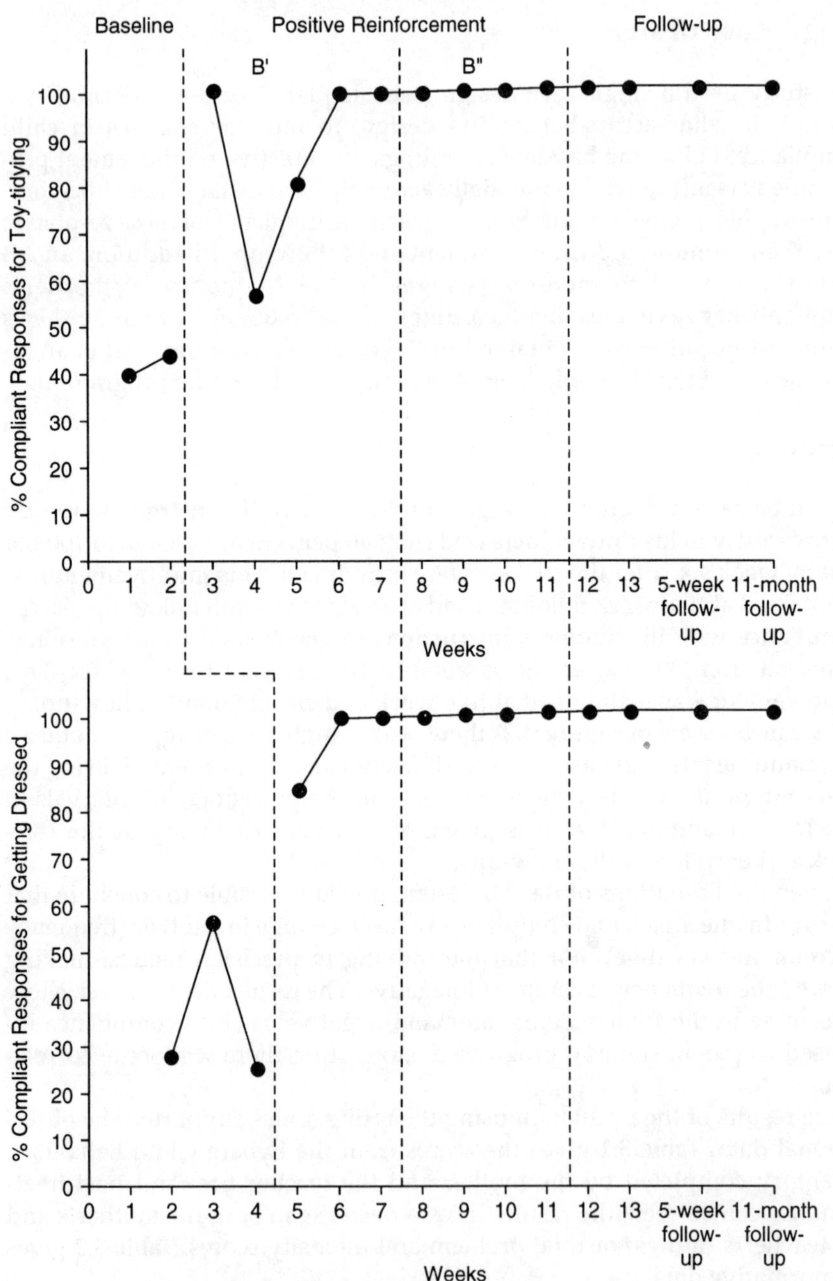

Figure 3.1 Percentage of compliance across baseline and treatment conditions for child toy-tidying and dressing

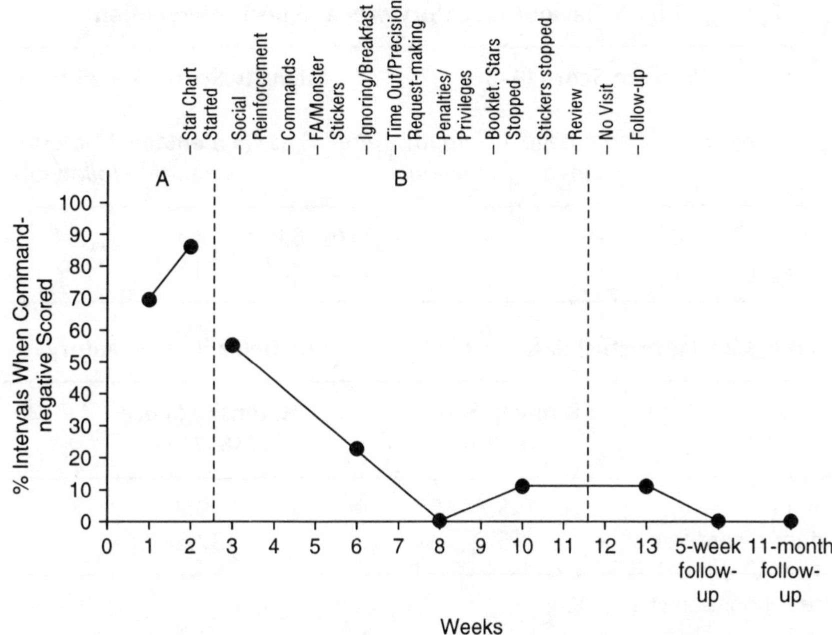

Figure 3.2 Percentage of mother's command-negative in baseline (A) and treatment (B) conditions

behaviour, and her confidence in tackling future problems. The problem severity decreased significantly. She rated her satisfaction in her relationship with her partner as high both pre- and post-intervention.

The ratings from the Conners Teacher Rating Scale showed an overall decrease in problem behaviours related to hyperactivity and conduct disorder factors identified by Trites et al. (1980). The number of items rated for low degrees of activity on these two factors changed from 13 pre- to 19 post-treatment.

Consumer and other feedback supported the data gathered by direct and participant observation and the rating scales. The mother reported increased personal satisfaction and confidence in her child management skills, a more positive relationship between herself and Scott, and improved child behaviour.

Observations showed that the mother's use of child management skills had generalised, in that she was seen to be using them with all four children. In addition, the father was observed by the key worker to be using 'Time Out' to manage the twins' temper tantrums by temporarily removing

Table 3.1 Total behaviour intensity scores and problem scores on the Eyberg Child Behaviour Inventory pre- and post-intervention

	Problem Score (0–36)				Intensity Score (36–252)			
	Pre-	*Post-*	*Percentage change*	*11-month follow-up*	*Pre-*	*Post-*	*Percentage change*	*11-month follow-up*
Mother	7	0	19.4	0	116	84	13	64
Teacher	15	11	11	–	120	92	11	–

Table 3.2 Normative data for the Eyberg Child Behaviour Inventory

	Problem Score (0–36)	Intensity Score (36–252)
Normal	5.8	99.2
Conduct-disordered	15	137.2

Source: Robinson et al. (1980)

Table 3.3 Rating by mother on the Life Aspects Questionnaire pre- to post-treatment on a scale of 1 (completely unhappy) to 5 (completely happy)

	Pre-treatment	Post-treatment
Problem severity (non-compliance)	2	5
Relationship with child	2	5
Relationship with partner	5	5
Understanding of child's behaviour	4	5
Confidence in tackling future problems	4	5
The help offered in past by social worker or during recent involvement	5	5
Total	22	30

Source: Bunyan (1984)

them to the hall, where the behaviour could not be reinforced. The father and aunt reported positive changes in Scott's behaviour, stating that he had 'calmed down' and was a 'different child'.

The key social worker reported that she found a significant change post-treatment, following her return after an absence of several weeks. She noted that the mother was looking more relaxed, describing what she was doing to manage Scott, and was positive about the changes in his behaviour.

Discussion and conclusions

The results showed that the intervention was successful in freeing mother and child from the negative reinforcement trap in which they were caught. It was also effective in reducing the risks of further incidents of over-chastisement of the children by their mother. Child compliance with maternal instructions increased. Previously ineffective parental commands had become events to which the child would respond with compliance in order to avoid 'Time Out'. The mother learned to be more consistent in tracking child behaviours, to use social reinforcers, small 'treats' and material rewards more consistently and frequently, and to ignore minor misbehaviour while appropriately punishing severe misbehaviour, including non-compliance and defiance by, for example, using 'Time Out'. Training in precision command-giving increased her skills in giving clear, positive instructions and requests, which she would then follow through, either to reward or sanction appropriately. An early emphasis on the use of positive reinforcement was aimed at making provision for the child's needs for positive attention in a tense and angry situation, and to stress the role of positive attention in learning new skills.

Once equipped with the skills with which to manage aversive child behaviour, there was a decrease in the level of stress experienced by the mother, a decrease in irritability, and an increase in confidence and problem-solving as new tactics were tried and proved successful. For example, when asked what she did instead of smacking Scott for misbehaviour or non-compliance, the mother said that she 'looks to see what he's doing, thinks "What's he doing? Yes, he's doing *x*, I'll warn him," says "Scott, if you don't do *y* you're going to Time Out"'; then she would 'go round again', that is, follow the request–consequence sequence until she had gained child compliance. This would suggest that she was observing and tracking child behaviour, and was problem-solving, using a complex range of skills learned during the parent training programme, to arrive at and implement a decision about the management of the behaviour. The Social Skills Model (Argyle 1983) suggests that a feedback loop is established when the individual perceives changes in the outside world as a result of his or her actions, which may be sufficient for response maintenance – in this case, continued use of child management skills.

Although the primary focus of the intervention was on skills acquisition and behavioural changes that could be monitored through observable behaviours, cognitive restructuring was an integral part of the intervention. Because individuals interpret and react to events in terms of their perceived significance, cognitive deficits and distorted thinking can cause emotional difficulties which may be shown behaviourally. Thus changes in a client's behaviour (including emotional behaviour) can be achieved by altering thought patterns, beliefs, attitudes and opinions; cognitive therapists would deal mainly with the client's verbal behaviour and images relating to the world around them.

In this case, dysfunctional cognitive processes and structures were challenged by the provision of new information and 'explanatory stories' (Herbert 1987). The mother was told the assessment results, and the negative reinforcement trap in which she and Scott were caught was explained to her with ABC examples. Developmental counselling and understanding that undesirable behaviour is learned and maintained in much the same way as desirable behaviour served to challenge her belief that the child was 'deliberately' misbehaving to wind his mother up.

Depression or learned helplessness (Seligman 1975) has been shown to be related to poor outcome in parent training. Herbert (1987) notes that repeated failure to modify child problem behaviour leads to feelings of demoralisation, hopelessness and helplessness as a parent perceives an absence of any relationship between his or her own efforts and the reinforcing nature of the successful management of child behaviour, and may 'give up', as had Scott's mother. It was hypothesised that an increase in the mother's child management skills, an increase in child compliance and a reduction in other problem behaviour would, appropriately perceived and reinforced, lead to increased self-efficacy beliefs as the mother increasingly came to perceive her effectiveness in dealing with child behaviour. Also, since it was recognised that the mother's environment, perhaps like that of many social work clients, might not offer much in the way of positive reinforcement, she was instructed in the importance of self-reinforcement and positive self-talk.

There were no major difficulties in retaining the client's interest as the programme progressed. As well as giving positive reinforcement and asking the key worker and family members to reinforce on-task behaviours, care was taken to ensure that tasks set were achievable, more frequent visits were made at critical points when early difficulties and misunderstandings could be ironed out, the parents were kept fully informed, a partnership was established, a simple contract was drawn up, and goals were made explicit and reflected the parents' priorities. Behavioural social workers and behaviour therapists stress the use of the core conditions of empathy, warmth and acceptance to promote a client's positive feelings about treatment: 'the behavioural social worker attempts to employ verbal and other types of reinforcers in treatment, in a conscious and deliberate manner, to encourage clients to continue in treatment, remain on-task and engaged during interviews, and to undertake any therapeutic tasks in their daily lives, outside of treatment sessions with the social worker' (Thyer 1992, p.9).

Single-case studies have traditionally been used by behavioural social workers and clinicians. Indeed, much of the evidence for the effectiveness of behavioural techniques comes from studies using reversal, multiple-baseline or other single-case designs. Based on repeated measurement with the same individual, single-case designs allow evaluation of the effectiveness of interventions. However, the major limitation of the single-case design is generalising the results from a single subject to other individuals or groups. In order to establish generality, the repeated, exact, direct replication of the results of a single case-study, or systematic planned alterations to study the effects, for example, of the variations in intervention, setting or client behaviour, is required (Hollin 1990).

There is no doubt that the anti-social behaviours associated with conduct disorder present a high cost to society and also cause individual distress, and there is no clearly effective treatment. Since child non-compliance may be central in the development of conduct disorder and its associated aggressive, disruptive and coercive behaviours, also having a knock-on effect in the failure to acquire social, reading and work skills, an earlier rather than a later intervention could help to prevent such deficits occurring at critical stages in child development. Social workers may be in a pivotal position to identify and intervene with families where such early, persistent difficulties are arising.

Hawkins and Weis (1985) suggest that the focus for the prevention of conduct disorders should be on the agents of socialisation: the parents, schools and peers, together with life and employment skills training and community development. Access to parent training programmes (with periodic 'booster' sessions or training and support at critical periods if required) and a network of community resources to decrease the social isolation and stress in vulnerable families with young children would be a significant part of such an approach. Similarly, such an intervention may be effective in reducing the risks of physical and emotional abuse where there are child protection concerns.

Acknowledgement

This material first appeared in *The British Journal of Social Work* by Diana Bourn (1993).

References

Argyle, M. (1983) *The Psychology of Interpersonal Behaviour*, Harmondsworth: Penguin.

Baum, C.G. and Forehand, R. (1981) 'Long-term follow-up of assessment of parent training by use of multiple outcome measures', *Behaviour Therapy*, 12, pp.643–5.

Bourn, D. (1993) 'Over-chastisement, child non-compliance, parenting skills: A behavioural intervention by a Family Centre social worker', *British Journal of Social Work*, 23, pp.481–9.

Bunyan, A. (1984) *The Behavioural Treatment of a Conduct Disordered Child within the Natural Home Setting*, University of Leicester, unpublished thesis.

Cigno, K. (1995) 'Helping to prevent abuse: A behavioural approach with families' in K. Wilson, and A. James (eds) *The Child Protection Handbook*, London: Ballière Tindall.

Conners, C.K. (1969) 'A teacher rating scale for use in drug studies with children', *American Journal of Psychiatry*, pp.884–8.

Dadds, N.K., Sanders, M.R. and James J.E. (1987) 'The generalisation of treatment effects in parent training with multi-distressed parents', *Behavioural Psychotherapy*, 15, pp.289–313.

Dangel, R.F. and Polster, R.A. (1988) *Teaching Child Management Skills*, Oxford: Pergamon Press.

Delfini, L.F., Bernal, M.E. and Rosen, P.M. (1976) 'Comparison of deviant and normal boys in home settings', in E.J. Mash, L.A Hammerlynck and L.C Handy (eds) *Behaviour Modification and Families*, New York: Brunner/Mazel.

Department of Health (1995) *Child Protection: Messages from Research*, London: HMSO.

Dumas, J.E. and Wahler, R.G. (1983) 'Prediction of treatment outcome in parent training: Mother insularity and socio-economic disadvantage', *Behavioural Assessment*, 5, pp.301–13.

Eyberg, S.M. and Johnson, S.M. (1974) 'Multiple assessment of behaviour with families: Effects on contingency contracting and order of treated problems', *Journal of Consulting and Clinical Psychology*, 42, pp.594–606.

Forehand, R. (1977) 'Child non-compliance to parental requests: Behaviour analysis and treatment', in M. Hersen, R.M. Eisler and P.M. Miller, *Progress in Behaviour Therapy*, New York: Academic Press.

Gambrill, E.D. (1983) 'Behavioural intervention with child abuse and neglect' in M. Hersen, R.M. Eisler and P.M. Miller, *Progress in Behaviour Modification*, 15, New York: Academic Press.

Gelfand, D.M., Jenson, W.R. and Drew, C.J. (1988) *Understanding Child Behaviour Disorders* (2nd edn), New York: Holt, Rinehart & Winston.

Gibbons, J., Conroy, S. and Bell, C. (1995) *Operating the Child Protection System*, London: HMSO.

Gough, D. (1993) *Child Abuse Interventions: A Review of the Literature*, Glasgow: Public Health Research Unit.

Green, K.D., Forehand, R. and McMahon, R.J. (1979) 'Parental manipulation of compliance and non-compliance in normal and deviant families', *Behaviour Modification*, 3, pp.245–66.

Griest, D.L., Forehand, R. and Wells, K. (1981) 'Follow-up assessment of parent behaviour training: An analysis of who will participate', *Child Study Journal*, 11, pp.221–9.

Gross, A.M. and Wixted, J.T. (1988) 'Assessment of child behaviour problems' in A.S. Bellack and M. Hersen, *Behavioural Assessment*, New York: Pergamon Press.

Hawkins, J.D. and Weis, J.G. (1985) 'The social development model: an integrated approach to delinquency prevention', *Journal of Primary Prevention*, 6, pp.73–9.

Herbert, M. (1987) *Conduct Disorders of Childhood and Adolescence: A Social Learning Perspective* (2nd edn), Chichester: John Wiley.

Herbert, M. (1988) *Working with Children and their Families*, Leicester: British Psychological Society.

Herbert, M. and Iwaniec, D. (1981) 'Behavioural psychotherapy in home settings: An empirical study applied to conduct disordered and incontinent children', *Behavioural Psychotherapy*, 9, pp.55–77.

Hollin, C.R. (1990) *Cognitive-behavioural Interventions with Young Offenders*, Oxford: Pergamon Press.

Jenson, W.R., Reavis, K. and Rhodes, G. (1987) 'A conceptual analysis of childhood behaviour disorders: a practical educational approach' in B. Scott and J. Gillam (eds) *Topics in Behaviour Disorders*, Austin, TX: Behavioral Learning Centre.

Kazdin, A.E. (1985) *Treatment of Anti-social Behaviour in Children and Adolescents*, New York: Dorsey Press.

Kazdin, A.E. (1987) 'Treatment of anti-social behaviour in children: current status and future directions', *Psychological Bulletin*, 102, pp.187–202.

Larrance, D.T. and Twentyman, C.T. (1983) 'Maternal attributions and child abuse', *Journal of Abnormal Psychology*, 92, pp.449–57.

McMahon, R.J. and Forehand, R. (1986) 'Parent training for the noncompliant child' in R.F Dangel and R.A Polster (eds) *Parent Training*, New York: Guilford Press.

Milne, D. (1986) *Training Behaviour Therapists: Methods, Evaluation and Implementation with Parents, Nurses and Teachers*, London: Croom Helm.

Patterson, G.R. (1976) 'The aggressive child, victim and architect of a coercive system' in E.J. Mash, L.A. Hamerlynck and L.C. Handy, *Behavior Modification and Families*, New York: Brunner.

Patterson, G.R. (1982) *Coercive Family Process: A Social Learning Approach*, Vol. 3, Eugene, OR: Castalia.

Reid, J.B., Kavanagh, K. and Baldwin, D.V. (1987) 'Abusive parents' perception of child behaviour problems: An example of parental bias', *Journal of Abnormal Child Psychology* 15, pp.457–66.

Roberts, M.W. (1985) 'Praising child compliance: Reinforcement or ritual?', *Journal of Abnormal Child Psychology*, 13, pp.611–29.

Robins, L.N. (1981) 'Epidemiological approaches to natural history research: Antisocial disorders in children', *Journal of the American Academy of Child Psychiatry* 20, pp.556–680.

Robinson, E.A., Eyberg, S.M. and Ross, A.W. (1980) 'The standardisation of an inventory of child conduct problem disorders', *Journal of Child Psychology*, Spring, pp.22–9.

Rutter, M., Cox, A., Tupling, C., Berger, M. and Yule, W. (1975) 'Attainment and adjustment in two geographical areas: The prevalence of psychiatric disorder', *British Journal of Psychiatry*, 126, pp.493–509.

Scott, M. (1989) *A Cognitive-behavioural Approach to Clients' Problems*, London: Tavistock/Routledge.

Sheldon, B (1980) *The Use of Contracts in Social Work*, Birmingham: BASW Publications.

Seligman, M.E.P. (1975) *Helplessness*, San Francisco, CA: Freeman.

Strain, S.P., Young, C.C. and Horowitz, J. (1981) 'Generalised behaviour change during oppositional child training: An examination of child and family variables', *Behaviour Modification*, 5, pp.15–26.

Thomas, A., Chess, S. and Birch, H.G. (1968) *Temperamental and Behaviour Disorders in Children*, London: University of London Press.

Thyer, B.A. (1992) 'Behavioural social work: It is not what you think', *Behavioural Social Work Review*, 13, 1.

Trites, R.L., Blouin, A.G. and Lapgrade, K. (1980) 'Factor analysis of the Conner Teacher Rating Scale based on a large normative sample', *Journal of Consulting and Clinical Psychology*, 50, pp.615–23.

Twentyman, C.T. and Plotkin, G. (1982) 'Unrealistic expectations of parents who maltreat their children: An educational deficit that pertains to child development' *Journal of Child Psychology*, 38, pp.497–503.

Wahler, R.G. and Afton, A.D. (1980) 'Attentional processes in insular and non-insular mothers: Some differences in their summary reports about child problem behaviours', *Child Behaviour Therapy*, 2, pp.25–41.

Webster-Stratton, C. and Herbert, M. (1995) *Troubled Families, Problem Children*, Chichester/New York: John Wiley.

Wells, K.C., Forehand, R. and Griest, D.L. (1980) 'Generality of treatment effects from treated to untreated behaviours from a parent training programme', *Journal of Clinical Child Psychology*, 51, pp.100–7.

Zeilburger, T., Sampen, S.E. and Sloane, H.N. (1968) 'Modification of a child's problem with the mother as therapist', *Journal of Applied Behaviour Analysis*, 1, pp.47–53.

4 Treating children who fail to thrive

Dorota Iwaniec

Failure-to-thrive (FTT) is associated with poor growth and development in infancy and early childhood for either organic or psycho-social reasons or a combination of both. It is far more common and widespread than was thought only about ten or fifteen years ago. Until the early 1980s, FTT was generally perceived as a paediatric problem, and was usually attended to by the medical profession. Growing research findings increased awareness about FTT, and helped to develop methods of intervention and treatment in order to help children and their carers (Iwaniec 1983; Iwaniec et al. 1985a and 1985b; Skuse 1988; Batchelor and Kerslake 1990; Iwaniec 1991 and 1995; Hanks and Hobbs 1993).

This chapter will describe behavioural assessment and treatment of combined FTT as an example of effective intervention led by a social worker in a multi-disciplinary team, using cognitive-behavioural methods.

Definition of failure-to-thrive

Failure-to-thrive is defined as failure to grow and develop according to the norms, in a healthy, vigorous and happy way. This has become a popular term to describe infants and young children whose weight, height, head growth and general psychosocial development are significantly below expected norms and whose well-being causes concern. It is conceived as a variable syndrome of severe growth-retardation, delayed skeletal maturation, and problematic psychomotor development, which is often associated with illnesses, inadequate caloric intake for normal growth, acute feeding difficulties, disturbed mother–child interaction and relationship, insecure or disorganised attachment, family dysfunctioning and poverty. The literature points out three possible types of FTT:

1 organic FTT
2 non-organic FTT
3 combined organic and non-organic FTT.

Organic failure-to-thrive presents a complex aetiology, including inadequate nutrition, malabsorption, chronic infection, major structural congenital abnormalities, and metabolic and endocrine defects. According to the latest findings, there are few children whose FTT is determined by physical illness alone (Skuse 1988; Batchelor and Kerslake 1990; Hanks and Hobbs 1993; Iwaniec 1995).

Non-organic failure-to-thrive (which is most commonly identified and is of primary importance for child care workers) is related to insufficient food intake due to neglect, acute feeding difficulties, problematic parenting, rejection, deprivation, emotional abuse and neglect, and poverty (Leonard et al. 1966; Fischhoff 1975; Pollitt 1975; Iwaniec 1983).

Combined failure-to-thrive occurs where organic and non-organic factors merge. This combination is more common than was thought, and is apparent when treatment of what had seemed to be a clear-cut organic condition does not produce the expected improvement. Emotional overlays and/or secondary gains are known to complicate so-called psychosomatic disorders, not least those which have a clear organic basis. On the other hand, a child who fails to thrive because of illness might also be rejected, neglected and severely deprived of attention and care, so the primary cause of FTT – illness – is exacerbated by parental maltreatment (Iwaniec 1983 and 1995; Hanks and Hobbs 1993).

Literature review

The hypothesis of a psychological aetiology for the non-organic failure-to-thrive syndrome has its roots in the extensive literature on the effects of institutionalisation, hospitalism and maternal deprivation in children. The introduction of maternal deprivation theory over four decades ago shed new light and increased understanding on why some children fail to grow and develop according to norms despite the absence of disease (Bowlby 1951). Some of the best early documentation of the failure-to-thrive syndrome was carried out by Goldfarb (1945), Spitz (1945), Talbot et al. (1947) and Widdowson (1951).

In the late 1950s and 1960s, studies of growth-failure and developmental delay (similar to that found in institutionalised children) were replicated in infants and young children living at home. These studies have shown that the most commonly identified forerunners to these growth problems are emotional disturbance, inadequate caloric intake and environmental deprivation, with the wide range of psychosocial disorganisation that these concepts imply. Deprivation often involves rejection, isolation from social contacts, and neglect. These associations with poor growth have been delineated in the context of maternal personality problems, often stemming from the mother's own early background and family dysfunctioning and other stresses, like poverty, unemployment and social isolation. Psychological difficulties have been found in the manner in which the mothers nurture their small infants (Coleman and Provence 1957; Leonard et al. 1966; Barbero and Shaheen 1967).

One of the early comprehensive studies of social development, emotional adaptation and functioning of mothers of FTT children was carried out by Pollitt et al. (1975). Results of this detailed study indicated that mothers of FTT children did not show overt psychopathologies. The largest differences between groups were found in the scores drawn from the mother–child interaction checklist. The mothers in the experimental group showed less frequent verbal and physical contact, and were less positively reinforcing and warm. Substantial differences were also noted in maternal affection, described as 'inoperant' in many of the index mothers. Similar findings emerged from the more recent studies (Iwaniec 1983; Iwaniec et al. 1985a, 1985b, 1994 and 1995; Powell et al. 1987; Wolfe 1988; Hanks and Hobbs 1993; Batchelor and Kerslake 1990). These studies indicated deficiencies in child-rearing practices, deviant parent–child interaction and feeding difficulties, rather than character disorders in the carers.

Early child-rearing difficulties such as feeding, sleeping, crying and absence of help and support are thought to prevent the development of physical and emotional closeness, mutual attachment and affectionate relationships. All the studies conducted over the last fifty years or so found one common feature – problematic feeding/eating behaviour; consequently, most FTT children are underfed, undernourished and underdeveloped, both physically and psychologically, for their age. Child-rearing practices in these cases tend to become tense and anxious, and if problems persist, hostility and rejection can result. Many of these children are observed to be apprehensive, fearful, withdrawn or attention-seeking. Causal factors, as outlined in the literature, are many and varied, so painstaking assessment is necessary.

Table 4.1 provides a profile of non-organic failure-to-thrive.

Table 4.1 Profile of children with non-organic failure-to-thrive

Failure-to-thrive
Child falls below expected norms for the chronological age in weight often in height and head circumference

Developmental retardation
- motor development
- language development
- social development
- intellectual development
- emotional development
- cognitive development

Physical appearance
Small, thin, wasted body, thin arms and legs, enlarged stomach, thin, wispy, dull and falling hair, dark circles around the eyes

Psychological description and behaviour
- sadness, withdrawal, and detachment
- expressionless face
- general lethargy
- tearful
- frequent whining
- minimal or no smiling
- diminished vocalisation
- staring blankly at people or objects
- lack of cuddliness
- unresponsiveness
- passivity or overactivity

Characteristic features
- feeding-eating problems
- vomiting, heaving
- refusal to chew and swallow
- diarrhoea
- frequent colds and infections

Insecure or avoidant attachment
Tense when in the mother's company; does not show interest and pleasure when with the mother or carer; does not show distress when mother leaves or is too clingy

Problematic behaviour
- whining and crying
- restlessness
- irritability
- apprehension
- anxiety
- resistance to socialisation
- poor sleeping pattern
- feeding and eating problems

Source: Iwaniec (1995)

Case history

Rebecca was 2½ years old at the time of referral. The referral came to the Student Training Unit from her father, who was desperately worried about his daughter and partner, but particularly about the deteriorating mother–child relationship, constant feeding battles with Rebecca, her poor physical growth and difficult behaviour, his partner's increased bouts of depression and strongly felt convictions that there was something organically wrong with the child, and that numerous medical examinations conducted privately and by the NHS were not accurate. Rebecca also had four admissions to hospital to investigate possible organic causes for her FTT. Over the intervening two years or so, the parents received varied and often contradictory advice as to how to manage their daughter. The mother became totally confused and exasperated as she tried different strategies suggested to her, none of which produced the desired outcomes.

Behavioural assessment

In order to understand how the problem developed over time and to establish what mechanisms controlled poor food intake leading to FTT, the medical and social histories (distal antecedents) need to be examined. They can have profound significance in planning appropriate treatment and intervention strategies.

History

Rebecca was born at 38 weeks, with a normal delivery. She was a planned and very much wanted child. Both parents were well educated with established professional careers and high standards of living. Rebecca's birth weight was on the 25th percentile. She was breast-fed. At 3 weeks she developed some colic and posseting, was sucking poorly, and had persistent vomiting. She stopped gaining weight at 5 months and fell below the third percentile at 7 months. Extensive investigations were carried out in the hospital, but no organic cause was found. The vomiting and feeding difficulties continued, and she had two further admissions to hospital, basically to deal with feeding difficulties. Her poor eating performance was seen as a result of high maternal anxiety level and mismanagement of feeding. Resistance to eating was perceived by nursing staff as manipulative behaviour which needed firm handling. She began to be force-fed, which resulted in Rebecca's complete food-avoidance behaviour. She was panic-stricken when food was presented to her: she would scream, push food away, heave, vomit and have diarrhoea.

This resistance to eating confirmed the parents' fears that there was something physically wrong with her, and they decided to seek private medical help. Further absorptive studies were carried out, and slight neuromuscular incoordination of the oesophagus was demonstrated. Surgery was carried out successfully, and it was then hoped that Rebecca would improve psychologically as the memory of the early discomfort when eating and being force-fed faded, but unfortunately this was not the case.

After being told that there was no longer anything wrong with Rebecca, the parents began to be more firm with her, expecting a quick improvement in eating behaviour, with subsequent weight gain. She continued to refuse food, and her physical appearance deteriorated, although her psychosocial development was within norms. The mother became depressed, feeling helpless, desperate, angry, frustrated and unable to cope with the daily struggle to feed Rebecca, which appeared to take over her life. Feeding-time became a major battle, and fluctuated between an angry, anxious and at times forceful feeding style to begging the child to eat, encouraging, bribing, giving up and allowing Rebecca to do anything in order to get some food into her. Rebecca's behaviour became extremely manipulative and oppositional as she learned how to get her own way, not only in relation to eating but in other areas of life. Since there was no improvement in weight gain, and intake of food was insufficient for the child's age (in spite of trying hard to feed her), the mother became totally demoralised and depressed. She began to believe very strongly that she was inadequate as a carer, and that she could not do anything right: her self-esteem was at rock-bottom.

At the point of referral, the situation became serious and needed immediate attention to prevent further deterioration in the mother–child relationship and increasing maternal depression, with family life becoming severely affected.

Assessment of eating behaviour

When assessing FTT, special attention should be given to the child's nutritional intake, feeding/eating behaviour, parent–child interaction during the act of feeding, and general physical and emotional care of the child. The following questions about nutrition should be explored and supported by direct observation:

1 Is the child fed regularly?
2 Is the child given enough food?
3 Are the signals of hunger or satiation properly interpreted?
4 Is the child given the right food?

5 Is the child handled patiently during feeding/eating?
6 Is the child held comfortably during feeding?
7 Is the child encouraged to eat?
8 Is there reasonable flexibility in feeding/eating routine?
9 Is there evidence of anger, frustration and force-feeding during the feeding/eating period?
10 Is the child punished for not eating?
11 Is food withheld as a means of punishment?
12 Is there awareness that the child is too thin and too small?
13 Is there concern about the child's health and well-being?
14 Is there evidence of seeking help and advice?
15 Is there evidence of responding to help and advice?

Observation of eating and mother–child interaction

Several observations of eating revealed a series of problems: refusal to eat, closing her mouth when being fed, spitting food, pushing the plate away, playing with food, and when pressed to eat, crying, screaming, pushing her mother away, running from the table. In all, only a few mouthfuls were taken. Eating-time from preparation to eventual end lasted one hour fifteen minutes on one occasion and one hour and thirty minutes on two other occasions.

The mother appeared to be anxious and apprehensive even before mealtimes, expecting a battle of wills, but desperately wanting Rebecca to take some nutrition. She would cook what Rebecca told her she would eat. When Rebecca refused to eat and left the table, her mother would run after her with the spoon, promise to read her a story if she ate, threaten to take all her toys away, plead with her, shout, forcibly sit her at the table, ignore her for a few minutes, then try to encourage her to eat, play with her and attempt to feed her at the same time. Once the mealtime was over, the mother immediately began to plan what she was going to prepare for tea, worrying how it was going to work next time round. She showed a tremendous preoccupation (to the point of obsession) with how to make her daughter eat so that she put on weight, to the point where she could think about nothing else.

Recording

The baseline of food intake over two weeks (which was meticulously recorded) proved insufficient in terms of calories. In addition, the tensions and anxieties occasioned by mealtimes clearly could not benefit the child (see Table 4.2).

Table 4.2 Daily eating record (a sample)

Date	Time	Food Amount	Method of Feeding	Time Taken	Mother's Feeling
Wednesday 20 October	8.30 a.m.	½ Weetabix, a little milk	Being fed	45 min.	Exhausted, depressed, bad start to the day
	10.00 a.m.	100 ml milk		10 min.	
	11.45 a.m.	½ potato, 2 pieces of carrot, few pieces of lamb, gravy	Began herself, but then refused to swallow meat. Mother ended up liquidising the child's lunch and feeding it to her, almost by force.	1 hour 20 min.	Angry and depressed
	3.00 p.m.	3 spoons of yoghurt, 1 biscuit	Fed herself	20 min.	Very tired
	5.30 p.m.	1 chip, 2 spoons of baked beans	Being fed, refused to eat fish		Gave up, asked her father to feed her
	7.00 p.m.	Cup of drinking chocolate		10 min.	

Child development and behaviour

In spite of Rebecca's poor physical growth and several admissions to hospital, her psychosocial development was within the upper range. She could speak fluently, using a large vocabulary, had good reasoning skills, could recognise some letters and words, could play in an imaginative way, and loved colouring and being read stories. She was fully toilet-trained, and her social behaviour and social skills were above average for her age. Emotionally, however, she was volatile. Her behaviour (apart from eating-related problems) was defiant and stubborn, but this was not perceived by the parents as something they would like to deal with. They were totally preoccupied with her poor eating and weight gain, and attributed her difficult behaviour to alleged health problems.

Parent–child interaction and relationship

Data on parent–child interactions and relationships were obtained by direct observation during home visits, and were supplemented by information provided by hospital staff, all of whom had the opportunity to observe the parents and Rebecca. Observation checklists (Iwaniec et al. 1985) were used to measure the nature and quality of interaction (see Tables 4.3).

Table 4.3 Observation checklist – child

Visit No.__________ Assessor______________ Name of Client____________

Child's Reactive and Proactive Behaviour	*Often*	*Seldom*	*Almost Never*
1 Playing freely			
2 Laughing/smiling			
3 Running			
4 Talking freely			
5 Coming for help			
6 Coming for comfort			
7 Cuddling up to parents			
8 Responding to affection			
9 Responding to attention			
10 At ease when parents are near the child			
11 Joining in activities with other children			
12 Not frightened when approached by parents or corrected			

Table 4.4 Observation checklist – parents

Father's/mother's Reactive and Proactive Behaviour	*Often*	*Seldom*	*Almost Never*
1 Talking to the child			
2 Looking at the child			
3 Smiling at the child			
4 Making eye contact (loving)			
5 Touching (gently)			
6 Holding (closely, lovingly)			
7 Playing			
8 Cuddling			
9 Kissing			
10 Sitting the child on the lap			
11 Handling the child in a gentle way			
12 Giving requests (as opposed to commands)			
13 Helping the child if it is in difficulties			
14 Encouraging the child to participate in play and other activities			
15 Being concerned about the child			
16 Picking the child up when it cries or when it is hurt			
17 Answering the child's questions			
18 Not ignoring the child's presence			
19 Emotionally treating the child the same as other children			
20 Handling children consistently			

Direct observation revealed that mother–child interaction during feeding-time was inconsistent, and ranged from allowing Rebecca to do whatever she wanted to becoming frustrated and putting pressure on the child. It became clear that Rebecca tended to get her own way all the time. In areas other than eating, interaction was more constructive and positive, although the father reported that their interaction (prior to assessment) was tense or indifferent, and their positive mutual activities of the past were fast disappearing. The maternal change of behaviour towards Rebecca was due to extreme worry about her survival, fits of depression and feelings of helplessness.

Functional analysis

Antecedent

Distal At 3 weeks developed colic, posseting and frequent vomiting, causing pain and discomfort. Acute parental anxiety and tension when child being fed. Child force-fed in hospital, and later at home. Surgery successful, but problem of eating unresolved. Maternal depression and helplessness led to inconsistent management. Eating associated with painful and anxiety-provoking experiences.

Proximal Tense, anxious atmosphere at meal times. Excessive worry about child's health and weight. Parents felt sorry for Rebecca, believing that there was something wrong physically with her in spite of surgery. Mother reinforced negative behaviour by complying with Rebecca's demands, just to make her take some food. Parental conflict regarding management.

Behaviour

Refusing to eat, crying when pressure is put on her, closing mouth when being fed, spitting, heaving, storing food in the mouth, screaming, pushing mother away, playing with food, walking away from the table, being distressed.

Consequences

Proximal Mother tries for a long time, and usually gives in. Rebecca allowed to do what she wants in order to get some food into her. Mother gets frustrated – screams and shouts – Rebecca cries, mother feels guilty, cuddles her, begs her to eat, plays with her – if she refuses, mother cries, gets depressed, and switches off from Rebecca.

Distal Rebecca might develop serious illness, parents worry that she might die. Her development might slow down or seriously deteriorate. She might develop anorexia nervosa when older. Mother might reject Rebecca if situation persists. Mother might have nervous breakdown. Father's work might suffer, as he has to care for both of them. Rebecca might develop serious behavioural and emotional problems.

Clinical formulation

Rebecca's acute and prolonged feeding/eating difficulties resulting in poor weight gain and height-growth are the results of undetected organic reasons for her condition early on. For two years, her parents were told that there was nothing wrong with her, and that her refusal to eat was behavioural. Rebecca was force-fed in hospital during two admissions, and her parents were advised to be firm when feeding her. Eventually, an organic cause was found, and surgery was performed to alleviate the problem. In spite of successful minor surgery, Rebecca's eating behaviour did not improve, which in turn brought about even greater anxiety, worry and tension in her parents. They felt that either there was still something physically wrong with her or she was manipulating them, which brought about frustration, anger, depression and a sense of inadequacy and helplessness.

Looking at her history, it can be seen how food-avoidance behaviour was learned and maintained over time. Due to a neuro-muscular incoordination of the oesophagus which had been present since birth, pain associated with eating and an accompanying high level of tension in the parents (especially the mother, who had tried all sorts of ways to make her eat), there was now in existence a phobic avoidance of eating. It seems likely that the child learned (on a classical/operant basis, see Chapter 1) to avoid food by associating it with physical pain and discomfort because of the illness and force-feeding, and she was now associating eating with painful and unpleasant events such as the mother's anxiety, tension, anger, frustration and the pressure put on her to make her eat. On occasion, the mother would cry while trying to feed her, beg her to eat, distract her by playing, or simply give up after an hour or even two hours of struggling to feed her. Confusion and ill-informed advice regarding management of eating behaviour led to feelings of helplessness in the parents, and persistent worry that Rebecca might die.

Cognitive-behavioural treatment

Treatment of FTT might involve several stages. This entails a multi-element package which depends for its final shape on the behavioural assessment. Treatment should be organised on a multi-disciplinary basis as input from different experts is required for well-informed intervention. The medical profession (GP, paediatrician, health visitor, dietician) provide help with measuring and monitoring child growth and development, and the dietician advises on an appropriate diet. A psychologist's help may be needed to assist with assessment, for example through psychometric testing. Psychiatrists can help to deal with acute depression or other mental health problems. Social workers can assist in psychosocial assessment, the provision of daycare resources and the implementation of co-ordinated treatment within the framework of childcare legislation. A case conference is a good forum to work out a care plan and task distribution among professionals and parents.

Stages of involvement

The following strategies should be observed to avoid misdiagnosis, as FTT can be caused by organic and psychosocial reasons, or both. Therefore, a multi-disciplinary approach is essential when dealing with such children.

- *Stage 1*: Identifying that the child's weight is below expected norms and its general well-being is questionable.
- *Stage 2*: Advice and help provided by the health visitor regarding feeding, caring and management.
- *Stage 3*: If there is no improvement, referral to the paediatrician to investigate any possible organic reason for the child's poor growth and development.
- *Stage 4*: Medical investigation.
- *Stage 5*: If a non-organic reason is found for FTT, referral to social services for psychosocial assessment.
- *Stage 6*: More serious cases (if there is evidence of rejection, emotional indifference or other damaging neglect) to be the subject of a case conference.
- *Stage 7*: Treatment/intervention programme to be worked out and negotiated with the caregivers.
- *Stage 8*: Monitoring of child's growth and development – out-patient clinic, GP, health visitor, etc.
- *Stage 9*: Monitoring by the social worker of child–care-giver interaction and relationship and general well-being of the child.
- *Stage 10*: Case closed when there is evidence of systematic improvement in the child's growth, development and relationship between child and carer.

Treatment of Rebecca and parents

The primary objective in this case (and one strongly expressed by both parents) was to resolve eating difficulties in terms of consuming food more quickly, taking a wider variety of food, and lessening resistant and food-avoidance behaviour. By increasing caloric intake and decreasing tension and anxiety during the process of eating it was hoped that Rebecca would begin to gain weight, become more relaxed and begin to enjoy food, thus benefiting from improved nutrition. In order to create harmony between mother and child during the act of eating, the mother needed to learn how to control anxiety and to learn new strategies to manage her own behaviour and that of her daughter. Because of the severity of the mother's emotional state, debilitated energy levels and growing resentment towards Rebecca, arrangements were made for nursery attendance three days a week. An eating programme was carefully negotiated with the nursery staff, parents and the social worker, in line with home treatment methods.

Resolving eating problems Eating was tackled in a structured (and thus directive) manner. Much effort was put into making mealtimes more relaxed. The mealtime arrangements and appropriate feeding behaviour were discussed and modelled by a social worker. By direct modelling (and later, when things began to improve, by rehearsal), the caregiver can learn by observation how to create a relaxed atmosphere prior to and during the mealtime. The child should be spoken to warmly, quietly and encouragingly, and should be taken to the kitchen (when eating at home) to observe the carer preparing the food and to assist the carer in this task: for example, asking the child to hand an object to the carer. Informing the child what the carer is doing, drawing the child's attention to food preparation, and generating interest around this activity can be helpful. The carer should kiss, hug, smile at the child and thank him or her for help from time to time, helping the child to relax and feel more at ease. Food should be put on a plate in an interesting and appetising way, for example in the shape of a smiling face, a flower, a tree, etc. A story should be told referring to the arrangement on the plate to generate more interest in food, as this tends to speed up eating. For example, Rebecca was told a story about 'smiley face':

> Once upon a time there was a nice little girl called Rebecca, but she was very small and was not growing quickly because she ate very little. The face on the plate became sad because it thought that Rebecca might not have the strength to go to school [Rebecca wanted to go to school] and play games with other children and learn a lot. The face said to Rebecca: You must eat all that you have on the plate, so you can be strong, grow fast and be the best at playing games with other children. I will be a very happy and smiley face again if you eat everything – see you tomorrow on the plate.

Rebecca ate every scrap in no time at all, and became fascinated and stimulated by this approach to food.

What needs to be stressed here is that the therapist needs to be actively involved in the process of feeding, in order to model the style and tone of the feeding interactions. Advice and instructions alone – a didactic approach – do not seem to work in difficult cases, especially when parents have earlier received a variety of advice and instructions which did not work for them, when they did not get sufficient support and encouragement, or when methods of working were not evaluated and modified according to needs. Treatment must therefore be based on sound theoretical knowledge and empirical evidence in order to be successful, and applied with confidence. Once the caregiver feels more confident and relaxed (due to some improvement), distant reassurance and rehearsal (over the telephone) is often sufficient.

Further reinforcements were used to improve eating behaviour, in the form of symbolic and activity rewards. A picture-chart of fairy-tale characters (with which Rebecca was familiar and which she liked) was used to reward her for eating the required amount (established by the hospital dietician) and when she ate her food within the required time. The chart was placed on the kitchen door so that everyone could see it and make positive comments (social reinforcement). If she met minimum requirements, she could pick a picture from the envelope of her choice and help her parents to stick it on the chart. A lot of fuss and praise was given by the family, neighbours and professionals involved. Activity rewards consisted of being read stories by the parents or playing games (which she loved). Being read an extra story or special game was contingent on the number of pictures she earned during the day or previous day. If she earned at least two pictures a day (which included performance in the nursery), she could choose a game or an outing to the park.

Parents and nursery staff were prepared for 'good' and 'bad' days, and how to react and behave when things were not going well. It must be remembered that conditioned avoidance behaviour to food is not going to be resolved quickly and without setbacks. Carers are advised not to pressurise the child, scream, shout or to run after the child trying to force food on them. Equally, when they feel tense or angry, they should leave the child for a while, try to relax, and have another attempt when both parties feel calmer.

Treatment at the nursery Treatment in the nursery was similar to that at home, but with the advantage of having 'good eater' models at her table. One nursery nurse was trained and supervised to implement treatment and to take responsibility for Rebecca generally, but always at mealtimes. Observation of the child's eating behaviour showed that she responded less favourably when a lot of attention was directed to her. She tended to push food away, play with food, store food in her mouth or walk away from the table. Attention was then redirected to other children who were eating well: comments like 'What a great eater you are, Robin. You are going to be a football player soon and win all the matches' or 'Susan has already finished her sausage. You are a champion – it was nice wasn't it?' can help. Rebecca was approached in a matter-of-fact way, and occasionally prompted. By removing pressure and attention, Rebecca began to eat more quickly, almost competing with other children, and showed a tremendous pride in emptying her plate. She was praised for her achievements by the nursery staff, and was allowed to choose a story for story-time.

Relaxation training and cognitive work with the mother Among the commonest characteristics of mothers of FTT children are self-defeating thoughts and beliefs about their parenting skills. They tend to run themselves down, saying that they cannot do anything right, they are useless as carers, they cannot even feed the child, and whatever they do goes wrong. These dysfunctional thoughts lead to dysfunctional feelings, and consequently to negative outcomes for the child and the parents.

The aim of cognitive work with parents is to help them to begin viewing things in a way which is rational, in order to generate positive thoughts, beliefs and feelings about their capabilities of finding a way out of a problem, and to generate emotional energy based on facts and the increased conviction that they will be able to produce the necessary change. This work points to the successful aspects of clients' lives so that they can take comfort from those examples and reappraise their thinking and feelings: being ineffective in one area or with one child does not mean that the carer is useless at everything. Parents are asked to record unhelpful thoughts which seem to recur frequently, and to link them to the feelings accompanying those thoughts in order to create a realisation of how such thoughts can influence behaviour and well-being and how exaggerated they are at times. On closer examination, these beliefs and feelings often prove to be untrue because they are falsely linked to other areas of child care or life (compare the discussion of depressive feelings and beliefs in Chapter 9).

Rebecca's mother was depressed as a result of her daughter's poor physical growth, her own inability to feed the child, and her firm belief that there was something physically wrong which remained undetected. Her self-esteem could not have been lower. She perceived herself as totally inadequate as a mother, and lately as a wife. Furthermore, she began to blame Rebecca for all the ills in the family, and began to distance herself physically and emotionally from the child. Work included exploration of negative thinking and depressive feelings, their rationality, and the identification of positive actions and outcomes. The mother was asked to produce a balance sheet of her perception of successes and failures regarding child-rearing and child care as well as other life activities.

The fact that Rebecca was well above average in her psychosocial development (not often seen in FTT children) was due to the mother's stimulation, engagement in various learning activities and caring mothering. The child was properly dressed and provided with toys and playing material; the house was clean and well-managed, and the mother had been a successful career woman, a good home-maker, a good cook, was gentle and had good relationships with people. The positives out-balanced the negatives, such as being anxious, inability to manage the feedings, being unable to support her husband in his business, pushing responsibility for Rebecca's eating onto her already overburdened husband, or failure to control her frustration and feelings of helplessness. This exploration helped the mother to think more positively and rationally about her level of competence and achievement. She was asked to practise positive statements by repeating time and time again what was good about her performance, especially during periods when things were not going well. As Rebecca began to eat more and she slowly but surely began to put on weight, the mother's self-esteem began to rise. She was strongly and systematically reinforced by the therapist, who attributed slowly increasing positive outcomes to the mother's hard work.

Relaxation exercises were introduced during the first day of treatment. The mother was asked to do them at least twice a day, and more often when feeling particularly tense and anxious. Since lunch time was almost always the most difficult, she was advised to do them before lunch, in order to feel more at ease and calm (a 20-minute relaxation tape was provided, and exercises were rehearsed with the mother).

Treatment evaluation and outcomes

The treatment programme was implemented over three months. The first two weeks showed little improvement in eating behaviour, in spite of the hard work of parents and the nursery staff. Rebecca was either uncooperative or extremely manipulative, expecting to get her way as she had in the past. Perseverance and reduced anxiety and pressure paid off. During the third week, Rebecca doubled the amount of food eaten, and the duration of feeding-time was reduced by 50 per cent (on average half an hour). She put on weight – 2 lb within one month – and her weight began to rise thereafter, slowly reaching the 25th percentile after two-and-a-half months of treatment. Nursery attendance was terminated as there was no longer a need for her to be monitored.

The most rewarding change was observed in the mother. She became optimistic, confident, sure of herself, persistent and consistent when dealing with Rebecca. The mother–child relationship became warm, humorous and mutually rewarding. For the next six months, the case was followed up by the paediatrician and social worker: the hard-earned change in eating behaviour was maintained, and her weight gain was within the normal limits.

Conclusion

Cognitive-behavioural work offers an encouraging and constructive approach to the problem of FTT. The basic principles of behaviour modification and cognitive restructuring are clear and relatively easily communicated to parents, other caregivers, professionals and para-professionals. This approach provides a sound theoretical framework and a wealth of methods and techniques to use as therapeutic tools. Because of limited space here, only some treatment methods have been described.

Rebecca's case demonstrated combined FTT (organic, and later non-organic) mechanisms, both respondent and operant, which controlled and maintained the problem behaviours. Assessment based on a functional analysis provided a clear guide to methods of intervention for this particular case. The results show favourable outcomes for the child and the family.

References

Barbero, G.J. and Shaheen, E. (1967) 'Environmental failure to thrive: A clinical view', *Journal of Paediatrics*, 71, pp.639–44.

Batchelor, J. and Kerslake, A. (1990) *Failure to Find Failure-to-thrive*, London: Whiting and Birch.

Bowlby, J. (1951) *Maternal Care and Mental Health*, Geneva: Bulletin of the World Health Organisation.

Coleman, R. and Provence, S. (1957) 'Environmental retardation (hospitalism) in infants living with families', *Paediatrics* 19, p.285.

Fischhoff, J. (1975) 'Failure to thrive and maternal deprivation' in E.J. Nathony (ed.) *Explanations in Child Psychiatry*, New York: Plenum Press, pp.213–25.

Goldfarb, W. (1945) 'Effects of psychological deprivation in infancy and subsequent stimulation', *American Journal of Psychiatry*, 102, p.18.

Hanks, H. and Hobbs, C. (1993) 'Failure to thrive: A model for treatment' in *Baillière's Clinical Paediatrics*, **1**, 1, February, pp.101–19.

Haynes, C., Cutler, C., Gray, J., O'Keefe, K. and Kempe, R. (1983) 'Non-organic failure-to-thrive: Decision for placement and videotaped evaluation', *Child Abuse and Neglect: International Journal* 7, pp.309–19.

Iwaniec, D. (1983), *Social and Psychological Factors in the Aetiology and Management of Children Who Fail-to-thrive*, PhD thesis, University of Leicester Department of Psychology.

Iwaniec, D. (1991) 'Treatment of children who fail to grow in the light of the new Children Act', *Newsletter of the Association for Child Psychology and Psychiatry*, 13, pp.21–7.

Iwaniec, D. (1994) 'Neglect and emotional abuse in children who fail-to-thrive', *Child Care in Practice*, 1, pp.15–27.

Iwaniec, D. (1995) *The Emotionally Abused and Neglected Child: Identification, Assessment and Intervention*, Chichester: John Wiley.

Iwaniec, D., Herbert, M. and McNeish., A.S. (1985a) 'Social work with failure-to-thrive children and their families – Part I: Psychosocial factors', *British Journal of Social Work*, 15, pp.243–59.

Iwaniec, D., Herbert, M. and McNeish, A.S. (1985b) 'Social work with failure-to-thrive children and their families – Part II: Social work intervention', *British Journal of Social Work*, 15, pp.375–89.

Leonard, M.F., Rhymes, J.P. and Solnit, A.J. (1966) 'Failure-to-thrive in infants: A family problem', *American Journal of Diseases of Children*, 111, pp.600–12.

Pollitt, E. (1975) 'Failure-to-thrive: Socio-economic, dietary intake, and mother-child interaction', *Federal Proceedings*, 34, pp.1,593–7.

Pollitt, E., Eichler, A.W. and Chan, C.K. (1975) 'Psychosocial development and behaviour of mothers of failure-to-thrive children', *American Journal of Orthopsychiatry*, 45, pp.525–37.

Powell, G.F., Low, J.F. and Speers, M.A. (1987) 'Behaviour as a diagnostic aid in failure-to-thrive', *Journal of Developmental and Behavioural Paediatrics*, 8, pp.18–24.

Skuse, D. (1988) 'Failure to thrive. Failure to feed', *Community Paediatric Group Newsletter*, 6, pp.14–20.

Spitz, R.A. (1945) 'Hospitalism: An inquiry into the genesis of psychiatric conditions in early childhood', *Psychoanalytic Study of the Child*, 1, pp.53–74.

Talbot, N.B., Sobel, E.H., Burke, B.S., Lindeman, E. and Kaufman, S.B. (1947) 'Dwarfism in healthy children: Its possible relation to emotional, nutritional and endocrine disturbances', *New English Journal of Medicine*, 263, pp.783–93.

Widdowson, E.M. (1951) 'Mental contentment and physical growth', *The Lancet*, 260, pp.1,316–18.

Wolfe, D.A. (1988) 'Child abuse and neglect' in E.J. Mash and L.G. Terdal (eds) *Behavioral Assessment of Childhood Disorders*, New York: Guilford Press, pp.627–69.

5 Children with severe learning disabilities

Peter Burke

The needs of children with learning disabilities may easily be subsumed by the wishes of verbally expressive individuals, usually parents, who articulate these needs for their children. The effect, if not the intent, can be to exclude the wishes and needs of the children themselves. In my research with Katy Cigno (Burke and Cigno 1996), which focused on support for families, every effort was made to avoid this situation. However, there are no easy ways to incorporate the views of people whose attempts at communicating are less easily understood or who are dependent on others to express a view on their behalf. It became evident that a theoretical framework is needed which recognises that children with learning disabilities often have difficulty communicating their ideas or expressing their feelings. In other words, any behavioural approach adopted should be understood by those it directly concerns: the children themselves.

In this chapter, behavioural methods are identified which are applied in two case illustrations. Exploring behavioural methods in relation to children with severe levels of learning disabilities is made more difficult by their conceptual and intellectual problems in identifying a link between cause and effect experiences: for example, at night we tend to go to bed to sleep. Where an association is difficult to make, then traditional rewarding or reinforcing mechanisms are less likely to be meaningful. The child who does not or cannot associate sleep with night-time will need greater help to overcome their difficulty with sleeping at night than those of us who have little difficulty with the association but nevertheless might have problems getting to sleep. In order to overcome some of these problems, it is useful to find a meaningful link between antecedents and consequences. In making this link, I introduce the *locus of control* to help clarify the nature of influences which are meaningful for the child and for the child's family.

The locus of control (Lefcourt 1976) is based on principles of social learning theory (Stainton Rogers 1993) and can also be used in cognitive-behavioural therapy (Sheldon 1995). This is because the locus of control can represent any situation which requires some form of action – whether this is from the professional or parental view, or is orientated to encompass the world of the child – in all forms of daily interactions. Understanding the world of the child helps to locate situations experienced within families from a child's view, and therefore aids our determination of reasonable and realistic goals. Motivational interviewing, originally developed in work with problem drinkers (Miller 1983; see also Chapter 10) can be used to increase the client's awareness of problem behaviours which, following the identification of reasonably attainable goals, enables realistic changes to be achieved.

In work with children with learning disabilities, it is important to consider the meaning of the label. The term 'learning disability', used throughout this chapter, is preferred in government policy (Department of Health 1991). It is seen as less stigmatising than 'mental handicap' and applies to children who attend a special or mainstream school and who have been subject to a Statement of Special Educational Needs under the Education Act 1981. The Statement identifies the educational and learning needs of the child concerned, and particular areas of difficulty which may require specialist help. These might relate to communication difficulties and the need for specialised equipment such as a laptop computer, or the need for one-to-one assistance, whether from a teacher's assistant or a non-teaching assistant, depending on whether the need is educational or related to physical co-ordination problems, which might include incontinence. Children who receive a Statement of Special Needs are also 'children in need' under the Children Act 1989, Section 17 (10)(c), which specifies qualifying conditions relating to disabilities in Section 17 (11), and includes, for example, 'mental disorder of any kind ... or ... other disability as may be prescribed'.

There is no absolute level for the 'difficulties' concerned, as each child has needs which suggest they are different from the norm and label them as 'learning disabled'. Clearly, labelling groups of children by characteristics of impairment is an acknowledgement that their differences mean they do not learn in the 'expected' way, but it risks a later assessment of ability which undervalues the potential within the individual. The continued growth of new specialist terminology is evident within the legislation, as demonstrated in attempts to characterise children as 'different'. This is necessary as long as the intent is to provide an enabling framework without disablist stigmatisation and ridicule. Indeed, the concept of normalisation recognises that all children and adults have similar needs, but that those with learning disabilities may require additional help to follow the expected route of others not so disadvantaged (Frost and Stein 1989). 'Disadvantage', in the sense used here, is intended to convey the difference in expectations of an identifiable group of children, whether in the classroom, at home or in the community.

The locus of control

The idea that people explain their experiences in terms of what happens to them is central to a model of social learning. The assumption, according to Brown and Christie (1981), is that abnormal behaviour is not different from normal behaviour in its development, and that it may therefore be modified. Further, cognitive-behavioural therapy is part of a holistic approach where it is recognised that the behaviour of one human being has an impact on the behaviour of others. The therapist, in agreement with the service user or their carers, aims to identify particular behaviours which are problematic, and to bring about change by increasing awareness of the interactions and their contingencies which cause concern (Ronen 1997). The concept of the locus of control of behaviour, as identified by Lefcourt (1976), suggests that control is viewed by the individual as either internal or external. Individuals with an internal locus of control take responsibility for their own actions, and see rewards as a consequence of their own efforts. Individuals with an external locus of control view situations and outcomes as beyond their influence, and believe their lives to be subject to the control of others.

Critics of the 'locus of control' (see Stainton Rogers 1993) suggest that its psychometric grounding is at fault, due to the limitations of a dichotomic framework, and because reality is never as simple as the either/or view implied by the internal or external locus of control. It is therefore an inadequate portrayal of the events that control the lives of people: it represents an artificial construct. Further, because no two people share the same experience, individual perceptions will vary regarding whether an internal or external locus of control serves to explain the events under consideration. Stainton Rogers seems to believe that for a locus of control to exist, everyone must share the same view as to its location, and this is necessary for a form of external reliability to be achieved. However, the construct is not meant to be mechanistic but explanatory and interpretative, and is intended to refer to events, and the way people interpret their actions and perceive the world around them.

Since perceptions vary, then so must the locus of control. An inactive individual, typified as dependent and waiting for events to happen, is thought to have an external locus of control. Alternatively, an active person, who, at the other extreme, may seem 'out of control', is viewed as having an internal locus of control.

Wallston et al. (1978) introduce the multi-dimensional health locus of control (MHLC) scales to signify the influence on health of internal and external factors, including the effect of other people in positions of power. These have the potential to alter individual perceptions of their own locus of control. A 'powerful others' group of people may influence a change from an internal locus to an external one. A person may respond differently if their perception of a situation is reconstructed. Different situations give rise to different reactions and perceptions: the locus of control is adaptive if perceptions of circumstances can be changed from being viewed negatively to being considered as a challenge with positive characteristics. The adaptation that is required represents the potential to be influenced. This means that people whose behaviour is considered to reflect an externality of control are susceptible to interactive influence. Modifying the perceptions of control – encouraging listening and understanding – should help the individual to develop an internal locus of control.

Children with learning disabilities may be dependent on others, and thus have an external locus of control. Behavioural interventions need to recognise this external control, and put into operation a means for redirecting and reinforcing desired behaviours within the individual. The aim of intervention should be to increase the child's repertoire of skills and choices, enabling a move towards self-determination. However, it will also be recognised – if the hypothesis that learning disability compounds the likelihood of external control for the child is correct – that the family dynamic will be affected once the child becomes less dependent. The family may react by wishing to withdraw from the new and regress to their old better known ground, despite its apparent unacceptability.

It is also important to bear in mind that the 'rewards' used to reinforce a child's desired behaviour are more effective if they are perceived as such by the child. A psychologist who advised a mother to wrap little presents in paper and give them to her child when he ate at the table without screaming did not take into account the fact that the child was not able to associate the reinforcer with the behaviour and, furthermore, was unable to unwrap the paper. Such an intervention would not be effective in changing the child's behaviour, and would probably cause the mother to lose confidence in the ability of the professional to help. An accurate and careful assessment is needed which considers the ability of the child to learn, and includes the child's likes and dislikes, before an intervention strategy is implemented.

In the two case illustrations which follow, the intent is to illustrate the model by using case material, followed by an examination of how the locus of control varies in each. The point of the examination is to reflect on the whole family's situation, without isolating the child or parent in the intervention that is to ensue.

Methodological issues

The two case illustrations are presented from the mothers' point of view. Mothers are usually the main carers of their children with learning disabilities (Cigno with Burke 1997). These two situations are not representative of a worse-case scenario, but have been chosen because they encompass problems common to many families where there is a child with learning disabilities.

The cases suggest that unmet need exists, and that the services which are offered are often insufficient to enable any choice to be made (Burke and Cigno 1996; Ford 1996). The loneliness experienced by Julie's mother is a significant feature for many single parents who have children with learning disabilities (Brimblecombe 1987). There is a need to look at implications for practice. A behavioural approach provides a way forward.

Julie

Julie is 13, and lives with her mother on a council estate in a remote village. Her brother Richard, aged 17, lives with his father. Mother and father are divorced, and they parted before Julie's first birthday.

Julie's learning difficulties were not initially identified, despite concerns expressed by her mother to the medical profession. Julie's mother felt 'something was wrong', but little credence was given to her view. At 10 months of age, Julie had a fit which was attributed to a high temperature. After this, when crawling, she dragged her left side. However, it was not until Julie was 3 years old, after persistent requests from mother, that the doctors acknowledged her concerns. Eventually, extensive tests revealed a chromosomal abnormality which confers varying degrees of handicap (the condition is not named, to protect client confidentiality).

Julie learned to talk at the age of 6 years. Now, aged 13, she can dress herself, but cannot read or write. She will eat anything that she can get her hands on, including earth, any loose substances and, of course, food. Julie is difficult to manage at home due to her clumsy co-ordination and poor balance. She is diagnosed as epileptic, and her fits are largely controlled by medication. Her behaviour can be difficult to manage: for example, she has managed to break a number of antique dolls collected by her mother, and generally seems to gain pleasure from breaking things. At home from school over the weekend period, Julie sleeps with her mother, who says that this helps Julie to settle down at night. She is a vulnerable child, and there are concerns that she may be seen as 'easy prey' for anyone who takes an interest in her: she would be vulnerable to abuse or exploitation. Problem behaviours identified include destructiveness, over-eating and bedtime difficulties.

Education

Julie is subject to a Statement of Special Educational Needs. However, getting the best for Julie has been difficult for her mother. She appealed three times over the services provided to meet Julie's educational needs before Julie was allocated a place in her current school. She has now attended this school for over a year as a weekly boarder, using the hostel facility for the occasional weekend stay. Prior to this, Julie had to leave home at 8 a.m., returning at 6 p.m., exhausted due to the demands of travelling and the school routine.

Support

Social services were approached for assistance, but did not offer much help. For example, Julie's mother asked for a stair-gate to stop Julie wandering from her room at night. The social worker who visited recommended a bolt on the door. Julie's mother was not happy with this suggestion because, as she put it, 'I need to see Julie, not lock her out of sight.' The incident typified a rather indifferent attitude from social services, whose staff also seemed to lack the necessary expertise. Useful support was provided by Julie's teacher during her early schooling, where she received much individual attention. In mother's words, 'Julie was loved to bits.' The teacher concerned is still in touch with the family, and offers advice and other help when required.

Julie's mother has cancer and spondylitis, and requires regular treatment for both. She feels that most professionals do not understand her own or her daughter's needs. For example, the mother's operation to remove her tumour was planned to take place at a local hospital, but had to be delayed because school transport could not be rearranged while she was in hospital. She had previously worked as a pub manager, but due to her daughter's needs, can now only work on a part-time basis as a salesperson.

Some practical help was given. A charity paid for a new washer/dryer to meet Julie's almost constant need for a change of clothing, but could not pay for a fence to make the rear garden safer for Julie. The fence was finally erected at the mother's expense, despite her low income.

At present, Julie's mother has many good friends who are her main source of support. She has some respite on her day off from work when Julie is at school, and when Julie's father occasionally takes her out. The demands of looking after Julie at the weekend, plus a busy work routine, make her day off each week, on her own, very special. The demands on her time would otherwise be excessively stressful.

Future needs

It is anticipated that Julie will probably end up in 'some institution' when her mother feels she cannot manage her and she finishes school. No one is certain about the future. Medical explanations about Julie's intellectual difficulties are characterised by the expression 'You cannot put a pint into a quarter pint pot', reflecting the inadequacy of explanations offered, oppressive and stigmatising attitudes held by others, and general uncertainties about Julie's developmental potential.

At present, additional help is needed at weekends. The family has no transport, and is restricted to local activities and watching TV. School holidays are difficult and stressful times, and other parents are not very helpful. Julie needs almost constant supervision if she is not to endanger herself in some way. She has few friends with whom she can play.

A comprehensive assessment of need would be useful, so that Julie's situation and family needs could be thoroughly reviewed. A behavioural assessment could help identify and prioritise problem behaviours for change (see Chapter 1). A functional analysis would help to specify behavioural antecedents and consequences. Julie's mother felt she needed practical and emotional support, but this did not seem to be available.

Comment

The gradual realisation that Julie had a learning disability was difficult for her mother to accept. Her recollections of problems experienced in the past raise concerns for the future, and difficulties seem never-ending. Gaining access to suitable education for Julie was complicated by resource problems, and resulted in three appeals about the levels of educational services provided. Julie's mother felt she had received little and impractical help from social services. Further, she had her own health problems. Transport problems were compounded by living in a remote village.

The circumstances fit the external locus of control because Julie's mother's perception was that the situation and outcome were beyond her control, and that her and Julie's lives were subject to the control of others. Behavioural work might have helped to reduce the frequency and severity of Julie's problem behaviours and helped to reduce the mother's stress. Positive reinforcement to help shape Julie's pro-social behaviours combined with the introduction of new skills could improve family interactions and patterns of reinforcement (Brigden and Todd 1995).

It is also apparent that Julie's mother views all professionals with some suspicion. In order to gain acceptance, the worker needs to demonstrate a positive interest and understanding through working in partnership with Julie and her mother. A cognitive-behavioural intervention, according to Ronen (1997), would help the child's mother to view the worker more positively, and would enable the worker to modify parent–child interaction and increase the mother's self-esteem and coping abilities within a framework of support.

Richard

Richard is 5½ years old. He has an older sister, Susan, who is 7. The family live in a large, terraced house in a market town. Richard was born in the Far East. The family returned to the UK when he was 18 months old, following the diagnosis that he had 'learning difficulties'. His father gave up his work abroad so that Richard could commence special schooling in Britain rather than risk, as the family thought, the uncertainty of early school experience in a foreign city where resources seemed less focused on children with special needs.

Richard's condition affects his motor neurological pathways, and makes him seem a clumsy child. The cause is uncertain, but medical tests showed that it was not of genetic origin. Richard has partial vision. He had surgery on his tendons to improve his ability to walk. He seems not to notice pain – a problem which places him at considerable risk, given his susceptibility to falling and hurting himself without any awareness of the injury sustained.

Richard's sister, Susan, experiences some difficulty at school, where derogatory comments are made about her brother, such as 'He's stupid.' This can be very upsetting for her. Richard dotes on his sister, and they play happily together.

Although both parents thought Richard was developmentally slower than average (for instance, one indication was that he would sleep from 5 p.m. to 10 a.m.), at first they did not realise the significance of this. Richard has attended a special school for one year since the age of 4.

It is doubtful that Richard will ever achieve independence, although his parents adopt a policy of 'wait and see', hoping for further improvements in his abilities. It is probable, though, that normal parental expectations – for example, that he will leave home at the age of 20 or thereabouts – will not apply.

Support

The family's impression of support services is that because Richard has borderline disabilities, demanding too much in the way of services amounts to 'being greedy'. Indeed, their impression is that resources have to be fought for: 'fighting for everything' is almost a family motto.

It has been difficult for the family to adjust to Richard's situation. There is a lack of knowledgeable people who can give advice and help. The medical profession does not seem to be able to indicate the probable outcome for Richard in the future. A counselling service or even a help line to talk to someone with experience of disability in the family might help his parents.

Education

Richard has been subject to five revised Statements of Special Educational Need. His parents refused to sign them because, in their opinion, the Statements did not properly reflect his needs. The Statementing process does not provide a mandate for health services, so, for example, speech therapy cannot be prescribed. As a result, his parents feel that their hands are tied, and that their child does not get the services he requires. Parents who are demanding can be seen by professionals as 'bad' or troublesome and 'pushing beyond their rights' (Burke and Cigno 1996).

Other factors

Caring for a disabled child can be stressful, and is made more difficult for the carers because professionals and service providers often lack sufficient detailed knowledge of the child's disability. Parents are not put in contact with each other. Self-help may be the only way to get a child's needs met.

Partner support is vital. Life can seem to consist of an exchange of angry letters with the Education Department, with little opportunity to talk with others or to relax. Friends may not understand or be able to help – carers need to talk to parents who have experienced similar problems. Respite care, such as that provided by a summer playscheme, may give carers time to think and allow the child's needs to be met.

The help from social services is insignificant, and is not proactively offered. Services need to be publicised: all too often parents don't know what to ask for because they do not know what is available. Less delay in responding to parents would make parents feel that they were being heard. Openness is necessary to improve the lot of children like Richard; indeed, all written information should be shared with carers.

Comment

Richard's learning disabilities, like Julie's, were slow to surface. His dependence is likely to continue beyond his teenage years. As a result of his prognosis, the family have fundamentally changed the course of their lives, resulting in a loss of prestige, change of address and recurring confrontations with authority figures as the parents tried to obtain services for their child and themselves.

Unlike Julie, Richard had a sibling for company, and while Susan experiences unkind comments about her brother, his needs for a supportive home environment appear to be met. Children with special needs may have their needs met to the detriment of other siblings, a situation confirmed by Kew (1975) and Powell and Ogle (1985). However, Beresford (1994) suggests that sibling relationships can be positive, as brothers and sisters feel valued when relied on for practical support.

Richard's family look upon his dependency and uncertain future as a child with special needs as a challenge which they may not overcome. The family experiences an external locus of control centred on the professional services offered by health, education and Social Services. Friendships appear not to be helpful to the family in maintaining their identity because their caring role, with its additional demands in responding to Richard's needs, leaves little time to develop and maintain informal social relationships. The family, successful and independent prior to their son's birth, has lost its internal locus of control, the locus of control changing from being self-driven towards an external reality where they are dependent on others to provide (or fail to provide) the services required. Both parents are assertive and are able to confront authorities, but gain little satisfaction and achieve minimal progress in the provision of resources to which they consider they are entitled.

Both parents appear to need much support. The first stage of intervention would be to offer them a listening service to help formulate their view of the difficulties that confront them and to begin to recognise their positive contribution to Richard's life, as typified by their return to the UK for his benefit. Although it is probably also the case that the matching reality produced disappointment and grieving over a changed lifestyle, recognition of the sacrifice they had made in their commitment to Richard would help his parents to acknowledge and value their contribution to his well-being, and might also help to extinguish the anger they have directed towards professionals.

Observations of Richard at play would provide the foundation for a detailed assessment of his abilities and vulnerability to injury. From this, it would be possible to plan how best to keep him safe while enabling him to play creatively. Susan could be helped to deal with derogatory comments about her brother at school by teaching her coping strategies. The locus of control would be directed back within the family to achieve a level of internalisation of appropriate behaviours in relation to the needs of both children.

Conclusion

The case illustrations show how two families were initially slow to realise that their child had learning disabilities, but once the realisation had set in, fundamental changes occurred: Julie ended up living on an isolated housing estate with her mother, Richard moved from the Far East back to Britain; both families confronted social, health and school professionals in seeking the best for their child.

It is hypothesised that the locus of control changes from a former internal level of control to an external locus as each family adjusts to caring for a child with a learning disability. A previously self-motivating and functioning family has to re-adapt and regain control over their life. Because previously independent, self-functioning families have shifted the internal locus of control to an external one since they need resources which only external bodies can provide, the change is resisted by means of misdirected activity, such as a show of anger or frustration at the delivery, or delayed delivery, of services. Indeed, the parental perception is that they have lost control and are struggling to regain their previous level of control, a necessary stage in their adjustment to the difficult and often frustrating experiences of caring for a child with a learning disability.

In these circumstances, the locus is heuristic in enabling the professional worker to hypothesise about the functioning of the family and in assisting the reframing of family activities. Work should be aimed at assisting the family to gain control over day-to-day experiences through positive reinforcement of their considerable achievements in taking care of their children. Training in anger management would also be useful for Richard's parents (see, for example, Scott 1989). Some features of the lives of these families may be present in any family undergoing change, but in the cases presented, there is in addition the child's disability, the limitations of resource provision and future uncertainty.

The advantage cognitive-behavioural methods bring to an examination of families who have a child with learning disabilities is that a detailed ecological assessment is made of family circumstances, including child–parent interaction, child management and parental skills in negotiating with gatekeepers of resources. The dynamic of the locus of control may then be considered – a device for identifying whether parents are subject to internal or external influences, reflected through their level of adjustment to their child's learning disability. The locus is unique in its family orientation, and behaviours are viewed as either internal or subject to external influence. The effect of identifying an external locus may deny the child's input into a situation, but redirecting that input through work with family members acts like an internal family adjustment mechanism, which enables the child's individuality to be regained and a first step to be made towards independence and control by both the child and other family members.

Acknowledgement

I would like to express my appreciation for the advice and assistance offered by Di Bourn and Katy Cigno, who were always willing to help during the drafting of this chapter.

References

Beresford, B. (1994) *Positively Parents: Caring for a Severely Disabled Child*, London: HMSO.

Brigden, P. and Todd, M. (1995) 'Behavioural Approaches' in M. Todd and G. Gilbert (eds) *Learning Disabilities: Practice Issues in Health Settings*, London: Routledge.

Brimblecombe, F. (1987) 'The voices of disabled young people: The Exeter Project', *Children and Society*, 1, pp.58–70.

Brown, B.J. and Christie, C. (1981) *Social Learning Practice in Residential Child Care*, Oxford: Pergamon Press.

Burke, P. and Cigno, K. (1996) *Support for Families: Helping Children with Learning Disabilities*, Aldershot: Avebury.

Cigno, K. with Burke, P. (1997) 'Single mothers of children with learning disabilities: An undervalued group', *Journal of Interprofessional Care*, 11, pp.177–86.

Department of Health (1991) *The Children Act 1989: Guidance and Regulations. Vol. 6,*

Children with Disabilities: A New Framework for the Care and Upbringing of Children, London: HMSO.

Ford, S. (1996) 'Learning difficulties' in G. Hales (ed.) *Beyond Disability: Towards an Enabling Society,* London: Open University/Sage.

Frost, N. and Stein, M. (1989) *The Politics of Child Welfare: Inequality, Power and Change,* London: Harvester Wheatsheaf.

Kew, S. (1975) *Handicap and Family Crisis: A Study of the Siblings of Handicapped Children,* Bath: Pitman Publishing.

Lefcourt, H.M. (1976) *Locus of Control: Current Trends in Theory and Research,* Hillsborough, NJ: Lawrence Erlbaum.

Miller, W.R. (1983) 'Motivational interviewing with problem drinkers', *Behavioural Psychology,* 11, pp.147–72.

Powell, T.H. and Ogle, P.A. (1985) *Brothers and Sisters: A Special Part of Exceptional Families,* Baltimore, MD: Paul Brookes Publishing.

Ronen, T. (1997) 'Cognitive behavioural therapy' in M. Davies (ed.) *The Blackwell Companion to Social Work,* Oxford: Blackwell.

Scott, M. (1989) *A Cognitive-behavioural Approach to Clients' Problems,* London: Tavistock/Routledge.

Sheldon, B. (1995) *Cognitive-behavioural Therapy: Research, Practice and Philosophy,* London: Routledge.

Stainton Rogers, W. (1993) 'From psychometric scales to cultural perspectives' in A. Beatie, M. Gott, L. Jones and M. Sidel (eds) *Health and Wellbeing,* London: Macmillan.

Wallston, K.A., Wallston, B.S. and De Vellis, R. (1978) 'Development of the multidimensional health locus of control (MHLC) scales', *Health Education Monograph,* 6, pp.161–70.

6 Behavioural work in residential childcare

Mansoor A.F. Kazi and Safina Mir

This chapter illustrates examples from two residential homes for children and young people where the approaches of social workers were influenced by social learning theory and where the social workers used empirical practice techniques to evaluate the impact of their interventions on the residents. The first is a home in Yorkshire where Safina Mir successfully completed a practice placement, and the second a home in Lancashire where Pat Powell and her staff were helped by Mansoor Kazi to apply single-case evaluation techniques in their work.

Behavioural approaches have developed as an important part of social work practice in the last three decades. Gambrill (1987) describes the wide range of emphases that exist within the behavioural perspective, ranging from applied behavioural analysis, which focuses on observable behaviours and related environmental factors, to cognitive behaviour modification, which focuses on altering thoughts presumed to be related to behaviours. Lying close to the latter end of the spectrum is social learning theory, although there is controversy regarding the exact relationship between cognitive approaches and procedures based on social learning theory:

> Symbolic processes such as modelling, vicarious learning, and the anticipation of consequences are critical components of social learning theory. Social learning theory is a social systems approach in which attention is given to the social cues and consequences related to behaviours (Gambrill 1987, p.185).

A full description can be found in Bandura (1977), and a summary in Sheldon (1995, pp.94–8; see also Chapter 1).

Thyer (1994) identifies three major forms of learning associated with social learning theory:

1 *respondent conditioning*, where a conditioned stimulus can lead to a conditioned response or respondent behaviours
2 *operant conditioning*, where the consequences of a past behaviour influence its present occurrence; something good may be presented (positive reinforcement), something bad may be taken away (negative reinforcement), something bad may be presented (positive punishment), or something good is taken away (negative punishment)
3 *modelling* or *imitation of others*.

'Over the time course of childhood development, most individuals develop strong imitative skills, skills that are durable in part because of the sometimes inconsistent occurrence of being rewarded for imitation' (Thyer 1994, p.138).

These three forms of learning are prevalent in most residential homes for children, and influence the behaviours and outcomes for children in various ways. A child's personality or behaviours develop as a result of social interaction within the residential home, including the ways in which the framework of rewards and punishments are formulated, and the ways in which they are carried out by staff in practice. The process of imitation and identification with role models can take place both with other residents and the individual members of staff themselves, therefore the personalities and behaviours of residential social workers can influence the outcomes for children in their care.

Behavioural approaches and evaluation of practice

Behavioural approaches enable residential social workers to be more aware of the social interactions within their homes, and to harness and influence these naturally occurring events in a planned way to generate positive outcomes for children in their care. The first case study illustrates the helpfulness of these approaches. First, they help social workers to lead by example, providing models of good behaviour and appropriate relationships between human beings. Second, they help to manage rewarding and punishing policies and practices in such a way that positive behaviour is encouraged and unacceptable behaviour is not unwittingly reinforced in the daily social interactions between staff and residents. Third, these approaches help to develop specific intervention plans and to review progress as required by legislation. Finally, the social workers are encouraged to use evaluation techniques which can be employed in the course of their daily practice to provide feedback on the performance of clients against agreed targets. One way to facilitate such ongoing evaluation is the use of single-case designs.

As an evaluation methodology, single-case designs have become more responsive to the needs of social work practice. The main requirements are that target problems – which are the object of the social work intervention(s) – should be specified, and suitable measuring instruments should be assigned and used repeatedly to enable systematic tracking of client progress over time. If appropriate standardised measures of proven reliability cannot be found (as in Fischer and Corcoran 1994), then practitioners can construct their own, provided due attention is paid to potential errors, and reliability is enhanced as much as possible. For example, practitioners can devise formats for observing frequency of behaviour or use rating scales to indicate whether a target problem is improving or deteriorating, provided the behaviours that are being observed are operationally defined in such a way that ambiguity or 'grey areas' are minimised, and that the rating scales are anchored so that definitions of what constitutes an improvement are applied consistently throughout the measurement period (see Thyer 1993; Kazi and Wilson 1996; Kazi 1996 and Kazi 1998 for a fuller description of single-case designs). The last two case examples in this chapter are from the home in Lancashire where the social workers took part in a study to consider the utility of these evaluation techniques. It should be noted that these evaluation procedures can be used to evaluate all types of intervention programmes, and not just behavioural approaches.

What happens when the principles outlined above are not followed, the effects of intervention are not evaluated and when the primary goal – the child's interests – is lost was seen in one of the worst examples of residential childcare in recent years: the so-called practice of pin-down. Here, a poorly-understood and questionably ethical process was employed without regard to its effects on children. The use of punishment became the main method of control (see, for example, Levy and Kahan 1991, and Howe 1992 for accounts of pin-down and childcare practices).

Case study: A residential home for children

As a student on the qualifying Diploma in Social Work, Safina Mir was placed in a local authority residential children's home whose main purpose was to prepare young people for fostering or adoption, or to rehabilitate them back to their own homes and families. The home had a capacity of eight residents, and was run along the lines of a large, single family unit, with minimal sub-divisions into age, sex and other characteristics of its client group. The organisation and structure of the unit was designed to facilitate the overall purpose of preparing residents to return to family life. A strong emphasis was placed on providing an environment in which children could develop and meet their social, emotional, physical and educational needs. The home's purpose was consistent with Part III (Section 20) of the Children Act 1989, which placed specific duties on local authorities to provide consumer-led services for children in need and their families – services to be delivered not as a means for the local authority to gain control over the child who is accommodated, but in order to help and serve the child. The local authority is also required to agree a plan with the parent and child, and to review the plan on a regular basis. The unit provided intensive, short-term work depending on the child's needs.

During the placement, there were seven residents, and the main reason for their admission was due to family breakdown or foster placement breakdown. These experiences often caused the children and young people to become resentful and anxious. They would vent their anger and frustration by displaying disruptive and challenging behaviour. These situations were usually dealt with in a positive and sensitive manner; however, there were occasions when sanctions were used inappropriately as a method of control. Policies relating to control, discipline and sanctions were clearly defined in accordance with Regulation 8(2) of *The Children Act 1989: Guidance and Regulations*, Volume 4. The home's stated policies recognised that a framework of controls was essential for the children in order for them to feel safe and secure and to develop self-control. The policies also stated that such control should essentially be maintained on the basis of good personal and professional relationships between residential staff and the children.

While on placement, Safina Mir observed that whenever a child was admitted to the unit, he or she was informed of the rules and regulations of the home. They were also informed verbally or in writing of the implications of behaviour which would demand staff intervention. The purpose was to provide choices for the children, and to instil responsibility for their own behaviour. Staff were also required to record the date and full particulars of the use of permitted methods of discipline, and to ensure that such records were signed by both the child and the staff member invoking the sanctions. Such records were made available for inspection by representatives of the local authority. Throughout Safina Mir's placement, there was only one occasion when she invoked these sanctions as a method of control, after three verbal warnings. Before sanctioning, she carefully informed the child of the reasons why he was being sanctioned, the purpose of the sanction, and how he could take control of his behaviour in future. In the main, Safina Mir's preferred approach was to use what she calls 'psychological punishment', as described below.

Residential homes attempt to influence children's behaviour by means of tangible rewards or some kind of praise for good behaviour, and sanctions or punishment for what is considered as bad, unacceptable or inappropriate behaviour. The reward and sanctions framework varies from home to home. At this home, sanctions took the form of loss of privileges, extra household jobs, or loss of part of pocket money to pay for damages, for example. However, it is argued that the use of sanctions is a highly inefficient and time-wasting way of socialising children, particularly since it increases the need to avoid being found out, and it does not stop the child from proceeding to do something equally bad, or even worse. The child tends to see the penalty as a price to be paid for a specific behaviour. With this form of punishment, the child does not need to take the responsibility or even feel guilty for his or her actions. A counter-argument is that, when faced with challenging and disruptive behaviour, the residential social worker needs to maintain control, and that order cannot be restored without sanctions.

Moreover, there are other ways of exercising control that do instil a sense of responsibility. The use of psychological punishment, for example, does not necessarily require any sort of tangible penalty – the child is 'punished' primarily in terms of awareness of the hurt they have caused to other people, and the act of apology can help to develop a stronger conscience than the use of physical forms of punishment. Gradually, this becomes internalised, so that rather than just saying 'sorry', the child comes to *feel* sorry, and later responsible or guilty (Hayes and Orrell 1987). This type of punishment was used by some members of staff within the home, but there was no set policy governing its use. (The importance of policy consistency in institutional care is discussed in Chapter 7.)

From the social learning perspective, imitation and identification are forms of observational learning, and their impact may be strengthened with the use of positive reinforcers such as praise or encouragement. Anything which strengthens a particular form of behaviour is a reinforcer. A child who exhibits challenging behaviour has his or her behaviour rewarded by attention of some kind. Moreover, typically he or she has not had the opportunity to learn alternative forms of behaviour. This was true for children in the home, as in the earlier stages of their stay they all exhibited behaviours which were considered extreme and difficult. They may well have been present in the child's own home prior to reception into care. For example, one child was sent to his family's home for a weekend visit. The parents reported that the child had been noisy and disruptive on Friday night and throughout Saturday, and behaved only on Sunday after a new computer game had been bought. The child was very pleased with the game, which was actually positive reinforcement for noisy and disruptive behaviour.

Thus, on return to residential care, the child's disruptive behaviour might escalate.

The impact of imitation and identification supports the need for residential social workers to act as positive role models. In addition, the staff need to have a sensitive approach if they are to deal appropriately with children from different cultural backgrounds, especially being aware of the different social expectations that children may have had placed upon them in the past. Social expectations placed upon a child will vary since, according to their family cultures, the 'ways in which working class children are brought up are often vastly different from the kinds of upbringing that middle class children have' (Hayes and Orrell 1987, p.303). Therefore, it is the responsibility of the residential care worker to be sensitive to the needs of the child and to have an awareness of cultural backgrounds so that unrealistic social expectations are not placed upon the child while being looked after in care.

Behavioural approaches: Case example 'A'

On one occasion while Safina Mir was on duty, one young resident, 'A', felt he had been unfairly sanctioned by a member of staff. His reaction was one of anger and outrage, along with further disruptive behaviour. This he displayed by climbing on to the roof of the outhouse. When he was approached and asked to come down, he proceeded to shout racist abuse at Safina, as well as other forms of abuse at the rest of the staff on duty. Safina's reaction was to remain calm, and she left the scene while the other members of staff helped to bring the child down.

After A came off the roof, he spent most of the evening avoiding Safina. She did not approach him, as she wanted him to calm down and to reflect on his behaviour. Eventually, at bed-time, she took the opportunity to discuss A's behaviour with him, in private. She began with emphasising the need to respect each other, and each other's feelings. She informed A that she was perhaps more offended than angry at his racist abuse. A responded by apologising, and went on to say that he understood how she felt as he had also experienced 'name-calling' and it was 'not nice'. Safina's approach to this incident was based on empowering A, through relating his feelings and experiences to her own. She conveyed respect by discussing this situation in private and by speaking to him in a quiet, normal manner. In this way, she also helped A deal with his own position with regard to racism.

If Safina's response had been to apply more tit-for-tat sanctions, the situation might have deteriorated still further. Instead, through modelling and imitation, a positive approach was demonstrated, and A responded in kind. The incident was not repeated, and there was no need to invoke further sanctions during A's stay at the Home. A was able to develop helpful relationships with both peers and staff, and received good reports from his school.

Single-case designs: Case example 'G'

'G' was accommodated at the Lancashire home at the request of her parents, who described her as beyond their control. They had expressed concern about her staying out late at night, mixing with an undesirable peer group, and drug abuse. G felt that her parents were being unreasonable in denying her the freedoms she was requesting, and that their attitude to her friends was biased. The parents appeared to have different attitudes towards dealing with these problems, and were unable to exercise any form of control or provide parental guidance for G.

As part of their assessment, the staff used standardised measures from Corcoran and Fischer (1987). Hudson's Child's Attitude Toward Father (CAF) and Child's Attitude Toward Mother (CAM) Scales indicated that there were significant problems with both the father and mother, although the score was a little better with the latter. At the same time, the Assertiveness Scale for Adolescents indicated a strong personality, with firmly held views and opinions. However, the Rosenberg Self-Esteem Scale indicated that G's perception of herself was significantly poor. The staff also used the Hare Self-Esteem Scale, which provides an indication of self-esteem in the areas of school, home and peer group, and found that self-esteem was very high in the peer group area, but very low in the areas of home and school, due to G's poor relationship with her parents, and also because she was unable to fulfil their expectations at school. Finally, the Children's Perceived Self-Control Scale indicated that G had a low perception of her own self-control, particularly in the company of her peers.

The staff's intervention programme was largely based on a social systems (social learning) approach in which due attention was paid to the social cues and consequences related to G's behaviours. In her first week at the home, G absconded for a weekend, and upon her return negative punishment was used, depriving her of participation in outside activities for a short period. Apart from this incident, G responded very positively to the home's intervention, with continuing good behaviour. The positive, one-to-one attention provided by the staff helped her to be more responsible for her own behaviour. The intervention was designed to lead by example, providing consistent management of behaviour, while at the same time giving G the freedom to make her own choices, and to make normal adolescent mistakes.

During the respite that was offered to G and her parents by the Home, G was able to develop self-control, raise her self-esteem and improve her relationship with her parents. The home visits were all very positive, and G's scores on all of the standardised measures used indicated significant improvements.

Case example: 'C' and 'S'

'C' and 'S' were two young brothers with learning difficulties, who were placed in the home to improve their ability to get up in the mornings, to wash and dress themselves, to reduce inappropriate swearing in social situations, and to develop appropriate table manners during meals. Specific behavioural interventions were used for each of these target problems, and the social workers used single-case designs to evaluate progress against each of these variables. In this case example, we illustrate two of these single-case designs.

The target problem – ability to wash and dress themselves – was measured with the use of a ten-point rating scale (see Figure 6.1). The tasks were identified as cleaning teeth, washing face and hands, combing hair, etc. and

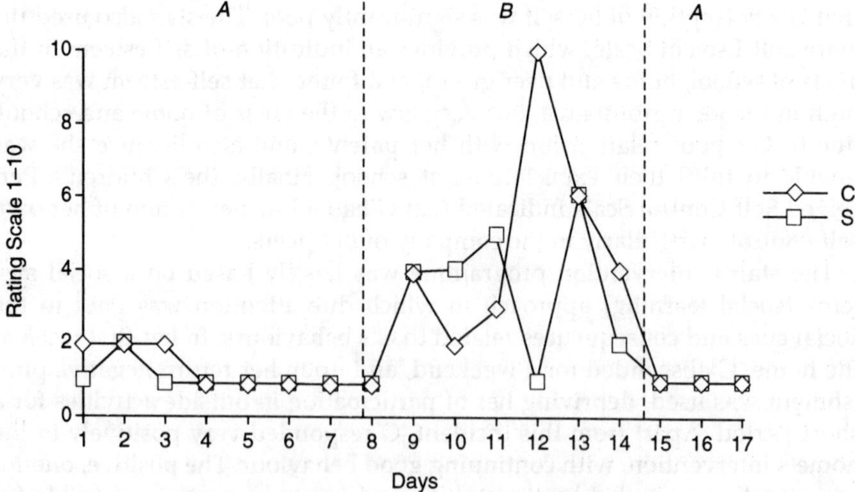

Figure 6.1 'C' and 'S': Washing and dressing ratings

the scale ranged from 1 = none of the tasks completed to 10 = all of the tasks completed. *A* represents the periods when the ability of the children was observed, and *B* the period of intervention when the social worker not only observed, but also intervened to demonstrate the appropriate ways of completing each task each time the children were unable to complete an activity themselves.

In the baseline period of the first seven days, both C and S scored very low on the scale. At the onset of intervention phase *B*, an immediate improvement took place, and the ratings for both children were higher than in the baseline phase. However, the follow-up observations at the end of the intervention indicate that there was an immediate deterioration, and the scores were very low again. The two 'coincidences' – that there was an improvement when intervention started, and a deterioration when it stopped – indicate that the intervention was probably responsible for the improvements during phase *B*. However, both C and S were unable to maintain the improvements without further intervention.

The second target problem was the incidence of swearing (see Figure 6.2). This was measured as the frequency of swearing per day, based on the social worker's observations. Although this measure did not take into account the severity of each incident observed, it was an easy measure to administer once 'swearing' was adequately defined, and it did provide some indication of the extent of swearing. The intervention in phase *B* was that once the incident was observed, the child responsible was given 'Time

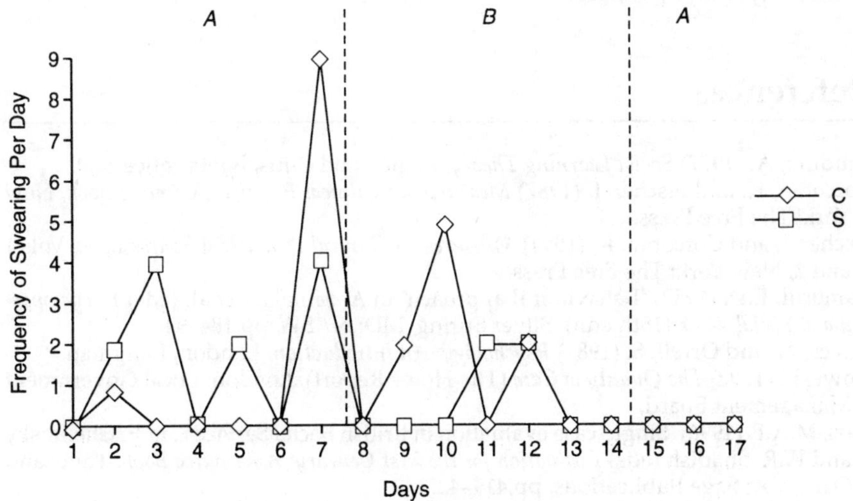

Figure 6.2 'C' and 'S': Incidence of swearing

Out' from the group or social situation in which swearing occurred, and was reminded that swearing was not appropriate. Figure 6.2 indicates that the incidence of swearing reduced at the onset of phase *B*, and continued to decline. Follow-up observations indicate that the incidence of swearing was reduced to zero even after the intervention finished.

Conclusion

The case study and the case examples from both residential homes indicate the utility of behavioural approaches in developing helpful interventions for children in residential care. Social learning theory does not focus on the child's behaviour alone; rather, it helps to locate the child as part of a system, and the child's behaviours as a function of social interaction between the child and other residents, and between the residents and the social workers caring for them. The behavioural approaches help to develop individual programmes for each resident within the framework of a home that is aware of its impact on the development of its residents – the impact may be positive in improving the child's functioning, or it could be negative in reinforcing inappropriate behaviours. Single-case designs help to evaluate this impact through systematic tracking of client progress. The method provides evidence in relation to the overall effectiveness of the residential home which can be of benefit both for the home and its residents in shaping future practice.

References

Bandura, A. (1977) *Social Learning Theory*, Englewood Cliffs, NJ: Prentice-Hall.

Corcoran, K. and Fischer, J. (1987) *Measures for Clinical Practice: A Source Book*, New York: The Free Press.

Fischer, J. and Corcoran, K. (1994) *Measures for Clinical Practice: A Source Book*, Vols 1 and 2, New York: The Free Press.

Gambrill, E.D. (1987) 'Behavioural approach' in A. Minahan et al. (eds) *Encyclopaedia of Social Work* (18th edn), Silver Spring, MD: NASW, pp.184–94.

Hayes, N. and Orrell, S. (1987) *Psychology: An Introduction*, London: Longman.

Howe, E. (1992) *The Quality of Care* (The Howe Report), London: Local Government Management Board.

Kazi, M.A.F. (1996) 'Single-case evaluation in British Social Services', in E. Chelimsky and W.R. Shadish (eds) *Evaluation for the 21st Century: A Resource Book*, Thousand Oaks, CA: Sage Publications, pp.419–42.

Kazi, M.A.F. (1998) *Single-case Evaluation by Social Workers*, Aldershot: Ashgate.

Kazi, M.A.F. and Wilson, J. (1996) 'Applying single-case evaluation in social work' in *British Journal of Social Work*, 26, pp.699–717.

Levy, A. and Kahan, B. (1991) *The Pin-down Experience and the Protection of Children: The Report of the Staffordshire Child Care Inquiry 1990*, Stafford: Staffordshire County Council.

Sheldon, B. (1995) *Cognitive-behavioural Therapy: Research, Practice and Philosophy*, London: Routledge.

Thyer, B.A. (1993) 'Single-system research designs' in R.M. Grinnell Jr (ed.) *Social Work Research and Evaluation* (4th edn), Itasca, IL: F.E. Peacock, pp.94–117.

Thyer, B.A. (1994) 'Social learning theory: Empirical applications to culturally diverse practice' in R.R. Greene (ed.) *Human Behaviour Theory: Diversity Applications*, New York: Aldine de Gruyter.

7 Working with young offenders

Clive R. Hollin

This chapter begins with an overview of cognitive-behavioural approaches to working with young offenders. The overview complements both existing reviews of the same topic (for example, Garrido and Sanchis 1991; Hollin 1993; Ross and Ross 1989) and reviews of delinquency prevention generally (for example, Farrington 1992; Gendreau et al. 1994; Hollin and Howells 1996; Mulvey et al. 1993). The chapter goes on to consider what is known about the general effectiveness of working with young offenders. The chapter concludes with a look at social and policy issues.

Cognitive-behavioural programmes

Cognitive-behavioural programmes are based on the application of both social learning theory and cognitive theory to inform therapeutic methods. This approach is marked by an emphasis on the role of social factors, together with a focus on changing emotion and cognition as well as overt behaviour. As discussed below, a range of cognitive-behavioural programmes for young offenders have been reported in the literature (Hollin 1990).

Self-control and self-instruction

Children gain self-control over their actions as their 'inner' speech develops. Such inner speech, in the form of self-statements or self-talk, serves several functions, including the child's self-observation, self-evaluation and self-reinforcement. The development of self-statements to achieve increased self-control can be achieved through *self-instructional training* (SIT: Goldstein and Keller 1987). SIT with young offenders has been found to increase self-control, and so lower rates of aggressive behaviour (Snyder and White 1979).

Anger control

An application of self-control procedures has been seen in interventions specifically designed for anger control. Most closely identified with the work of Novaco (1975 and 1994) there are anger control programmes specifically for adolescent populations (Feindler and Ecton 1986). A typical anger management programme consists of three stages – cognitive preparation, skill acquisition, application training – with the aim of reducing aggressive behaviour through increasing control over angry arousal.

There have been several studies of anger control with young offenders. McDougall et al. (1987), working with young offenders in custody, found that anger control assisted in lowering levels of institutional offending. Lochman (1992) reported a three-year follow-up of aggressive young men participating in a school-based anger control programme. The findings were encouraging in showing that, compared with young men not taking part in treatment, the treated group had lower rates of substance abuse and higher levels of self-esteem and social problem-solving skills. However, there was no evidence that the programme had a significant long-term effect on delinquent behaviour.

Role-taking

Chandler (1973) describes a programme designed to help male young offenders to see themselves from the perspective of other people, and so to develop their own role-taking abilities. This work was a clear success when judged in terms of enhancing the young offenders' role-taking skill. A similarly successful programme in social perspective-taking skills, carried out with female delinquents, has been reported by Chalmers and Townsend (1990).

Social problem-solving

Spivack et al. (1976) suggested that several cognitive problem-solving skills are necessary for successful social interaction. These cognitive skills include sensitivity to interpersonal problems, the ability to choose the desired outcome of a social exchange ('means–end thinking'), considering the likely outcomes of one's actions ('consequential thinking') and generating different ways to achieve the desired outcome ('alternative thinking'). In social problem-solving skills training, a variety of techniques, including modelling, role-play and discussion, are blended with cognitive techniques, principally SIT. Several studies have provided clear evidence that social problem-solving skills training can lead young offenders to generate more solutions to social problems (see, for example, Hains 1984).

Moral reasoning development

It is clear that immature moral reasoning is a characteristic of some juvenile delinquents (Nelson et al. 1990). Thus, several programmes have attempted to increase moral reasoning in young offenders. In a typical study, Gibbs et al. (1984) conducted an intervention in the form of small-group discussions about socio-moral dilemmas: the young offenders not only gave their views, but were required to justify their opinions and to attempt to reach a consensus on the best solution. The intervention led to a significant gain in moral reasoning ability. More recently, the development of the EQUIP programme has proved a significant step in this area of work (see Gibbs 1996).

Multimodal programmes

Some programmes have incorporated a variety of techniques to form a 'multimodal' programme. Gross et al. (1980) used a combination of social skills training (SST), behaviour therapy and self-management training with ten female young offenders. The programme improved self-control, reduced problem behaviour and reduced school absenteeism. Similarly, Aggression Replacement Training (ART: Glick and Goldstein 1987; Goldstein and Glick 1996) uses structured learning training, including SST and social problem-solving training, anger control training and moral education. The outcome studies show that ART does lead to improved skills, greater self-control and improved institutional behaviour (Goldstein and Glick 1996). Other multimodal programmes include the popular Reasoning and Rehabilitation (R&R) programme developed by Ross and Fabiano (1985). The R&R programme aims to develop a wide range of the offender's cognitive skills, including self-control, problem-solving and empathy.

The STOP Project (see also Chapter 8) conducted by Mid-Glamorgan Probation Service in Wales, was based on the Reasoning and Rehabilitation Programme (Knott 1995; Ross and Fabiano 1985; Ross and Ross 1989). At a one-year follow-up, the findings showed that those offenders (not all juveniles) who completed the STOP programme showed lower rates of reconviction than comparable offenders who had received custodial sentences (Raynor and Vanstone 1994). Indeed, the use of intensive probation and supervision schemes, sometimes incorporating treatment elements, as an alternative to custody is a focus of attention (Brownlee and Joanes 1993; Gendreau et al. 1994).

In addition to these individually focused programmes, there are several notable attempts to work on a wider scale while, in the main, maintaining a cognitive-behavioural stance.

Family-based intervention

Parent management training (PMT) PMT aims to modify, through training, the way in which parents interact with their children. Typically, this training aims to guide parents to reappraise their style of parenting so as to reinforce the child's appropriate behaviour and to use fitting methods of discipline for inappropriate behaviour. Some studies have been carried out looking at the effects of PMT with young offenders and their families (Bank et al. 1987). The findings clearly show that PMT has beneficial effects on family communication and family relationships, with some indication of a reduction in offending. A study by Kazdin et al. (1992) evaluated the combined effects of problem-solving skills training and PMT targeted at children showing severe anti-social behaviour. They found that the combined treatments were highly effective in reducing aggression and anti-social behaviour, as well as having positive effects on parental stress and depression.

Functional family therapy (FFT) While there are some similarities between PMT and FFT, in the latter the emphasis is much more explicitly focused on family interaction. Several studies have used *contingency contracting* as a means of changing family interaction in cases of young offenders, with benefits in reducing offending (Stumphauzer 1976; Welch 1985). Other studies, in sympathy with a multimodal approach, have used a broader range of techniques: Henderson (1981) used behavioural, cognitive and FFT methods in a programme that was successful in reducing stealing. Similarly, Alexander and Parsons (1973) used skills training, contingency contracting and problem-solving training to improve family interaction. The follow-up studies showed that for the families participating in FFT, the young offenders had lower rates of offending (Alexander et al., 1976), as did the offenders' younger siblings (Klein et al. 1977). The findings from the FFT studies strongly suggest that this approach can have a beneficial effect on family interaction and reduce recidivism. It is increasingly evident that work with families must be an important ingredient in working with young offenders (see for example, Henggeler et al. 1993; Kazdin 1987).

Residential establishments

The Achievement Place style of residential provision has generated a great deal of interest for its innovative use of 'teaching-parents' alongside the use of more traditional behavioural methods of change. Achievement Place itself is based on a collection of family-style homes, each run by a trained (usually married) couple, for about six young offenders per home. The couple have the role of *teaching-parents:* they have responsibility for specific behaviour change programmes, such as skills training, together with the less structured task of parental childcare. The behaviour change system progresses from a reward system to a 'merit system', with a peer management system, alongside which individually based programmes in social, educational and self-management skills also take place (Braukmann and Wolf 1987; Burchard and Lane 1982).

The first major outcome study of Achievement Place compared 13 Achievement Place homes with 9 group homes that had not used a teaching-parent approach (Kirigin et al. 1982). It was found that *during* the period in which the programme was running, the young offenders at Achievement Place were at a significant advantage with regard to offending but this advantage was not maintained after a one-year period. At least two other outcome studies have reported similar findings (Braukmann and Wolf 1987; Weinrott et al. 1982). It seems that the Achievement Place model is successful in reducing offending in the short-term, but that this success does not always transfer to the community in the longer term.

Obviously, residential practice continues to develop. Hagan and King (1992) describe an intensive treatment programme conducted in a correctional facility for young offenders. This programme combined a range of interventions, including individual cognitive-behavioural treatment and psychotherapy, a residential management programme, education, family therapy and an independent living programme. At a two-year follow-up, there were encouraging findings with regard to the success of the programme in reducing return to further correctional placements. Similar examples of successful residential outcomes, generally incorporating elements of cognitive-behavioural work, even with the most difficult and disadvantaged young people, can be found (for example, Bullock et al. 1990; Epps 1994; Haghighi and Lopez 1993).

This overview of the literature leads us to the important issue: 'Does treatment work?' In the discussion above, it was evident that on some occasions some approaches were successful, although not always in terms of reducing offending. What sense can we make of the outcome studies to help us to consider what elements are contained in programmes that are successful in reducing offending among young offenders?

Making sense of the evidence

The problem of making sense of any large body of research evidence is very much one that academics should be able to solve. In the field of offender rehabilitation, for example, there are many different types of intervention, conducted in different settings, with different measures of 'success'. As there are literally hundreds of outcome studies, how can meaningful conclusions be drawn from this literature about what works, for whom, and under what conditions?

The traditional approach to making sense of a large body of research evidence is for a reviewer to conduct a traditional narrative or qualitative literature review. Now, as several authors note (for example, Cook et al. 1992; Gendreau and Andrews 1990), such an approach to understanding the messages embedded in a large empirical literature can be problematic, not least because of the risk of author bias in the conclusions drawn from the review. Thus, we can read some narrative reviews of offender rehabilitation that are pessimistic in concluding that nothing works (for example, Lipton et al. 1975; Martinson 1974), while other narrative reviews advance the claim for successful treatments (for example, Gendreau and Ross 1979 and 1987; Ross and Gendreau 1980).

The development of the analytical technique of *meta-analysis* has provided a means by which to produce a standardised summary of a large number of studies.

Meta-analysis

As Izzo and Ross (1990) explain, meta-analysis is:

> A technique that enables a reviewer to objectively and statistically analyse the findings of each study as data points ... The procedure of meta-analysis involves collection of relevant studies, using the summary statistics from each study as units of analysis, and then analysing the aggregated data in a quantitative manner using statistical tests (p.135).

For example, in a typical meta-analytic study, Garrett (1985) included in her analysis 111 studies reported between 1960 and 1983, involving a total of 13,055 young offenders. The results of such a meta-analysis allow conclusions to be drawn about whether treatment works, and allow estimates to be made of what type of intervention works best in what setting.

There have been several meta-analytic studies of the offender treatment literature (Andrews et al. 1990; Garrett 1985; Gottschalk et al. 1987; Lipsey 1992; Lösel and Köferl 1989; Izzo and Ross 1990; Roberts and Camasso 1991;

Whitehead and Lab 1989), and several summaries are now available (Gendreau and Andrews 1990; Lipsey 1995; Lösel 1995a, 1995b and 1996). As with most research, later studies can build upon and avoid the criticisms levelled at earlier efforts, therefore the conclusions listed below are based mainly on the two most recent meta-analytic studies reported by Andrews et al. (1990) and by Lipsey (1992).

The first point to make, importantly, is that the overall conclusion from the meta-analyses is that treatment does have a positive effect in terms of reducing offending. Compared with offenders who do not participate in a treatment programme, the net effect of treatment is a small but significant reduction in offending. However, the real impact of the meta-analyses has been to highlight the factors associated with high treatment effects. In other words, firmer conclusions can be made about 'what works' in terms of reducing offending.

What works?

It is important to note that the points given below relate to *reduced offending* as a treatment outcome. It is crucial to understand that this focus on offending says nothing about the effects of any therapeutic orientation or method in bringing about clinical or personal change. Nevertheless, it is clear that psychological, educational and behavioural treatment programmes are effective in bringing about more general clinical change (Lipsey and Wilson 1993).

The initial point to take from the findings of the meta-analyses is that indiscriminate targeting of treatment programmes may be counterproductive in reducing recidivism. Andrews and Bonta (1994) suggest that the *risk principle* states that important predictors of success are that offenders assessed (by criminal history or a standarised measure) as of medium to high risk of recidivism should be selected for intensive programmes.

The type of treatment programme is important: 'More structured and focused treatments (e.g., behavioral, skill-orientated) and multimodal treatments seem to be more effective than the less structured and focused approaches (e.g., counseling)' (Lipsey 1992, p.123). Indeed, Andrews et al. (1990) suggest that some therapeutic approaches are not suitable for general use with offenders. Specifically, they argue that: 'Traditional psychodynamic and nondirective client-centred therapies are to be avoided within general samples of offenders' (p.376). This view leads Andrews and Bonta (1994) to the *responsivity principle:* the need to deliver programmes in a way that is congruent with the style of service delivery to which young offenders will be likely to respond.

However, the most successful studies, while behavioural in nature, include a cognitive component in order to focus on the 'attitudes, values, and beliefs that support anti-social behaviour' (Gendreau and Andrews 1990, p.182). Further, Roberts and Camasso (1991) stress the importance of working with families to reduce recidivism. The focus on offending is in keeping with the *need principle*, as Andrews and Bonta (1994) explain:

> Many offenders, especially high-risk offenders, have a variety of needs. They need places to live and work and/or they need to stop taking drugs. Some have poor self-esteem, chronic headaches or cavities in their teeth. These are all 'needs'. The need principle draws our attention to the distinction between *criminogenic* and *noncriminogenic* needs. Criminogenic needs are a subset of an offender's risk level. They are dynamic attributes of an offender that, when changed, are associated with changes in the probability of recidivism. Noncriminogenic needs are also dynamic and changeable, but these changes are not necessarily associated with the probability of recidivism (p.176).

With respect to setting, treatment programmes conducted in the community are likely to have stronger effects on delinquency than residential programmes. While residential programmes can be effective, they need to be linked with community-based interventions. Further, programmes that help the young offenders to gain real employment in the community have a significantly enhanced chance of success.

Finally, the meta-analyses strongly suggest that the most effective programmes have high 'treatment integrity'. In essence, this means that the programmes are conducted by trained staff, while those individuals responsible for the management and supervision of treatment are involved in all the operational phases of the programme (Hollin 1995; Hollin et al. 1995; Lösel and Wittmann 1989).

Given the above, Lipsey (1992) concludes that treatment can produce decreases in recidivism of the order of 20–40 per cent above the baseline levels from mainstream criminal sanctioning of offenders. It is fair to conclude that it is not true that 'nothing works' when it comes to the treatment of offenders: intervention – particularly cognitive-behavioural intervention – can have an impact on a range of target behaviours, including criminal behaviours.

The impact of the meta-analyses has been seen in several areas. There has been a willingness to reassert the potential effectiveness of intervention, and to place rehabilitation of young offenders back on the political agenda (for example, Palmer 1991 and 1992). Finally, efforts are being made to bridge the research–practice divide by distilling the complexities of the meta-analysis into blueprints for the design of effective programmes (Antonowicz and Ross 1994; Coulson and Nutbrown 1992; Gendreau 1996; Lösel 1995a and 1996).

It would be a mistake, however, to assume that there is a consensus in the field, with everyone moving in the same direction. As always, there are barriers to be overcome to get to where we might like to be.

Barriers to success

There are four key areas of resistance that provide barriers to success: client resistance, institutional resistance, resistance to treatment integrity, and social resistance.

Client resistance The idea of client resistance relates to the reluctance of young offenders to engage in rehabilitation programmes. With particular emphasis on problem drinking, Miller (1985) described a range of variables – including client characteristics, environmental factors and therapist characteristics – to account for a client's lack of motivation for engaging in a clinical programme. However, Miller also suggested that motivation to engage in treatment can be encouraged by attention to these characteristics of the reluctant client. Miller's ideas led to the development of intervention techniques specifically designed to increase the likelihood of people entering, continuing in and taking the benefits from behaviour change programmes. These techniques have been grouped under the title of 'motivational interviewing' (Miller and Rollnick 1991; see also Chapter 10). Perkins (1991) and Mann and Rollnick (1996) have used motivational techniques with sex offenders, who are generally characterised by high levels of denial of both their offence and the need to change. A similar development of motivational techniques for working with young offenders would be a welcome step.

Institutional resistance This type of resistance refers to the obstacles – in a community or residential setting – that hinder and impede the progress that might be made with a properly implemented treatment programme. Laws (1974) has described the barriers he faced in attempting to set up a residential behavioural programme with offenders. Essentially, the barriers were about control: control over admission to the programme, offenders leaving the programme before its completion, control over finances, and control over staff training. Laws, as have others, documented professional clashes both with administrators and fellow practitioners. Overcoming such institutional resistance implies a need for greater political and organisational awareness and ability by behavioural practitioners. As Burchard and Lane (1982) comment: 'With respect to resistance to change ... behavior-modification advocates who do not recognize that much of their time will be spent trying to change the behavior of staff and policy and administrators are in for a rude awakening' (p.616).

Resistance to treatment integrity The third barrier lies in making real the concept of treatment integrity. As the meta-analyses show, any treatment programme, whatever its theoretical base, can only stand a chance of being successful if it is rigorously and properly implemented. Solid and effective treatment programmes do not magically appear overnight: they require planning for both content and resources, trained personnel to conduct assessments and deliver treatment, and the flexibility to cope with the varying demands and problems presented by different clients. The development and maintenance of systems to support treatment programmes is a management task that demands attention before treatment begins (Hollin et al. 1995).

Social resistance The final barrier lies in the frequently observed *social resistance* to the idea of working constructively with young offenders. Two strands to social resistance can be identified: the first is public and political resistance; the second is academic resistance, or what Gendreau (1996) terms 'theorecticism', or 'knowledge destruction' as preferred by Andrews and Wormith (1989).

There is a great deal of rhetoric to the effect that the public at large has no heart for rehabilitation, and is more concerned with retribution and punishment. However, as Gardiner (1956) said so eloquently: 'To some politicians, too, it may not be unfair to say that public opinion is "the clamour of the ignorant mob" when they do not support the politician's view, and the "voice of the people" when they do' (p.68). Indeed, it is interesting that empirical studies suggest that while the public are far from being against punishment, there is a view that rehabilitation should be one of the goals of the criminal justice system (Cullen et al. 1990). As Cullen et al. note, the tenacity of a belief in the need for rehabilitation is probably pragmatic, in that offenders 'should be given the education, training, employment experiences, and, perhaps, counselling that will enable them to become productive citizens' (pp.15–16). It is probably the case that most victims of crime simply want their property back, want not to be re-victimised, want their friends and neighbours not to suffer in the same way, and finally want the offender to be caught and not to reoffend in the future. Accepting the need for some degree of retribution, it is a matter of debate whether there would be strong public support for harsh punitive measures of doubtful effect on reoffending (Gendreau et al. 1993; Macallair 1993; Mathlas and Mathews 1991).

Academic resistance to working with offenders is not hard to find. As Gendreau (1996) notes, there are two main tactics used in knowledge destruction (see also Andrews 1989; Andrews and Wormith 1989): the first is to ignore or to dismiss on spurious grounds any research findings that are not in keeping with one's own favoured position; the second is to mount broad-scale 'philosophical' arguments against rehabilitation.

The 'philosophical' objections, which many will have witnessed or faced in conferences and seminars, generally run along the lines of statements such as 'human problems are intractable', 'rehabilitation is about social control not freedom', and 'positive findings do not have an answer to every possible question about every possible criminal group'.

Conclusion

There are growing grounds for optimism in the field of working with young offenders. If barriers can be overcome, there is every indication that methods are available that will allow interventions to have a significant impact on recidivism. It is true that there are other challenges to be met by practitioners. Legislative changes will continue to exercise practitioners, who must rightly design treatment programmes to accommodate legal requirements. Similarly, technical advances, as with the application of functional analysis to offending histories in single-case analysis (Gresswell and Hollin 1992), will continue to inform the field. Nevertheless, there is now a firm base from which to design effective programmes. Such an achievement is to the advantage of all concerned – the offenders and their families, the potential future victims, and the public who have to bear the costs of offending.

References

Alexander, J.F. and Parsons, B.V. (1973) 'Short-term behavioral intervention with delinquent families: Impact on family processes and recidivism', *Journal of Abnormal Psychology*, 81, pp.223–31.

Alexander, J.F., Barton, C., Schiavo, R.S. and Parsons, B.V. (1976) 'Systems behavioral intervention with families of delinquents: Therapist characteristics, family behavior, and outcome', *Journal of Consulting and Clinical Psychology*, 44, pp.656–64.

Andrews, D.A. (1989) 'Recidivism is predictable and can be influenced: Using risk assessments to reduce recidivism', *Forum on Corrections Research*, 1, pp.11–18.

Andrews, D.A. and Bonta, J. (1994) *The Psychology of Criminal Conduct*, Cincinnati, OH: Anderson Publishing.

Andrews, D.A. and Wormith, J.S. (1989) 'Personality and crime: Knowledge destruction and construction in criminology', *Justice Quarterly*, 6, pp.289–309.

Andrews, D.A., Zinger, I., Hoge, R.D., Bonta, J., Gendreau, P. and Cullen, F.T. (1990) 'Does correctional treatment work? A clinically relevant and psychologically informed meta-analysis', *Criminology*, 28, pp.369–404.

Antonowicz, D.H. and Ross, R.R. (1994) 'Essential Components of Successful Rehabilitation Programs for Offenders', *International Journal of Offender Therapy and Comparative Criminology*, 38, pp.97–104.

Bank, L., Patterson, G.R. and Reid, J.B. (1987) 'Delinquency prevention through training parents in family management', *The Behavior Analyst*, 10, pp.75–82.

Braukmann, C.J. and Wolf, M.M. (1987) 'Behaviourally based group homes for juvenile offenders' in E.K. Morris and C.J. Braukmann (eds) *Behavioral Approaches to Crime and Delinquency: A Handbook of Application Research and Concepts*, New York: Plenum.

Brownlee, I.D. and Joanes, D. (1993) 'Intensive probation for young adult offenders', *British Journal of Criminology*, 33, pp.216-230.

Bullock, R., Hosie, K., Little, M. and Millham, S. (1990) 'Secure accommodation for very difficult adolescents: Some recent research findings', *Journal of Adolescence*, 13, pp.205–16.

Burchard, J.D. and Lane, T.W. (1982) 'Crime and delinquency' in A.S. Bellack, M. Hersen and A.E. Kazdin (eds) *International Handbook of Behavior Modification and Therapy*, New York: Plenum.

Chalmers, J.B. and Townsend, M.A.R. (1990) 'The effects of training in social perspective taking on socially maladjusted girls', *Child Development*, 61, pp.178–90.

Chandler, M.J. (1973) 'Egocentrism and anti-social behavior: The assessment and training of social perspective-taking skills', *Developmental Psychology*, 9, pp.326–32.

Cook, T.D., Cooper, H., Cordray, D.S., Hartmann, H., Hedges, L.V., Light, R.J., Louis, T.A. and Mosteller, F. (eds) (1992) *Meta-analysis for explanation: A Casebook*, New York: Russell Sage Foundation.

Coulson, G.E. and Nutbrown, V. (1992) 'Properties of an ideal rehabilitative program for high-need offenders', *International Journal of Offender Therapy and Comparative Criminology*, 36, pp.203–8.

Cullen, F.T., Skovron, S.E., Scott, J.E. and Burton, V.S. (1990) 'Public support for correctional treatment: The tenacity of rehabilitative ideology', *Criminal Justice and Behavior*, 17, pp.6–18.

Epps, K.J. (1994) 'Treating adolescent sex offenders in secure conditions: The experience at Glenthorne Centre', *Journal of Adolescence*, 17, pp.105–22.

Farrington, D.P. (1992) 'Psychological contributions to the explanation, prevention and treatment of offending', in F. Lösel, D. Bender and T. Bliesener (eds) *Psychology and Law: International Perspectives*, Berlin: De Gruyter.

Feindler, E.L. and Ecton, R.B. (1986) *Adolescent Anger Control: Cognitive-behavioral Techniques*, New York: Pergamon Press.

Fishman, D.B., Rotgers, F. and Franks, C.M. (eds) (1988) *Paradigms in Behavior Therapy: Present and Promise*, New York: Springer.

Gardiner, G. (1956) *Capital Punishment as a Deterrent: And the Alternative*. London: Victor Gollancz.

Garrett, C.J. (1985) 'Effects of residential treatment on adjudicated delinquents: A meta-analysis', *Journal of Research on Crime and Delinquency*, 22, pp.287–308.

Garrido, V. and Sanchis, J.R. (1991) 'The cognitive model in the treatment of Spanish offenders: Theory and practice', *Journal of Correctional Education*, 42, pp.111–18.

Gendreau, P. (1996) 'Offender rehabilitation: What we know and what needs to be done', *Criminal Justice and Behavior*, 23, pp.144–61 .

Gendreau, P. and Andrews, D.A. (1990) 'Tertiary prevention: What the meta-analyses of the offender treatment literature tells us about "what works"', *Canadian Journal of Criminology*, 32, pp.173–84.

Gendreau, P. and Ross, R.R. (1979) 'Effective correctional treatment: Bibliotherapy for cynics', *Crime and Delinquency*, 25, pp.463–89.
Gendreau, P. and Ross, R.R. (1987) 'Revivification of rehabilitation: Evidence from the 1980s', *Justice Quarterly*, 4, pp.349–407.
Gendreau, P., Cullen, F.T. and Bonta, J. (1994) 'Intensive rehabilitation supervision: The next generation in community corrections', *Federal Probation*, 58, pp.72–8.
Gendreau, P., Paparozzi, M., Little, T. and Goddard, M. (1993) 'Does "punishing smarter" work? An assessment of the new generation of alternative sanctions in probation', *Forum on Corrections Research*, 5, pp.31–4.
Gibbs, J.C. (1996) 'Sociomoral group treatment for young offenders' in C.R. Hollin and K. Howells (eds) *Clinical Approaches to Working With Young Offenders*, Chichester: John Wiley.
Gibbs, J.C., Arnold, K.D., Chessman, F.L. and Ahlborn, H.H. (1984) 'Facilitation of sociomoral reasoning in delinquents', *Journal of Consulting and Clinical Psychology*, 52, pp.37–45.
Glick, B. and Goldstein, A.P. (1987) 'Aggression Replacement Training', *Journal of Counseling and Development*, 65, pp.356–67.
Goldstein, A.P. and Glick, B. (1996) 'Aggression Replacement Training: methods and outcomes', in C.R. Hollin and K. Howells (eds) *Clinical Approaches to Working with Young Offenders*, Chichester: John Wiley.
Goldstein, A.P. and Keller, H. (1987) *Aggressive Behavior: Assessment and Intervention*, New York: Pergamon Press.
Gottschalk, R., Davidson, W.S., Gensheimer, L.K. and Mayer, J. (1987) 'Community-based interventions' in H.C. Quay (ed.) *Handbook of Juvenile Delinquency*, New York: John Wiley.
Gresswell, D.M. and Hollin, C.R. (1992) 'Towards a new methodology for making sense of case material: An illustrative case involving attempted multiple murder', *Criminal Behaviour and Mental Health*, 2, pp.329–41.
Gross, A.M., Brigham, T.A., Hopper, C. and Bologna, N.C. (1980) 'Self-management and social skills training: A study with pre-delinquent and delinquent youths', *Criminal Justice and Behavior*, 7, pp.161–84.
Hagan, M. and King, R.P. (1992) 'Recidivism rates of youth completing an intensive treatment program in a juvenile correctional facility', *International Journal of Offender Therapy and Comparative Criminology*, 36, pp.349–58.
Haghighi, B. and Lopez, A. (1993) 'Success/failure of group home treatment programs for juveniles', *Federal Probation*, 57, pp.53–8.
Hains, A.A. (1984) 'A preliminary attempt to teach the use of social problem-solving skills to delinquents', *Child Study Journal*, 14, pp.271–85.
Henderson, J.Q. (1981) 'A behavioral approach to stealing: A proposal for treatment based on ten cases', *Journal of Behavior Therapy and Experimental Psychiatry*, 12, pp.231–6.
Henggeler, S.W., Melton, G.B., Smith, L.A., Schoewald, S.K. and Hanley, J.H. (1993) 'Family preservation using multisystemic treatment: Long-term follow-up to a clinical trial with serious juvenile offenders', *Journal of Child and Family Studies*, 2, pp.283–93.
Hollin, C.R. (1990) *Cognitive-behavioural Interventions with Young Offenders*, Elmsford, New York: Pergamon Press.
Hollin, C.R. (1993) 'Advances in the psychological treatment of delinquent behaviour', *Criminal Behaviour and Mental Health*, 3, pp.142–57.
Hollin, C.R. (1995) 'The meaning and implications of "programme integrity"' in J.

McGuire (ed.) *What Works: Effective Methods to Reduce Reoffending*, Chichester: John Wiley.

Hollin, C.R. and Howells, K. (eds) (1996) *Clinical Approaches to Working with Young Offenders*. Chichester: John Wiley.

Hollin, C.R., Epps, K.J. and Kendrick, D.J. (1995) *Managing Behavioural Treatment: Policy and Practice with Delinquent Adolescents*. London: Routledge.

Izzo, R.L. and Ross, R.R. (1990) 'Meta-analysis of rehabilitation programs for juvenile delinquents: A brief report', *Criminal Justice and Behavior*, 17, pp.134–42.

Kazdin, A.E. (1987) 'Treatment of antisocial behavior in children: Current status and future directions', *Psychological Bulletin*, 102, pp.187–203.

Kazdin, A.E., Siegel, T.C. and Bass, D. (1992) 'Cognitive problem-solving skills training and parent management training in the treatment of antisocial behavior in children', *Journal of Consulting and Clinical Psychology*, 60, pp.733–47.

Kirigin, K.A., Braukmann, C.J., Atwater, J. and Wolf, M.M. (1982) 'An evaluation of Achievement Place (Teaching-Family) group homes for juvenile offenders', *Journal of Applied Behavior Analysis*, 15, pp.1–16.

Klein, N.C., Alexander, J.F. and Parsons, B.V. (1977) 'Impact of family systems intervention on recidivism and sibling delinquency: A model of primary prevention and program evaluation', *Journal of Consulting and Clinical Psychology*, 45, pp.469–74.

Knott, C. (1995) 'The STOP Programme: Reasoning and rehabilitation in a British setting' in J. McGuire (ed.) *What Works: Reducing Reoffending*, Chichester: John Wiley.

Laws, D.R. (1974) 'The failure of a token economy', *Federal Probation*, 38, pp.33–8.

Lipsey, M.W. (1992) 'Juvenile delinquency treatment: A meta-analytic inquiry into the variability of effects', in T.D. Cook, H. Cooper, D.S. Cordray, H. Hartmann, L.V. Hedges, R.J. Light, T.A. Louis and F. Mosteller (eds) *Meta-analysis for Explanation: A Casebook*. New York: Russell Sage Foundation.

Lipsey, M.W. (1995) 'What do we learn from 400 research studies on the effectiveness of treatment with juvenile delinquents?' in J. McGuire (ed.) *What Works: Reducing Reoffending*, Chichester: John Wiley.

Lipsey, M.W. and Wilson, D.B. (1993) 'The efficacy of psychological, educational, and behavioral treatment: Confirmation from meta-analysis', *American Psychologist*, 48, pp.1181–209.

Lipton, D.N., Martinson, R. and Wilks, D. (1975) *The Effectiveness of Correctional Treatment*, New York: Praeger.

Lochman, J.E. (1992) 'Cognitive-behavioral intervention with aggressive boys: Three-year follow-up and preventive effects', *Journal of Consulting and Clinical Psychology*, 60, pp.426–32.

Lösel, F. (1995a) 'Increasing consensus in the evaluation of offender rehabilitation: Lessons from recent research syntheses', *Psychology, Crime and Law*, 2, pp.19–39.

Lösel, F. (1995b) 'The efficacy of correctional treatment: A review and synthesis of the meta-analyses' in J. McGuire (ed.) *What Works: Reducing Reoffending*, Chichester: John Wiley.

Lösel, F. (1996) 'Working with young offenders: The impact of meta-analyses' in C.R. Hollin and K. Howells (eds), *Clinical Approaches to Working with Young Offenders*, Chichester: John Wiley.

Lösel, F. and Köferl, P. (1989) 'Evaluation research on correctional treatment in West Germany: A meta-analysis' in H. Wegener, F. Lösel. and J. Haison (eds) *Criminal*

Behaviour and the Justice System: Psychological Perspectives, New York: Springer-Verlag.

Lösel, F. and Wittmann, W.W. (1989) 'The relationship of treatment integrity and intensity to outcome criteria' in R.F. Conner and M. Hendricks (eds) *International Innovations in Evaluation Methodology: New Directions for Program Evaluation*, No. 42, San Francisco, CA: Jossey-Bass.

Macallair, D. (1993) 'Reaffirming rehabilitation in juvenile justice', *Youth and Society*, 25, pp.104-25.

Mann, R.E. and Rollnick, S. (1996) 'Motivational interviewing with a sex offender who believed he was innocent', *Behavioural and Cognitive Psychotherapy*, 24, pp.127–34.

Martinson, R. (1974) 'What works? Questions and answers about prison reform', *The Public Interest*, 35, pp.22–54.

Mathlas, R.E. and Mathews, J.W. (1991) 'The boot camp program for offenders: Does the shoe fit?', *International Journal of Offender Therapy and Comparative Criminology*, 35, pp.322–7.

McDougall, C., Barnett, R.M., Ashurst, B. and Willis, B. (1987) 'Cognitive control of anger' in B.J. McGurk, D.M. Thornton and M. Williams (eds), *Applying Psychology to Imprisonment: Theory and Practice*, London: HMSO.

Miller, W.R. (1985) 'Motivation for treatment: A review with special emphasis on alcoholism', *Psychological Bulletin*, 98, pp.84–107.

Miller, W.R. and Rollnick, S. (1991) *Motivational Interviewing: Preparing People to Change Addictive Behavior*, New York: Guilford Press.

Mulvey, E.P., Arthur, M.W. and Reppucci, N.D. (1993) 'The prevention and treatment of juvenile delinquency: A review of the research', *Clinical Psychological Review*, 13, pp.133–67.

Nelson, J.R., Smith, D.J. and Dodd, J. (1990) 'The moral reasoning of juvenile delinquents: A meta-analysis', *Journal of Abnormal Child Psychology*, 18, pp.231–9.

Novaco, R.W. (1975) *Anger Control: The Development and Evaluation of an Experimental Treatment*, Lexington, MA: D.C. Heath.

Novaco, R.W. (1994) 'Anger as a risk factor for violence among the mentally disordered' in J. Monahan and H.J. Steadman (eds) *Violence and Mental Disorder: Developments in Risk Assessment*, Chicago, IL: University of Chicago Press.

Palmer, T. (1991) 'The effectiveness of intervention: Recent trends and current issues', *Crime and Delinquency*, 37, pp.330–46.

Palmer, T. (1992) *The Re-emergence of Correctional Intervention*, Newbury Park, CA: Sage.

Perkins, D. (1991) 'Clinical work with sex offenders in secure settings' in C.R. Hollin and K. Howells (eds), *Clinical Approaches to Sex Offenders and their Victims*, Chichester: John Wiley.

Raynor, P. and Vanstone, M. (1994) *STOP: Straight Thinking On Probation: Third Interim Evaluation Report*, Bridgend, Mid-Glamorgan: Mid-Glamorgan Probation Service.

Roberts, A.R. and Camasso, M.J. (1991) 'Juvenile offender treatment programs and cost-benefit analysis', *Juvenile and Family Court Journal*, 42, pp.37–47.

Ross, R.R. and Fabiano, E.A. (1985) *Time to Think: A Cognitive Model of Delinquency Prevention and Offender Rehabilitation*, Johnson City, TN: Institute of Social Sciences and Arts.

Ross, R.R. and Gendreau, P. (1980) *Effective Correctional Treatment*, Toronto: Butterworths.

Ross, R.R. and Ross, B.D. (1989) 'Delinquency prevention through cognitive training', *Educational Horizons*, Summer, pp.124–30.

Snyder, J.J. and White, M.J. (1979) 'The use of cognitive self-instruction in the treatment of behaviorally disturbed adolescents', *Behavior Therapy*, 10, pp.227–35.

Spivack, G., Platt, J.J. and Shure, M.B. (1976) *The Problem-solving Approach to Adjustment: A Guide to Research and Intervention*, San Francisco, CA: Jossey-Bass.

Stumphauzer, J.S. (1976) 'Elimination of stealing by self-reinforcement of alternative behavior and family contracting', *Journal of Behavior Therapy and Experimental Psychiatry*, 7, pp.265–8.

Weinrott, M.R., Jones, R.R. and Howard, J.R. (1982) 'Cost effectiveness of teaching family programs for delinquents: Results of a national evaluation', *Evaluation Review*, 6, pp.173–201.

Welch, G.J. (1985) 'Contingency contracting with a delinquent and his family', *Journal of Behaviour Therapy and Experimental Psychiatry*, 16, pp.253–9.

Whitehead, J.T. and Lab, S.P. (1989) 'A meta-analysis of juvenile correctional treatment', *Journal of Research in Crime and Delinquency*, 26, pp.276–95.

8 Adult probationers and the STOP programme

Peter Raynor and Maurice Vanstone

The purpose of this chapter is to describe an experimental programme which has attempted to apply cognitive-behavioural methods in the supervision of male offenders on probation, and to present some information about its results. The programme, known as STOP (Straight Thinking On Probation), represented the first systematic attempt to provide and evaluate a cognitive-behavioural programme for persistent offenders in the context of a British probation service. It has played a significant part in the movement towards evidence-based practice in probation (Knott 1995; Raynor 1996) which has been gathering momentum since the emergence of new evidence about the impact of appropriate methods on offending (Andrews et al. 1990; Lipsey 1992), and its results (both good and not so good) have much to teach us about the practical business of introducing and sustaining effective innovations in established agencies like the Probation Service.

Background

The STOP programme, which is based on the Reasoning and Rehabilitation (R & R) programme developed by Robert Ross and his colleagues in Canada (Ross et al. 1986), was established in the Mid-Glamorgan Probation Service in 1991. The decision to embark on an experimental programme of this kind emerged from management concerns not about the quality of work then being undertaken in the service, but about the degree to which that work was informed by empirical studies of the effectiveness of helping people to stop offending. Although during the fifteen years or so prior to this decision Mid-Glamorgan probation officers, like their colleagues throughout

England and Wales, had been practising against the background of discouraging research findings (for example, Folkard et al. 1976; Martinson 1974), they had continued to work optimistically to reduce offending. They had been attempting this through one-to-one supervision, offending behaviour groups and the more intensive supervision structures available in the statutory day centre (Vanstone 1993). Much of that work had been informed by the problem-solving approach promulgated by Priestley and McGuire (Priestley et al. 1978; McGuire and Priestley 1985), and was based on a range of methods and materials gathered from the fields of education, psychology, social work and industry.

They had therefore been accustomed to working with groups of probationers and to using methods drawn from cognitive-behavioural psychology such as role-play, role rehearsal, problem checklists and positive reinforcement. What distinguishes STOP, however, is that it is based on a well-researched and validated programme, and requires training which is aimed specifically at preparing the officers to deliver that programme so that it meets the requirements of programme integrity: that the programme is delivered as prescribed. The choice of the R & R model was based partly on its demonstrated success with Canadian probationers (Ross et al. 1988).

Planning and organisation

In attempting to describe how STOP was established, we will refer mainly to the experimental period that comprised the first twelve months of the project, and therefore will describe it in this section in the past tense, although the programme continues to operate in Mid Glamorgan.

Helping probation officers to move from innovative but arbitrarily applied practice to implementing consistently a predetermined programme within an evaluative framework required a change in the culture of the organisation, and this in turn demanded detailed and meticulous preparation and organisation. This process began with a paper prepared by the Chief Probation Officer which contained the following objective:

> That we should systematically apply an agreed challenging programme of social work inputs which are drawn from proven best practice and which are applied by staff who are enthusiastic and well trained in the delivery of that programme. Any such programme will be rigorously monitored to enable us to evaluate its effectiveness regarding either reducing or slowing down re-offending (Sutton 1990, p.1).

This proposal was examined critically in a two-day management meeting, and agreement was reached about the principle of undertaking the project. A further decision was made to circulate the paper to each probation field team, along with that written by Ross and his colleagues evaluating the original Reasoning and Rehabilitation experiment (Ross et al. 1988). Following this, the Chief Probation Officer solicited the support of the probation committee, who agreed to the necessary funding. Simultaneously, negotiations were opened with Robert Ross for the purchase of the manuals, and the Chief Probation Officer and the co-ordinator visited teams to explain the project and gain their commitment to it. Generally, the responses of the teams were positive, but some reservations were expressed: these were focused on several factors, including the failure of previous innovations, the implications for workload, and a lack of clarity about how the project would unfold organisationally. Indeed, at one stage in this process a growing sense of the enormity of the commitment led the management group to express strong doubts about whether to proceed. With hindsight, these can be seen to be part of a process invariably connected to change of the magnitude involved in a project of this kind. In the event, the organisation as a whole recovered its nerve and moved on.

A further unique feature of this project was the collaborative relationship that was established between the Mid Glamorgan Probation Service and the University of Wales, Swansea, to ensure evaluation of the project. One consequence was that the research design could be worked out as part of the process of setting up the project and with the participation of the service itself. This created a sense of ownership of and involvement in evaluation, and in the long term was to play a significant part in shifting the culture of the organisation towards evidence-based practice (Deering et al. 1996).

The practical work of organising and structuring the project was undertaken by a number of cross-grade working groups: programme construction, training, research and evaluation, targeting and finally resources. In addition to bringing the original concept to life, these groups fulfilled the essential purpose of sustaining officers' commitment and sense of ownership. The key components of planning and preparation, which spanned a period of six months, were:

- appointing a research consultant
- appointing a project consultant
- revising the Canadian manuals so that they were appropriate to the local cultural context
- producing publicity materials for the courts, combined with meetings with magistrates and judges

- appointing five additional officers to help resource the project
- setting up a staff conference to ensure full dissemination of information
- organising and delivering a five-day training programme for 45 officers
- ordering supplementary materials
- developing a research and evaluation design
- developing guidance for practitioners about who was suitable for referral to the project
- producing an agreed format for the delivery of the programme which included number of hours, type of group leadership, the appropriate environment for group sessions and arrangements for video recording
- piloting a demonstration session with volunteer probationers which was recorded on video for the staff conference and for meetings with magistrates
- formulating a policy on failure to comply with the programme
- providing two days' training for managers to assist them in their supervisory role.

All of this activity was informed by what the service had learned about successful projects, and by a determination to avoid the 'charismatic but unsupported project leader' syndrome so characteristic of previous Probation Service innovation. Attempts were therefore made to ensure that the project was properly resourced, supported by management, run by well-trained, enthusiastic and committed staff, structured within an evaluative framework and based on reputable research findings.

Implementation

As can be deduced from the fact that three-quarters of the service's officers were trained in the approach, an early decision was made to deliver the programme in each of the six field teams. The motivation for this lay in a desire not only to avoid the problems of elitism and remoteness associated with specialist units, but also to influence the culture of the whole organisation towards critically informed practice. Inevitably, this increased the complexity of the experiment and heightened the difficulties of ensuring consistency of application and uniform quality of performance. On the other hand, it contributed positively to increased skills, knowledge and confidence in groupwork across a wide range of officers.

Although each group session was run by two officers, the content of the session was delivered by one leader at a time, the other sitting 'off stage'. This teaching style demanded quite significant adjustments from practitioners whose previous experience had been in running groups in which there was greater emphasis on working with process and dynamics and on personal problems. In this programme, although an understanding of group process and dynamics was germane to the facilitation of the session, the overriding emphasis was upon the teaching of the particular skill in focus at the time.

The programme itself was run over an 18-week period with two sessions per week each lasting two hours, and delivered in a classroom situation, in stark contrast to the more familiar therapeutic groupwork environment of easy chairs and closed circles. Every session was recorded on video, and a random sample was scrutinised by one of the researchers to ensure that the programme was adhered to in both its structure and content. Such formalisation required adjustment not just from the group leaders, but also the probationers themselves. Observation of the sessions and subsequent interviews with the participants suggested that a majority made this adjustment without any great difficulty, though a few said it was 'like school'.

The programme

Based as it is on the Reasoning and Rehabilitation model, STOP draws on research findings which suggest that some people who persistently offend are impulsive in their responses to problems, attribute blame to others rather than to themselves, and have difficulty in empathising with others: in other words, they have poor problem-solving and thinking skills. Underpinning the programme, therefore, is a cognitive-behavioural theoretical model which (according to Ross and Fabiano 1985) is not a theory of crime, but a model of rehabilitation. It does not purport to provide a complete explanation of why people offend, but instead suggests that thinking and values are closely linked to criminal behaviour. As a result, it has attracted criticism from practitioners and others who prefer to emphasise the role of social factors such as poverty and inequality: ideological critics such as Neary (1992) allege that it focuses on the individual to the exclusion of social and cultural contexts.

While this might be fair comment on the preoccupation with individual wickedness and neglect of social context which have characterised the development of criminal justice policy in the mid-1990s (for example, Home Secretary Michael Howard's speech to the Conservative Party conference in

1993), programmes such as STOP are more plausibly seen as empowering rather than blaming (for a fuller discussion of this issue, see Raynor and Vanstone 1994a). Indeed, the importance of social factors was explicitly recognised by the original proponents of the Reasoning and Rehabilitation approach: 'factors such as poverty, lack of opportunity ... and a host of other environmental, experiential, and familial factors can profoundly influence both the individual's cognitive development and the likelihood that he will engage in anti-social behaviour' (Ross and Fabiano, 1985, p.11).

The term 'cognitive-behavioural' has come to include quite a wide range of approaches. Within this range, the R & R model emphasises cognition more than behaviour, with the effect that the programme content is weighted more towards discussion and reflection than rehearsal and role-play. The programme itself is drawn from an amalgam of methods from child development to philosophy and in this sense is not original. Its uniqueness, certainly in British probation practice, lies in the fact that it is neither offence- nor problem-focused: it involves discussion of offences and personal problems, but only as materials and stimuli for the enhancement of thinking skills. This was a major departure for probation officers working in a service whose history is steeped both in the attempted resolution of problems and in the analysis of offences. The programme was also unusual in having a coherent knowledge base: probation officers in Britain during the 1970s and 1980s had applied a range of methods enthusiastically and with optimism that they could influence people's behaviour, but largely they had done this without a theory of effectiveness, in spite of the efforts of some criminologists to draw research evidence to their attention (for example, McGuire and Priestley 1985).

The original R & R programme was based on a review of a wide spectrum of work that had demonstrated some impact on recidivism rates (Ross and Fabiano 1985). Subsequent analyses have broadly confirmed the features of successful programmes identified in that review (Andrews et al. 1990; Lipsey 1992; McIvor 1990; McGuire and Priestley 1995). These are programmes in which there is a sound conceptual model, a variety of methods, a focus on factors linked to offending such as problem-solving and self-control, a match of teaching and modes of service styles to the learning styles of participants, and an emphasis on techniques liable to have an impact on people's thinking. They stand in contrast to programmes associated with ineffectiveness, such as those premised on shocking people into going 'straight', traditional psychodynamic intervention, non-directive client-centred therapy, and attempts to increase self-esteem without challenging values or behaviour (McLaren 1992).

Probation officers who led the STOP groups used a manual and materials based on the original R & R model, amended to make them more appropriate to the cultural setting in which the participants lived. While not prescribing all the material used, the manual is highly prescriptive of those factors vital to what has been described as 'programme integrity': 'that the programme is conducted in practice as intended in theory and design' (Hollin 1995, p.196). While it was permissible for the group leaders to change some of the materials being used, it was considered vital that they adhered to the use of dialogue as opposed to didactic teaching (the ideal interactions being between participants, rather than between leader and participant), that the process of reasoning was regarded as more important than the content of discussion, that the correct sequence of the sessions and of the skills in focus was adhered to, and that the participants were encouraged to lead the group at appropriate moments. It became clear that the knowledge and expertise of the group leaders were important in the maintenance of programme integrity, and that they should have an above-average level of verbal and inter-personal skills, the ability to relate empathetically without compromising key values, an understanding of group dynamics, leadership skills, and an understanding of the theoretical model.

The programme is designed so that the participant's learning is graduated and reinforced. This is achieved by repetition and the building and integration of one skill with another so that the participant emerges with a repertoire of skills and strategies. In all, there are seven modules that encompass broad skill areas: problem-solving, social skills, negotiation skills, management of emotions, creative thinking, values enhancement, and critical reasoning. These are in turn broken down into specific and manageable micro-skills: for example, problem-solving covers the ability to recognise the existence of a problem, the capacity to identify the nature of the problem, information-gathering, the skill of generating ideas about the problem, verbal and non-verbal communication, alternative ways of thinking about the problem, thinking about the consequences, and assertiveness. The other modules are similarly broken down into manageable skills. Limitations of space preclude a fuller account of the programme itself and its methods here; however, we hope we have accurately conveyed the basic features of a programme which used a variety of methods in a broad application of cognitive-behavioural principles, and was delivered as a requirement of a Probation Order in an attempt to reduce people's offending. Readers interested in a fuller account of the programme will find it in the original manual (Ross et al. 1986).

Much of the discussion about this programme has understandably centred on its effect or otherwise upon the people who were subjected to it, and this is the main theme of the remainder of this chapter. However, it is important to remember that the programme was established not simply as an additional option for probation officers to use, but as a deliberate strategy to change the service culture in the direction of evidence-based practice. An important part of the programme's effect has been its impact upon policy and practice within the Mid-Glamorgan Probation Service, and the fact that this can be covered only briefly in this chapter risks understating its long-term significance. This falls broadly into three areas. First, the knowledge base and skill level of a majority of officers increased. The degree to which this has influenced their other work cannot be measured precisely, but there is some evidence available in the current standard Probation Order experiment designed and implemented by practitioners (Deering et al. 1996), and in the work of the service's Resource, Research and Development Unit. Second, attitudes to evaluation and research changed, as demonstrated by the development of a well-resourced research unit. Third, managers became aware of the need for management to take responsibility for innovation and adequate resourcing.

Programme integrity and staffing

The research carried out in and around the STOP programme developed into one of the most comprehensive evaluations of a probation programme so far carried out in Britain, and the full results have been embodied in a series of reports and articles (particularly Lucas et al. 1992; Raynor and Vanstone 1994b; Raynor et al. 1995; Raynor and Vanstone 1996; Raynor 1998). This chapter aims to summarise only those findings likely to be of particular interest to readers of this book.

Part of the purpose of the evaluation study was to find out whether British probation services and probation officers were capable of delivering a programme of this kind. A random sample of videotapes of sessions (amounting to 11 per cent of all programme time delivered in the first year) was examined for departures from the programme. We found only 18 examples of changes, most of which did not erode programme integrity as they were successfully incorporated into the design of the session. Typically, they involved the use of either additional or different games, exercises and illustrative material, the non-repetition of exercises when it was evident that participants had grasped the learning point, and the selective use of items of equipment. In three of the observed sessions, however, the changes made were judged to have seriously weakened the design and thereby impeded the achievement of the session's objectives: for example, a social skills training session in which there was no use of role-play. It is reasonable to conclude from these findings that officers involved in the experiment mainly delivered the programme as it was intended. When they made innovations, this usually increased the relevance and attractiveness of the programme to the participants.

As well as being able to deliver the programme, a survey of officers' views indicated that they responded quite positively to the opportunity to do so. All of the officers who had experience of running the programme understood its aims, which they described as improving decision-making and reducing offending. Most officers also expressed increased confidence in their ability to practise within groups, and increased optimism about the feasibility of pursuing such aims within a group programme; 93 per cent of officers reported an increase in skills, and 43 per cent an improvement in confidence. A significant proportion (62 per cent) experienced an increase in job satisfaction.

The views of programme members

All participants in the programme who completed it successfully during the research period (a total of 64) were interviewed within two weeks after the termination of their groups. They were asked a range of questions regarding the causes of their offending and their views on the STOP programme. For the purposes of this chapter, we concentrate on their views of the programme.

A considerable majority (89 per cent) viewed the programme as helpful, and a similar majority (91 per cent) indicated that the programme had affected their thinking in problem situations. Such generally positive reactions to probation are not uncommonly reported in 'consumer' studies (Day 1981; Bailey and Ward 1992), but in this study we aimed to discover what specifically the participants believed they had learned, and whether they could give examples of how this affected their behaviour outside the programme groups. The impact on thinking is evident both from the factors identified as being helpful in the programme and from the specific changes in thinking reported. It can be seen from Table 8.1 that nearly all of the group indicated that the focus on thinking skills had been helpful to them and made specific reference to a range of skills such as thinking of others, controlling anger, and assertiveness (numbers in the table total more than 64 as more than one choice of response was allowed).

Table 8.2 provides a more detailed breakdown of specific types of thinking applied to problem-solving. These show a link with target skills in the programme, for example controlling impulsiveness. Some participants stated that as a result of the programme they think more before taking action, and

Table 8.1 What STOP programme participants said they had found helpful

	No.	%
Thinking skills	28	44
Thinking of others/seeing others' viewpoint	15	23
Coping with or solving problems	14	22
Controlling anger	11	17
Thinking in relation to offending	11	17
Having a different perspective on life	5	8
Increased confidence	3	5
Increased assertiveness	3	5
Improved inter-personal skills	3	5
Keeping out of trouble	2	3
General understanding of learning	2	3

Table 8.2 Self-reported changes in thinking among STOP programme participants

	No.	%
Thinking before acting, speaking or offending	16	28
Thinking a problem through	15	26
Thinking of consequences	14	24
Talking and explaining to people	10	17
Thinking of others	8	14
Thinking about who can help/involving others	6	10
Prioritising/sorting out options	4	7
Understanding and/or listening to other viewpoints	4	7
Thinking positively	3	5
Dealing with a problem immediately	3	5
Thinking more clearly	2	3
More open and assertive	2	3
Less aggressive	2	3

consider the consequences of their actions. Significantly, some participants also reported that they now think more about the effects of their actions on others. Others highlighted an increase in the use of problem-solving techniques and a decrease in aggression.

Predicted and actual reconvictions

As in the original Canadian probation experiment (Ross et al. 1988), an important aspect of the evaluation of the STOP programme has been a reconviction study of those passing through it compared with broadly similar male offenders receiving other sentences. At the start of the project and the evaluation study, the relevant comparison groups were identified as offenders sentenced to other Probation Orders, mainly without any special requirements; Community Service Orders; suspended prison sentences, and custodial sentences of moderate severity, including sentences to Young Offender Institutions (YOI) and prison sentences of up to 12 months for adults.

In order to avoid 'contamination' of the study by low-risk offenders, the probation and community service groups were limited to offenders with a measured 'risk of custody' (ROC) score of 55 or more (the ROC scale was the main measure of seriousness and risk level in use in probation services at that time: see Bale 1987). This method of ensuring comparability was only partly successful, as the STOP group turned out in practice to contain offenders with more previous convictions than other groups in the study: with an average age of 23 years, they had an average of nine previous convictions, and the majority had served at least one custodial sentence (Lucas et al. 1992). A better way of controlling for differences between groups had to be devised, as described below. The reconviction study so far has been based on 655 offenders residing in Mid Glamorgan and sentenced in the first ten months of the experiment up to April 1992. This includes 107 sentenced to the STOP programme, and 548 members of the comparison groups.

Information on 'standard list' convictions (excluding the most trivial offences, which are not centrally recorded) was obtained from the National Identification Bureau and from the Offenders Index maintained by the Home Office. A small number of offenders had to be dropped from the study because of the unavailability of offending data or unreliability of identification, but these losses were spread fairly evenly across the groups, and are unlikely to affect the findings significantly. The use of nationally collected data avoids the problems arising from varying local recording practices.

By the time the 12-month follow-up was undertaken (Raynor and Vanstone 1994b), it was possible to adopt a new approach to the problem of comparability between groups, as the Home Office had developed the 'national risk of reconviction predictor', based on a sample of 37,711 recently active offenders in the Offenders Index (Copas 1992; Home Office 1993). This allowed us to calculate a predicted risk of reconviction for all groups in the study, using a locally calculated adjustment to convert the 24-month predicted rate yielded by the predictor into a 12-month rate (this adjustment factor has now been checked against the more recent actuarial tables developed by the Home Office which enable prediction of reconviction risk at any point in the two years following release from prison: Copas et al. 1994; this results in a very slight improvement in accuracy over the version used in Raynor and Vanstone 1994b, so 12-month predicted rates in this chapter incorporate this correction). The predicted reconviction rates for each group were then compared with actual reconviction rates at 12 and 24 months from sentence or release, as appropriate, based on the first recorded 'standard list' reconviction. The analysis also included two further groups, one containing all immediate custodial sentences (the Young Offender Institution and adult custodial groups combined) and a sub-group consisting of those STOP group participants who actually completed the programme. This group is included on the assumption that, as the programme is designed and delivered as a coherent whole, any influence on behaviour would be presumed to affect primarily those who undertook the whole programme.

Some further comment on this latter group should be made at this point. First, because it is drawn from the early months of the programme, it should not be taken as an indication of the normal completion rate, which was 62 per cent during the full first year, or 75 per cent if those who dropped out for 'legitimate' reasons such as health or employment are discounted (Lucas et al. 1992). This compares reasonably with the national completion rate of 71 per cent for Community Service Orders (Home Office 1994). Second, the 'STOP completers' group is not fully comparable with the other groups in the study, which are based on sentence rather than completion, even in the case of custodial sentences, since those who receive a custodial sentence have little option but to complete it. Any group which completes the requirements of a community sentence will tend to show a lower rate of post-sentence reconviction than the whole group of those sentenced to that option, since reasons for non-completion can include reconviction. However, the group which completed the STOP programme nevertheless represents the best source of information on what happens if the whole programme is completed, and is therefore included in the tables.

The figures have also been adjusted to include a correction relating to 'false positives' or pseudo-reconvictions. Neither predicted nor actual rates derived from central sources make allowance for convictions after the target sentence which relate to offences committed before the sentence was imposed. In practice, such convictions are not infrequent. More important, they are more likely to occur in community sentences than after custodial sentences, where any 'clearing up' of outstanding offences is more likely to be done while the offender is in custody than after release. File sampling in Mid Glamorgan covering over 700 offenders was undertaken to estimate the extent of this phenomenon. This indicated that a correction factor was needed for predicted and actual rates to eliminate the 'false positive' effect. Such correction factors will differ from area to area depending on local police and prosecution practice, and will also differ from national rates used in national reconviction studies (such as Lloyd et al. 1994). Correction factors for Mid Glamorgan are calculated as 0.9 for community sentences and 0.97 for custodial sentences on a 12-month follow-up, and 0.93 and 0.98 respectively at 24 months. Table 8.3 shows predicted and actual rates adjusted to eliminate pseudo-reconvictions, and subsequent discussion is based mainly on these figures.

Table 8.3 Predicted and actual reconviction rates adjusted to eliminate 'false positives'

	By 12 months		**By 24 months**	
	Predicted %	*Actual* %	*Predicted* %	*Actual* %
STOP (n=107)	44	44	63	65
Other probation (n=100)	41	40	59	61
Community Service (n=194)	35	32	52	49
Suspended imprisonment (n=90)	26	27	41	41
Immediate imprisonment (adults) (n=82)	38	44	55	56
Young Offender Institutions (n=82)	47	54	65	73
Combined custodials (n=164)	42	49	60	65
STOP completers (n=59)	42	35	61	63

Several features of these figures are of interest. The general tendency to fairly high reconviction rates in the high-risk groups is characteristic of the area, and probably reflects the endemic poverty and male unemployment resulting from the destruction of heavy industry in South Wales during the 1980s. Within this general picture, and concentrating particularly on the higher-risk groups, community sentences are performing at or near predicted levels, whereas custodial sentences, particularly for young people, result in higher than predicted rates. Of the two highest-risk groups (STOP and YOI), the outcomes for STOP are better, and the STOP completers perform better than the combined custodial group.

Those who completed STOP orders show an interesting pattern, with better than predicted reconvictions at 12 months, but results comparable to other community sentences at 24 months. A similar pattern appears in another recent evaluation of an intensive probation project (Brownlee 1995), and a dissimilar pattern in an earlier study (Raynor 1988). In the latter case, differences evident at 12 months had increased at 24, and it may be relevant to note that this was a project which continued to involve and support programme participants after the end of the formal programme.

The seriousness of reconvictions

In addition to simple counting of first reconvictions, a further analysis was undertaken of the extent of serious offending, defined as violent or sexual offences and burglaries. These offences cause great public concern, and affect victims directly and personally. Hence they are relevant to one of the goals of the Reasoning and Rehabilitation programme, which includes attempts to improve victim awareness and understanding of other people's point of view. Another possible measure of seriousness is the extent to which reconvictions are regarded as serious enough to attract custodial sentences.

Table 8.4 shows the proportions originally convicted of serious offences and those subsequently reconvicted of serious offences, with the proportion sentenced custodially on reconviction for the whole STOP group, the combined custodial comparison group and those who completed the STOP programme. The combined custodial comparison group is selected here because it is a close comparison in terms of initial risk, and because STOP was intended to offer an alternative disposal for those who would otherwise be likely to receive custodial sentences.

These figures again show a marked difference in the pattern between the 12-month and 24-month follow-ups. In the first year, STOP group members

Table 8.4 Serious offences and custodial sentences on reconviction

	Serious Offences on Original Conviction	**Serious Offences on Reconviction at**		**Custodial Sentences on Reconviction**
		12 months	*24 months*	
Sentenced to STOP (n=107)	42 (39%)	19 (18%)	29 (27%)	21 (20%)
Combined custodials (n=164)	67 (41%)	34 (21%)	41 (25%)	25 (15%)
STOP completers (n=59)	21 (36%)	5 (8%)	13 (22%)	1 (2%)

committed fewer serious offences than the custodial comparison group, and those who completed the programme committed very few. Their reconvictions indicated instead a higher proportion of offences which damaged things rather than people (criminal damage), or perhaps themselves rather than other people (drugs). By the end of the second year, the rates of apparent serious offending were more similar, though the STOP completers were still lower. What is very striking, however, is that the STOP completers continued to receive very few custodial sentences. No other group in the study showed less than 12 per cent receiving a custodial sentence within two years, and the average for the whole study was 17 per cent. The most likely explanation is that the vast majority of new offences committed by the STOP completers were seen as not serious enough to require a custodial sentence. Although this does not emerge as strongly from the counting of offence categories at 24 months as it did at 12 months, it remains a clear feature of the courts' response.

Changes in attitudes and problems

By the end of the 1980s, managers and practitioners in Mid Glamorgan had identified a need for an assessment instrument which could be administered to probationers to identify changes in attitudes believed to be contributory factors in offending. In 1990 the service began to use the CRIME-PICS questionnaire (Frude et al. 1990). This allowed information from CRIME-PICS to be incorporated in the evaluation of STOP. A full account of the CRIME-PICS instrument, its development and psychometric evaluation based on a sample of 422 probationers can be found in the manual issued to support the revised version of the scale, CRIME-PICS II (Frude et al. 1994), which has been used in a number of probation services and Scottish social work departments.

The original version used in the STOP study differed little from the revised version. It consisted of 28 questions to which respondents were asked to indicate agreement or disagreement. These yielded scores from 0 to 9 on five scales: awareness of the costs of crime (C), acceptance or denial of responsibility for offending (R), impulsiveness (I), moral attitudes to crime (M) and awareness of effects on victims (E). These were combined to form a CRIME index which summarised the extent to which the respondent's attitudes were supportive of offending. The questionnaire also included a problem inventory covering 15 problem areas (P) for self-rating on a scale of 4 (big problem) to 1 (no problem), and provided further scores indicating how far the respondent held a criminal self-concept (identity as criminal, IC) and a self-prediction about future offending (S). (These last two scores and the problem inventory did not form part of the CRIME index in the original version.) It should be noted that CRIME-PICS was not designed to predict offending, but to provide a practical instrument for assessing attitudes and problems likely to be connected with offending.

Of the 655 offenders included in the reconviction study, 401 were involved in various forms of community supervision: the STOP programme, 'standard' Probation Orders and Community Service Orders. Within these groups, initial CRIME-PICS data were available on 85 STOP members, 48 other probationers and 47 offenders subject to Community Service Orders. In the latter two groups, it was not possible to cover as large a number of offenders as in the STOP group, but the resulting samples can be taken as broadly representative. Administration was by probation staff who had received the small amount of training required for CRIME-PICS, but not by the supervisor of the offender concerned. Re-test scores could not be obtained in all cases for various practical reasons, including some offenders' failure to complete programmes, changes of residence and resource difficulties, but end-of-programme scores were obtained for 47 STOP members, and end-of-order scores for 15 other probationers and 37 of the Community Service group. All re-test groups are therefore biased to some degree in favour of those who completed orders or programmes successfully, with or without a reconviction along the way, and coverage of the 'standard probation' group is particularly low, so that re-test data in this group should be regarded with caution. It should be noted throughout this section that a *low* crime index score indicates a *high* level of attitudes and beliefs favourable to offending (this scoring rule was reversed for CRIME-PICS II), while a low problem score indicates a low level of self-reported problems.

The available pairs of initial and end-of-programme or end-of-order scores were examined to determine how far offenders were indicating changes during supervision. Briefly, both STOP group members and other probationers showed improvements in attitudes and beliefs, while offenders on Community Service Orders did not. There is also an indication of a substantial reduction in problems in the STOP group, and some reduction in the probation group, with no change in the Community Service group. Most of the changes do not reach statistical significance: the exception is the reduction in problems in STOP (T-test: $p<.01$). These results are consistent with the expectation that STOP and other probation orders should have more impact than Community Service on offenders' attitudes; what is particularly striking is the greater change in self-reported problems for STOP members, which adds to the positive findings generated by other components of the STOP evaluation.

Comparisons were also made between available reconviction data and initial scores on both 'crime index' and self-reported problems, and between reconviction data and information about changes in scores during supervision. Both high initial 'crime index' scores and low initial problem scores were associated with avoidance of reconviction: the association was significant in the case of problem scores ($p<0.1$).

The relationship between the CRIME-PICS problem profiles and reconviction is also apparent if we consider those whose scores showed changes between the beginning and end of their programmes or orders. Those whose 'crime index' increased (their attitudes and beliefs became more pro-social) were somewhat less likely to be reconvicted than those whose 'index' decreased, but the differences in reconvictions between those whose problems decreased and increased were greater, particularly during the first year of the reconviction follow-up. Table 8.5 illustrates the relationship: the association between reduced problem scores and avoidance of reconviction is significant ($p<.05$).

Table 8.5 Changes in CRIME-PICS scores and reconvictions within 12 months (all community sentences)

Component and Direction of Change	% Reconvicted
Attitudes and beliefs become more pro-criminal (n=40)	38
Attitudes and beliefs become more pro-social (n=55)	27
Self-reported problems increase (n=31)	48
Self-reported problems decrease (n=45)	22

In view of the evidence that STOP programme participants were the group most likely to show changes during supervision and also showed evidence of some programme effect on reconviction, it is interesting to consider what changes occurred in the CRIME-PICS components for the 47 STOP group members who provided two scores. Most items show some change in a positive direction. Of the 'crime index' items, the largest change is in impulsiveness, which is consistent with feedback from the offenders themselves. It is also interesting that some of the Canadian evaluations of Reasoning and Rehabilitation programmes report substantial change in the area of impulsiveness (for example, Robinson et al. 1991). Among the problem inventory items, the largest reported improvements concern a mixture of external and internal problems: money, employment, getting into trouble, depression, and not feeling good about oneself.

Conclusion

Overall, the evidence now available from the STOP evaluation is broadly encouraging. It shows that probation services can implement this kind of programme, and can achieve some useful impact on offending, particularly through the reduction of offences serious enough to qualify for custodial sentences. The evidence also suggests that improved selection for the programme (to increase completion rates) and improved follow-up (to reinforce learning and reduce 'relapse' after the end of the formal programme) would probably improve effectiveness further. Changes in attitudes and self-reported problems are in the intended direction, with changes in self-reported problems showing some association with reduced offending.

Together, these findings make a strong case for the continuing development and implementation of cognitive-behavioural programmes which make a systematic attempt to help offenders learn problem-solving skills. They also offer one way for the Probation Service to demonstrate a positive link between helping and crime reduction, instead of being caught uneasily between the welfare traditions of its social work past and the correctional emphasis of its probable criminal justice future.

References

Andrews, D.A., Zinger, I., Hoge, R.D., Bonta, J., Gendreau, P. and Cullen, F.T. (1990) 'Does correctional treatment work? A clinically relevant and psychologically informed meta-analysis', *Criminology*, 28, pp.369–404.

Bailey, R. and Ward, D. (1992) *Probation Supervision: Attitudes to Formalised Helping*, Belfast: Probation Board for Northern Ireland.

Bale, D. (1987) 'Using a risk of custody scale', *Probation Journal*, 34, pp.127–31.

Brownlee, I.D. (1995) 'Intensive probation with young adult offenders: A short reconviction study', *British Journal of Criminology*, 35, pp.599–612.

Copas, J.B. (1992) 'Statistical Analysis for a Risk of Reconviction Predictor', report to the Home Office, University of Warwick (unpublished).

Copas, J.B., Ditchfield, J. and Marshall, P. (1994) 'Development of a new reconviction prediction score', *Research Bulletin*, 36, pp.30–7.

Day, P. (1981) *Social Work and Social Control*, London: Tavistock.

Deering, J., Thurston, R. and Vanstone, M. (1996) 'Individual supervision and reconviction: An experimental programme in Pontypridd', *Probation Journal*, 43, pp.70–76.

Folkard, M.S., Smith, D.E. and Smith D.D. (1976) *IMPACT, volume II: The Results of the Experiment*, London: HMSO.

Frude, N., Honess, T. and Maguire, M. (1990) *CRIME-PICS Handbook*, Cardiff: Michael and Associates.

Frude, N., Honess, T. and Maguire, M. (1994) *CRIME-PICS II Manual*, Cardiff: Michael and Associates.

Hollin, C.R. (1995) 'The meaning and implications of programme integrity' in J. McGuire (ed.) *What Works: Reducing Reoffending*, Chichester: John Wiley, pp.195–208.

Home Office (1993) *The National Risk of Reconviction Predictor*, London: Home Office Research and Planning Unit.

Home Office (1994) *Probation Statistics England and Wales 1993*, London: Home Office.

Knott, C. (1995) 'The STOP programme: Reasoning and Rehabilitation in a British setting' in J. McGuire (ed.) *What Works: Reducing Reoffending*, Chichester: John Wiley, pp.116–26.

Lipsey, M. (1992) 'Juvenile delinquency treatment: A meta-analytic enquiry into the variability of effects' in T. Cook, H. Cooper, D.S. Cordray, H. Hartmann, L.V. Hedges, R.L. Light, T.A. Louis and F. Mosteller (eds) *Meta-analysis for Explanation: A Case-book*, New York: Russell Sage, pp.83–127.

Lloyd, C., Mair, G. and Hough, M. (1994) *Explaining Reconviction Rates: A Critical Analysis*, Home Office Research Study 136, London: HMSO.

Lucas, J., Raynor, P. and Vanstone, M. (1992) *Straight Thinking On Probation One Year On*, Bridgend, Mid-Glamorgan: Mid-Glamorgan Probation Service.

Martinson, R. (1974) 'What works?', *The Public Interest*, March, pp.22–54.

McGuire, J. (ed.) (1995) *What Works: Reducing Offending*, Chichester: John Wiley.

McGuire, J. and Priestley, P. (1985) *Offending Behaviour: Skills and Stratagems for Going Straight*, London: B.T. Batsford.

McGuire, J. and Priestley, P. (1995) 'Reviewing What Works: Past, present and future', in J. McGuire (ed.) *What Works: Reducing Reoffending*, Chichester: John Wiley, pp. 3-34.

McIvor, G. (1990) *Sanctions for Serious or Persistent Offenders*, Stirling: University of Stirling.

McLaren, K. (1992) *Reducing Reoffending: What Works Now*, Wellington, NZ: Penal Division, Department of Justice.

Neary, M. (1992) 'Robert Ross, Probation and the Problems of Rationality', paper distributed at the 'What Works' conference, Salford University (unpublished).

Priestley, P., McGuire, J., Flegg, D., Hemsley, V. and Welham, D. (1978) *Social Skills and Personal Problem Solving*, London: Tavistock.

Raynor, P. (1988) *Probation as an Alternative to Custody*, Aldershot: Avebury.

Raynor, P. (1996) 'Evaluating probation: The rehabilitation of effectiveness' in T. May and A. Vass (eds) *Working with Offenders: Issues Contexts and Outcomes*, London: Sage, pp.242–58.

Raynor, P. (1998) 'Attitudes, social problems and reconvictions in the STOP probation experiment', *Howard Journal of Criminal Justice*, 37, pp.1–15.

Raynor, P. and Vanstone, M. (1994a) 'Probation practice, effectiveness and the non-treatment paradigm', *British Journal of Social Work*, 24, pp.387–404.

Raynor, P., and Vanstone, M. (1994b) *Straight Thinking On Probation: Third Interim Evaluation Report – Reconvictions within 12 Months*, Bridgend, Mid-Glamorgan: Mid-Glamorgan Probation Service.

Raynor, P. and Vanstone, M. (1996) 'Reasoning and Rehabilitation in Britain: The results of the Straight Thinking On Probation (STOP) programme', *International Journal of Offender Therapy and Comparative Criminology*, 40, pp.279–91.

Raynor, P., Sutton, D. and Vanstone, M. (1995) 'The STOP programme' in R.R. Ross and R.D. Ross (eds) *Thinking Straight*, Ottawa: AIR Training and Publications, pp.313–39.

Robinson, D., Grossman, M. and Porporino, F. (1991) *Effectiveness of the Cognitive Skills Training Program: From Pilot to National Implementation*, Research Brief B-07, Ottawa: Correctional Service of Canada.

Ross, R.R. and Fabiano, E.A. (1985) *Time to Think: A Cognitive Model of Delinquency Prevention and Offender Rehabilitation*, Johnson City, TN: Institute of Social Sciences and Arts.

Ross, R.R., Fabiano, E.A. and Ewles, C.D. (1988) 'Reasoning and rehabilitation', *International Journal of Offender Therapy and Comparative Criminology*, 32, pp.29–35.

Ross, R.R., Fabiano, E.A. and Ross, R.D. (1986) *Reasoning and Rehabilitation: A Handbook for Teaching Cognitive Skills*, Ottawa: University of Ottawa.

Sutton, D. (1990) 'The search for quality work with high risk offenders', Mid-Glamorgan Probation Service, (unpublished).

Vanstone, M. (1993) 'A "missed opportunity" reassessed: The influence of the Day Training Centre experiment on the criminal justice system and probation practice', *British Journal of Social Work*, 23, pp.213–29.

9 Working with carers using the birthday exercise

Albert Kushlick, Dave Dagnan and Peter Trower

A major advance in the behavioural approach to 'severe challenging behaviours' has been the shift towards a behavioural analytic approach in which interventions are based upon an understanding of the functions of challenging behaviours (Horner et al. 1990; Remington 1991; see also Chapter 1). Increasingly, we recognise that challenging behaviour may serve a range of possible communication functions (although very inefficiently), for example: 'I feel', and 'I want' or 'I don't want ...'. Interventions may then teach carers to respond to challenging behaviour as if the person had communicated their preferences more appropriately. Carers may also begin to teach the person presenting the challenges to communicate these preferences more appropriately (Carr and Durand 1985; Carr 1988). These approaches can be considered constructional in that they build upon existing repertoires and offer alternative, adaptive behaviours in place of severe challenging behaviours (Goldiamond 1974). This chapter addresses how these advances can be supported in the work of people undertaking front-line care responsibilities in a range of settings: parents at home, day centre staff and teachers in social service, health and educational settings. It is particularly relevant for managers of these services who are responsible for providing and maintaining high-quality environments for users and those who work with them.

LaVigna and Donnellan (1986) describe a systematic constructional approach that involves celebrating and extending each person's current valuable repertoire of behaviour. Aspects of this approach include positive programming of a rich and comprehensive range of activities of daily living, and arranging contingencies of reinforcement to maintain behaviours other than the identified challenging behaviours. They also highlight the importance of a range of reactive strategies to keep clients and carers safe, and to limit any damage caused when destructive behaviours do occur. Such packages are complex, systematic and demanding, and people working with individuals who present severe challenges will need considerable support and guidance to implement them. Without such support, they are more likely to revert to using existing widespread practices that are likely to trigger or maintain the severe challenging behaviours of the client (Hall and Oliver 1992; Hastings and Remington 1994a).

Given the length of time that challenges are likely to have been present in a person's repertoire (see, for example, Emerson 1992) and been responded to ineffectively by others, changes that make a real difference in the quality of people's lives will take long periods to test and refine. Inevitably, there will be both successes and setbacks. It is important that setbacks are expected and understood. It is also important that we respond to them with well-tested reactive procedures, and by reassessment and problem-solving strategies. If we do not, it is likely that setbacks will be interpreted as evidence that the new procedures are completely useless and had better be abandoned in favour of the old, traditional, ineffective but more familiar procedures.

When clients have used severe challenging behaviour to gain their 'wants' and 'not wants' staff may experience a range of unhealthy negative emotions (Dagnan et al. 1998; Hastings and Remington 1995). They may also believe that these emotions and the actions that accompany them are fully justified by the 'condemnable' behaviour and the low worth of the person. Staff may believe that there is no hope of effecting changes (Dagnan et al. 1998). It is important that they are helped to discover that they have a much wider range of choices of how to respond to the client's behaviour than they have believed until now. While discovering this, they will be creating a high-quality life for themselves and their clients. However, they may also sometimes feel very uncomfortable when they do so. Much of this discomfort will be related to their unfamiliarity with the new practices, and to the extra work involved in implementing the new procedures. Without support, the chances of abandoning new approaches under these circumstances are very high.

Because of these very fallible tendencies of all humans, it seems reasonable to conclude that all of us, and especially those working with groups of people with severe impairments, will need support in implementing the detailed, multi-component procedures of the constructional behavioural approach. This support will help us work through setbacks and successes in implementing these procedures over long periods. Consequently, we have developed a new training approach that combines elements of Rational Emotive Behaviour Therapy (Ellis and Harper 1975; Ellis 1979) and Cognitive Behaviour Therapy (Beck et al. 1979) with training in constructional behavioural interventions for carers working with people with severe challenging behaviours.

We describe an experiential exercise – 'The Birthday Exercise' – that introduces the basic ideas of cognitive therapy to carers working with people with learning disabilities and severe challenging behaviour. The exercise described here can be used with individuals, but is even more powerful with groups, where it may take up to three hours. Groups can be made up of paid carers, family carers, managers, and people with learning disabilities themselves. The description here assumes that we are carrying out the exercise in a group. The application of this will give participants the tools to address the long-term task of working creatively to improve the quality of their own and others' lives as calmly and effectively as possible. The preparation for this exercise and its place in teaching constructional behavioural skills is described in more detail in Kushlick et al. (1997).

Implementing constructional behavioural interventions and training can facilitate working towards a common goal. However, this goal is not often made explicit. Throughout this exercise we identify the common goal for carers and clients as that of working towards a high quality of life for ourselves and for others. This process of identification brings together the goals of cognitive therapy (Ellis and Harper 1975; Ellis 1979; see also Chapter 1), definitions of challenging behaviour as behaviour that prevents inclusion in integrated activities of daily living (Emerson et al. 1987) and a frequently identified target of services for people with learning disabilities (Kushlick 1975; Kushlick et al. 1983; Felce and Perry 1995; Felce 1996; Dagnan et al. 1995).

Some patterns of thinking explored in this chapter obstruct achieving a high quality of life. Global rating and labelling in 'tautologous explanation' of human behaviour is a major example (Skinner 1972). To help us 'understand' and accept with humour why people continue to use such patterns of thinking, we introduce the idea of people as 'fallible human beings'. We expand on and stress throughout this chapter that the only predictable thing we can say about people in general is that they will sometimes get things right and sometimes get things wrong.

The birthday exercise

The main aims of the exercise are to help participants:

1 to distinguish the widely believed and culturally accepted A-C theory of the origin of emotions from the alternative cognitive ABC theory (in the

cognitive-behavioural paradigm, A represents activating events, B represents beliefs about A or C, and C represents the consequences (behaviour and feelings). In operant behavioural terms, A represents the antecedents of the behaviour under focus, B represents the behaviour and C represents the consequences of the behaviour. In 'front-line' practice we have not found it necessary to elaborate on this difference).

2 to distinguish feelings (usually described in one word) such as 'sad, concerned, depressed, hungry, sexy' from beliefs (usually described in several words and which usually include a verb) such as 'I am being rejected' or 'You don't love me.'

3 to identify and name negative and positive feelings

4 to clarify that there are healthy negative feelings that protect us and had better be celebrated. These negative feelings highlight situations where we are not getting what we want, or are getting what we do not want. If we are anaesthetised, and so do not recognise such feelings, we are in danger of suffering injury without being aware of it

5 to distinguish healthy from unhealthy negative feelings; healthy negative feelings help us defend and expand our high quality of life and the high quality of life of those we care about; with unhealthy negative feelings, we tend to destroy and sabotage a high quality of life

6 to recognise that there are also unhealthy positive feelings, these mislead us to conclude that we are getting what we want when we are not, and to deny that we are experiencing what we do not want when we are; under these conditions, we are likely to undertake projects for which we lack the skills or to remain in unsafe situations.

To illustrate the difference between the A-C theory of emotion and the cognitive ABC theory, participants are asked to rate their own feelings as they are then. We tell them:

> Rate yourself 0 if you are feeling such that you are considering suicide as a solution to your problems. Rate yourself 10 if you are feeling so energised that you are looking forward to making this workshop the best you have created.

All participants are encouraged to speak. Their usual responses illustrate the A-C theory of emotion and behaviour: A (the activating event) causes C (the consequence – what the person feels and how they behave). For example, they may say: 'This morning my score is nine. The baby slept all night. When I got up, the sun was shining. My partner smiled at me, and passed me the butter when I asked for it. The car started the first time, and there were no traffic jams on the way to work. I really like workshops.' Others may say: 'My score is two. The baby didn't sleep last night. My partner was in a foul mood at breakfast. The car didn't start for an hour, and the Inland Revenue had sent an account for £500 which we owe. Also, I hate workshops.'

We suggest that the A-C view of emotion has a disadvantage. If A is the cause of C, then until A is changed, the score at C cannot change. However, it is everyone's experience that the score does change during the day, though the As remain the same (partners remain grumpy, the Inland Revenue continues its demands, and traffic continues to build up on the roads). We then introduce participants to the ABC theory of emotion and behaviour. There are still activating events and consequences like those above. However, between A and C, we now consider B: our beliefs (or thoughts) about A or C. At its simplest level, this theory suggests that if one's beliefs about A or C are positive, one feels 'cheery' and does 'cheery' things; if one's beliefs about A or C are negative, one feels 'yukkie' and does things characterised as 'yukkie'.

However, we warn participants not to accept any theory – this or any other – without some experimental evidence, preferably from their everyday lives. We then invite them to join in an experiment to test the theory. We tell them that to do this we will need volunteers, and that the early volunteers will get the easy jobs. We tell them that we will give them an activating event (A) that occurs regularly in everyone's life. We will ask volunteers to share with the group their beliefs or thoughts in relation to this A.

The first volunteer will be asked to give us depressed thoughts in relation to the A. We explain that depressed thinking is offered to the earliest volunteer because most people are very good at it. We also reassure them that if they have any difficulty, they will be helped by the presenter, who is also an expert in depressed thinking. When the first person has volunteered, we seek a person for the equally easy task of offering anxious and panicky thoughts. We reassure participants that, like depressed thinking, this is a well-developed skill in most people. We then recruit volunteers for angry, calm, loving and excited thoughts. Volunteers for loving thoughts are usually the most difficult to recruit.

For each emotion, the task is first to generate thoughts appropriate to the emotion. In this part of the task, we may use 'inference chaining' to help clarify beliefs. Volunteers can be asked to imagine that the thing predicted has occurred, and to think what this means to them. For example, we could ask them, 'What's the worst aspect of that?' or 'What would it mean if that happened?' or '... and then ...?' We use these techniques to elicit and explore the later chains of beliefs and emotions which follow the earlier ones. We then dispute these beliefs together. (For an introduction to cognitions associated with different emotions, see, for example, Wessler and Wessler 1980 or Dryden 1987.)

Depressed thoughts

We tell participants that the A for the experiment is: 'It's your birthday, and it is five o'clock in the morning.' We tell the 'depressed' volunteer: 'You have woken up with depressed thoughts. Tell us some.' The volunteer usually starts with: 'I'm a year older. I haven't done the things I had wanted to do. No one has remembered my birthday. I'm a year closer to death. I have wrinkles on my face, and I'm getting bald.'

We point out that, surprisingly, such beliefs are not depressogenic. Scientifically accurate thinking supported by evidence may be accompanied by healthy feelings of sadness, concern or even annoyance, but are not accompanied by unhealthy emotions such as depression. Table 9.1 shows the healthy emotions and associated unhealthy emotions considered in this chapter. Healthy emotions had better be celebrated, because they highlight problems and set the occasion for healthy problem-solving. If I am aware of healthy emotions, I may choose to take steps to change what I can and to do high-quality things despite the things I cannot change. Experience suggests that if I do this, then some aspects of the quality of my life will improve. Thus, accurate beliefs will not succeed in the task of creating 'depression'. Participants will need additional effort for this. They are told that they will be given a recipe for having a 'great depression' because if they know how to create one, they will also know how to get out of it.

Table 9.1 Associated healthy and unhealthy emotions

Healthy	Unhealthy
Sadness	Depression
Concern	Anxiety/panic
Annoyance	Anaesthetised
Loving	Dire need for love
Excited	Euphoric

Depressive ingredient number 1

If no one has already offered this, we prompt participants towards global low self-ratings as the core belief leading to 'depression' (as opposed to healthy sadness or concern). They note that fallible human beings like us link accurate observations (for example, 'People have forgotten my birthday', 'I have not attained my targets', 'I am now nearer death') by a simple explanation: 'I am a failure, a loser, a nobody, a fool or a doormat.' Other cruder animal, psychiatric or sexually related labels may be also be used to describe ourselves. After asking permission from the participants to use a crude term that covers all of the above negative terms, we suggest the general label of 'worthless shit'. If anyone feels uncomfortable with this term, we substitute 'worthless slob'. Participants often find that the use of the generic term 'worthless shit' injects some humour into the proceedings. It is also an accurate self-descriptor that fallible people sometimes use to describe themselves.

Depressive ingredient number 2

We point out that most of the remaining 'depressed' beliefs follow 'logically' from the global self-rating, 'I am a worthless shit.' We can ask the volunteer and other participants, 'what is the future for us worthless shits?', and answers come in the form: 'The future is bleak and hopeless.'

Depressive ingredient number 3

We can then ask: 'How *should* the future be?' The answers will include, 'It should be good and easy', 'I should perform well and get the things I want', 'I shouldn't perform poorly, or get the things I don't want.' We may add: 'It should be like this for me because it is already like this for everyone else.'

Depressive ingredient number 4

We may then add 'poor me' as the fourth ingredient to the recipe. This arises from the assumption that everybody else is having a great time at five o'clock in the morning on their birthday.

Depressive ingredient number 5

The participants complete the prompt 'I can't ...' with 'I can't cope' or 'I can't stand it.'

We suggest that fallible human beings can repeat these five beliefs many thousands of times during their waking hours. The beliefs will probably be accompanied by 'yukkie' feelings labelled 'depressed'. This sequence may be reinforced by expressions of 'sympathy' and other special forms of attention from friends. People who practise the above thoughts may increase the intensity of their negative feelings by frequent repetition of additional beliefs such as 'I should feel normal' and 'I shouldn't have these depressed beliefs.' Ellis (1979) has pointed out that this tendency to 'upset ourselves about being upset' or about 'being upset about being upset' seriously interferes with working towards high-quality living, and is a major component of severe emotional distress.

Disputing depressive beliefs

We now ask the participants to address systematically the evidence supporting or challenging the five ingredients.

Disputing ingredient 1

We ask participants if they know a 'worthless shit'. We point out that people like us, who behave 'shittily some of the time', are not eligible. We suggest that although everyone does it, it is silly and ill-informed to give a global rating to the 'inherent value' of any object, however simple that object is. It is even sillier to rate a complex object as 'worthless' and to condemn it absolutely. It is very silly indeed to apply this rating to, and to condemn something as complex as a human being who has lived and will continue to live and change in a wide range of contexts in ways we cannot predict over many years. If the rating 'totally worthless' were to be used meaningfully, it would have to be applied only to humans who behave worthlessly all the time (24 hours a day, 365 days a year). Even if people were highly committed to behaving in such a worthless manner all the time, they could not possibly succeed in doing so. Fallible human beings would inevitably, by mistake, get something 'right' and do something 'worthy' some of the time. Like seriously depressed clients, most participants see the humour in this. We suggest that the only generalisation that can be usefully made about all people is that we are fallible human beings who sometimes get things right and sometimes get things wrong.

When humans apply global ratings to humans, they are playing at being gods. We note some of the difficulties of playing this role, including the pain it brings to most fallible human beings who try it, as well as to others who may be judged by these people. It is much more advantageous to fallible human beings to view themselves and others as fallible people who sometimes get things wrong and sometimes get things right. It is equally unhelpful to view ourselves or others as always worthy. One consequence of viewing oneself as always worthy is that when we do note ourselves or others performing poorly (as all fallible human beings do at some time), we will be more likely to apply the rating 'worthless shit' to ourselves or others. Globally rating ourselves worthy or as 'on the right-hand side of God' is almost as unhelpful as globally rating ourselves as 'worthless shits'.

Disputing ingredient 2

We take the same approach to disputing the belief that 'the future is hopeless'. Participants usually agree that they cannot predict the future, as they do not have a crystal ball or a time machine. While things could get much worse, they might also improve as people start working more actively towards their own high-quality life and for that of others. Despite setbacks, we control our own performance in key, predictable aspects of high-quality living. These include activities such as getting up in the morning, washing and dressing, getting children up and fed, buying and preparing food, and arranging leisure activities for ourselves. If we are to keep succeeding in those aspects of our lives that we control, we had better keep practising these activities even when we feel 'yukkie' and are faced with unfair obstacles and criticism. Participants may agree that when we have been feeling 'yukkie', we have often felt better when engaged busily in things that interest us. We stress the value of giving up the habit of globally rating ourselves and others. Instead, we stress the value of rating performances and behaviours which lead to high-quality lives. This is different from making a global rating of our value as human beings. If, instead of making global ratings of our value, we accurately value the things that we do, we will tend to experience healthy emotions, and this will raise the quality of our lives.

Participants also note that our own high-quality behaviour (such as getting up, washing, toileting, dressing and eating) are both predictable and controllable. On the other hand, the behaviour of others is very much more difficult to predict, let alone to control. We strongly suggest that we are our own best friends, as no one else is as uniquely committed to and aware of the quality of our lives as we are. Where necessary, we encourage participants to seek help creatively in problem-solving. We may suggest that they are doing this by attending the workshop.

Disputing ingredient 3

The belief that the future should be great, and that I should get everything I want and nothing that I do not want is addressed by asking participants for evidence that this is so. We can ask participants to look out of the window to check whether it is written in the sky that they should have a great life. They usually agree that it is not. Some may join in the spirit by humorously remarking that it was written there, but that someone has rubbed it out.

Disputing ingredient 4

The belief 'poor me' depends on belief number 3 that 'I should get more of what I want, and less of what I don't want' and that 'Everybody except me is getting what they want, and avoiding the things they don't want.' In order to check that everyone else is having a better time than I am at five o'clock in the morning, we would need a telephone or door-to-door survey. One reason why 'others' do not seem to depress themselves when we see them is that, like us, when they are in public, they wisely continue to work for high-quality lives despite their feeling upset. As there is no evidence for the belief associated with 'poor me', they may change it to the more healthy 'I'm not getting all that I want, and I'm getting some things that I don't want. Therefore, I feel healthily sad, and I am committed to work, with help if necessary, for my high-quality life despite this.'

Disputing ingredient 5

The belief 'I can't stand it', 'I can't cope' or 'I can't manage' is also challenged by the evidence. If I really could not 'stand it', I would not be here. Since I am indeed here, I can stand it even if I do not like how I feel. The belief 'I can't cope' is challenged by discussing what I have already done today. This always shows that I am 'coping'. For example, I woke up, got up, got dressed and washed, got the children up and washed and dressed and fed, and took them to school. All this was done despite feeling 'yukkie', and despite being criticised while doing so by fallible children and a fallible partner. We might even suggest that this deserves more celebration than doing these things while feeling cheery with co-operative children and partners. For some people, evidence of 'not coping' is tearfulness. We celebrate the value of tears and the sadness they may express, pass the tissues, and note the value of problem-solving despite tearfulness.

Depressed behaviour alongside the beliefs

We ask the first volunteer: 'If you were rehearsing the five depressogenic beliefs energetically at five o'clock in the morning, which room of the house would you be in, and what would you be doing?' The volunteer generally replies: 'In my bedroom. I would probably be in bed, looking very gloomy, the curtains would be drawn, the floor would be covered with dirty clothes, unwashed cups and plates, filled ashtrays, empty beer cans, unopened mail and unread newspapers.' Asked what arrangements they would have made about the birthday if they were rehearsing depressed beliefs, volunteers usually shake their heads and say 'None.'

They may even add that they hope that no one else has remembered either.

We then go on to the other volunteers, and work through beliefs and behaviours associated with their emotions. We have considered depression in detail because it is possible to show how the beliefs associated with other unhealthy emotions can be related back to those beliefs associated with depression.

Anxious and panicky beliefs

The 'anxious' volunteer lists 'awful' things that could happen on their birthday. They say: 'No one will come to the party, and I will not have enough food for those that do come.' We point out that experts in anxious thinking can catastrophise in both directions, for example: 'No one will turn up' or 'There will be too many people', and 'There won't be enough food and drink' or 'There will be too much.' These thoughts can lead to two forms of anxiety. The first is *ego anxiety*, characterised by thoughts such as: 'Whatever happens, people will discover what I have been hiding until today; they will know that I'm a worthless shit.' The second is *discomfort anxiety*, characterised by thoughts such as: 'I will feel awful, I'll have palpitations and a pain in the chest, and I'll feel breathless, sweaty, shaky and nauseous' (Ellis 1979).

We ask the volunteer to imagine that the worst predictions have occurred, hordes of people have arrived, they have all got drunk, eaten all the food and left none for other guests. Asked what that would mean to them, volunteers may say: 'My friends will go home leaving me alone, I will feel isolated and get depressed or I'll have a nervous breakdown.' However, we remind people that there are good things that can be done by oneself. We also remind them that we will only feel depressed if we add to these thoughts the five depressogenic beliefs without checking them for accuracy and correcting those that are inaccurate. The thought 'I am going to have a nervous breakdown' is rephrased as: 'I feel healthily yukkie about not getting what I want, and getting what I don't want. I'm starting to tell myself I'm a worthless shit ... As this is not compulsory, I can choose to do some problem-solving, alone or with help.'

Anxious or panicky behaviour

When asked to describe anxious or panicky behaviour, people describe themselves as moving from task to task without completing any, making mistakes, and frequently 'changing their minds'. For example, they start phoning people (at five o'clock in the morning!) and then put the phone down to tidy up; they then change to making sandwiches and return to phoning. They go to the toilet frequently. Smokers smoke, and overeaters eat. They may eventually give up all activities, go to bed and depress themselves.

Distinguishing healthy concern from unhealthy anxiety or panic beliefs

Healthily concerned beliefs are distinguished from anxious or panicky beliefs by using the example of crossing a dangerous road. Concerned thinking would be: 'I'd like to get safely to the other side of the road despite my discomfort. I will therefore wait till the traffic stops before moving quickly but carefully to the other side.' These healthily concerned beliefs accompany careful crossing behaviour. Panicked thinking would include: 'This feeling is awful [discomfort anxiety]. I'll faint and get knocked over. Casualty staff will see my dirty underpants, and then they'll know that I am a worthless shit [ego anxiety], and treat me badly.' With thoughts like these, I am more likely to misjudge the traffic and have an accident. Anxious and panicky thoughts are accompanied by increasingly destructive behaviour.

Angry thoughts

Asked to think angry thoughts about someone who has let them down on their birthday, volunteers may say: 'Joe didn't send me a card or got the wrong present, so I won't send him a card, or I'll send him an inappropriate present.' Asked what will it mean if they do not take this revenge, they may reply: 'I will be a worthless shit.' Revenge is believed essential if angry 'victims' who believe themselves to be completely in the right are to avoid being 'wound up', 'made a fool of', 'getting depressed', or receiving more bad treatment from the worthless shit who deserves total condemnation.

Angry 'victims' also specialise in catching 'guilty' people getting things wrong not only now but in the past: 'You didn't get me a card. Also, you forgot the food yesterday. Last week, you finished the milk and didn't replace it. Last month, you left the car without any petrol. Last birthday, you came late for my special dinner. Three years ago, you went to a conference on my birthday. Ten years ago, you gave the present I wanted to your sister. You take after your psychopathic father!'

Asked how they lay tables or shut doors when feeling angry and thinking angry thoughts, volunteers report: 'I bang things down on the table and slam doors.' Asked what they do if the offending person comes into the room asking 'What's going on?', they may shout, 'What the hell are you doing here?' Alternative healthy annoyed thoughts can be suggested: 'I'll tell him I feel really annoyed, give him a cuddle, and remind him of my birthday early and often next year.'

Calm thoughts

Volunteers who think calmly may say: 'I have everything prepared for today's celebrations. The invitations, the food and the house are organised.' Such thinking may be accompanied by going back to sleep or other preferred activities. Calm thoughts can often be maintained despite setbacks such as: 'You have prepared for a barbecue in the evening and rain is forecast.' Calm thinkers may respond: 'Never mind, we'll grill the food inside.' We may then say: 'But there has been no card from your partner', and again a calm thinker may respond: 'The post is late, or she probably forgot because she's arranging a surprise party.'

Loving thoughts

The volunteer for loving thoughts is told that there are two components to this: 'loving of oneself' and 'loving of others'.

Loving thoughts about oneself

To help people, they are asked to list three things they have done in the last year about which they are proud. This may prove difficult, as people may not be used to saying good things about themselves. We can point out that we seem better at listing 'depressed' and 'anxious' thoughts than talking about the positive things we have done. This may be because we are often more supported and comforted by others when we put ourselves down or express anxieties. When we list our positive features, we may even be criticised for 'boasting', 'grandiosity' or even for being 'worthless shits'.

The early reluctance of people to volunteer for 'loving thoughts' is discussed in this exercise. Men tend to find expressing all loving thoughts difficult. Women tend to list loving thoughts about others as loving thoughts about themselves. For example, they may say 'I have a supportive partner' or 'My friends are understanding.' They are encouraged to list and praise their own successes as friends, parents or colleagues, and to act out of the belief 'me first, and others a close second'. Eventually, when pressed, volunteers can list three performances in the last year that they have been proud of. Examples often include things they have done for other people: 'I have supported my son when he raised problems with me' or 'I have visited my parents and helped them to find alternative housing.'

We ask: 'Given that you have done these loving things for others during the last year, what special treat would you like to give yourself on your birthday?' The volunteer may say: 'I'll take the morning off' or 'I'll take a long bath with scented oil' or 'I'll get my hair done, have a massage and buy some new clothes for myself.'

Loving thoughts about others

Asked about people who have done nice things for them during the year, the volunteer may give examples such as: 'One of my children has supported her younger sister through difficulties at school.' Asked 'How will you communicate today that you appreciate what they have done?', the volunteer may say: 'I'll give them a hug and tell them.' We list other ways of expressing love to others; these may include phoning, sending cards, cuddling, making food for the person, inviting them out, performing chores or sending flowers.

We suggest that it is also easy and appropriate to express love towards people about whom we also have angry thoughts. What often stops us doing this is the unhelpful belief 'If I think loving thoughts and do loving things to someone I feel angry with, I am automatically two-faced, insincere, a doormat, and a worthless shit!'

The belief that 'others must love me'

No harm generally follows expressing love and helping oneself or others actively to attain the high-quality lives we prefer. However, healthy, active loving is usefully distinguished from unhealthy demands that others must express love to us if we are to avoid depression. Ellis has called this the 'dire need for love' (Ellis 1979). We remind participants that while we are fallibly able to control our own thoughts and performances, we are unable to control those of others. If we believe that our worth as humans depends on expressions of love by another fallible human being, then we are likely to upset ourselves seriously when they fail to express it to us, or express it to others. On the other hand, if we healthily prefer others to express love towards us, we will feel healthily sad, annoyed or jealous when they do not. These healthy discomforts may motivate creative ways of either accepting or changing other people's responses to us. Discomfort felt alongside this is usefully described as 'healthy jealousy'.

Excited thoughts about my birthday

The relationship between excited beliefs, emotions and behaviour is illustrated as the volunteer rubs their hands, grins and jumps up and down while saying: 'Hooray, I've survived another year, I'm getting up to look at my cards and presents, I'll have a great time and try on my party things before having a bath.'

Some conclusions from this exercise

First, we check that participants agree that it is possible to think, and therefore to feel and to act, in a very wide range of ways about any event, internal or external. An important point to be made from this exercise is that the behaviour of people thinking unhealthy, depressed, anxious or angry thoughts is often limited and destructive. However, when people think healthy, calm, loving or excited thoughts, they seem to behave more creatively and flexibly.

We then round off by recalling that we have been testing the hypothesis that our beliefs or thoughts (B) have a profound influence on how we feel and act (C) about activating events (A). We suggest that the evidence we have examined has supported this. We can then begin to get more feedback from participants by asking them to apply the process to a wider range of antecedents in their home and work lives.

Continuing the birthday exercise

In this chapter, for reasons of space, we illustrate the continuation of the exercise with two examples from work settings. In the full exercise, we would use examples from both home and work life.

First, we take the antecedent 'I get no feedback from my supervisor.' We ask people to think about this event from the different emotional perspectives. Participants may offer angry thoughts such as: 'She doesn't give a damn. The next time she asks me to do overtime I'll tell her to get lost.' Depressed thoughts may include: 'I'm obviously doing so badly she is avoiding me. I'd better look for another job in a different type of work.' Loving thoughts about the supervisor might be: 'She's probably overworked and stressed. I'll give her a call and check out if she wants some help.'

Next, we take the antecedent 'My client kicks me for the fifth time today.' Participants may give angry thoughts such as: 'How can she do this to me after all the nice things I have done for her? She is clearly an attention-seeking and jealous person having a go at me. If I let her get away with this, she has made a fool of me and she will continue to dominate me. I must ignore her more effectively and do something to let her know who's boss around here.' Depressed thoughts might include: 'She has made a fool of me, and that's because I really can't handle her the way others can. Now everybody knows how hopeless I am.' Healthy sad and annoyed thoughts with healthy problem-solving might include: 'I really don't like it when my ankle gets kicked or I am spat on. I feel lousy, and I will never feel other than lousy about that. But I haven't yet worked out the functional communication of these behaviours. Until I have done so, I will work out better reactive procedures to keep me and others safe from assault and spitting. Meanwhile, I will ask for more support and training to continue to provide a high quality of life environment despite the possibility that I will get kicked or spat at some of the time. I know it's not me alone triggering the responses because I have noticed that other staff are also victims some of the time.' In each case, unhelpful thoughts can be challenged and associated behaviours identified. Several publications have begun to identify staff emotional, behavioural and cognitive responses to different types of challenging behaviour (for example Hastings and Remington 1994a and 1994b; Hall and Oliver 1992; Dagnan et al. 1998). These may be useful in providing material for discussion.

The approach described above is then supported in supervision of staff groups working with individual clients.

Case example: Helen

Thirty-year-old Helen arrives home and immediately goes to the notice board, points to the menu and asks 'What's for dinner?' or 'Who's on tonight?' Staff currently take time politely to give her the information she wants, paying particular attention to the replies that highlight her preferences. When staff move on to the next activity, believing that they have given Helen what she wanted, she may strike out at them or other residents.

Initially, staff see this as happening for 'no apparent reason', and believe she must be doing this to 'wind them up'. Given time to think about this during supervision, staff firm up a tentative suspicion that Helen wants to spend time with staff, and does not have the more direct assertive behaviour of saying: 'I feel a bit uncomfortable and I'd really like to spend some time working with you.' Given this as a hypothesis, they can plan to test it by telling her what is on the menu, and then warmly inviting her to work with them. If the hypothesis is right, she will appear cheery and work along with them. If it is wrong, she will continue with the original behaviour.

Staff can reflect upon the workshop material and note that their feelings of sadness, frustration, annoyance and guilt are signs of a healthy response to this challenge, and that they offer the opportunity for healthy problem-solving about Helen's behaviour. They may then work calmly and lovingly, despite the healthy negative feelings and the occasional bruise, on keeping themselves, Helen and other residents safe with agreed and practised reactive strategies. They can also spend time reviewing new data and planning alternative approaches.

Case example: Tom

Tom links arms with a support worker, and queues for his lunch in a dining room seating eighty people. He repeats 'I'm hungry', and appears upset. Staff know that if he does not get what he wants, he escalates to hitting staff, running off and pushing frail clients. Staff are committed to responding to his earliest and most appropriate communication before it escalates, and have been getting good results by doing so. However, on this occasion they choose to encourage Tom to wait in the queue. The beliefs accompanying this are: 'He must learn to wait. If he is allowed to go to the front of the queue, he will increase his level of demands. We will also be faced by other clients, support staff and managers complaining that Tom is getting treatment that is unfair and an ill-informed soft option which will have the effect of bringing about poor-quality lives for both him and us.'

If support workers are going to appraise critically both what they are doing and the comments made on it by others, they will need time to reflect on their own behaviour and to consider a range of options for enabling Tom to collect his food successfully, express his discomfort, and escape from it without escalating to the point of injuring staff or clients. In our experience, staff will need to set aside about three hours every two weeks away from the front line to problem-solve and plan how they will turn the situation around. They will need to make alternative arrangements for Tom and their other clients while problem-solving takes place. In the problem-solving situation, they will need to face active listening from the facilitator. They will need to do so in front of their colleagues, and possibly other professionals from other settings who also work with Tom. They will need to reflect on the possibility that any prediction (for example, that things will get much worse if we give in to Tom's demands) is a hypothesis which can only be tested if an experiment is done to check it. They need to accept that if the news is bad and Tom's behaviour does get worse, they, like all fallible human beings, have a tendency to exaggerate its extent. They may then describe it in ways that make it virtually impossible to respond to except by avoidance or neglect (with or without specifically planned and 'justified' punishment). We believe that without the support and training described here and in Kushlick et al. (1997), an environment like this is, and will remain, potentially dangerous (compare the case of Miss 'B', Chapter 12).

Supervision, training and staff development

To make things work and attain a high-quality life for carers and clients, staff had better recognise that some of the things they are doing as part of their current practice are not working. They will need to commit themselves to finding and practising new alternatives. These will feel additionally uncomfortable at first because they are new, unfamiliar and often quite different from their current well-practised habits.

In supervision, this process is encouraged through celebrating the 'good news' of the things that are working, and reviewing the conditions under which this occurs. They will also be encouraged to note with healthy sadness and concern the same level of detail about the 'bad news' of the things that are not working. They will then be helped to choose a prioritised aspect of the 'bad news' on which to focus, agree and describe alternative high-quality life activities which will need to occur for the label 'good news' to be justified, and finally, to agree and describe who will do what to arrive at the 'good news' option and monitor the steps along the way.

Problems arising from 'getting better'

Paradoxically, important difficulties may arise out of success following on from these strategies. The absence of outbursts or threats of violence may deprive people of opportunities to practise addressing these challenges in real life. People may also become reluctant to role-play interventions, due to the beliefs: 'The person has changed and the sooner the "bad" behaviour is forgotten the better' or 'People don't like doing role-plays, and doing them is likely to bring back the "bad" behaviour by provoking them or reminding them of it.'

A further problem created by success can be that setbacks may then not be associated with healthy sadness, concern and continuing development of problem-solving, but with panic and catastrophising: 'We are back to square one.' These obstacles to continuing problem-solving, if not addressed as we have described above, may result in good work by both clients and staff being devalued or condemned, and may present subsequent barriers to high-quality lives for carers and clients.

Conclusions

All fallible human beings upset themselves unnecessarily, and will continue to do so some of the time. This will happen despite workshops where they learn how they do it and how to give it up. Giving up well-practised old habits and practising new thinking, behaving and feeling takes time. It is more likely to take place where people's new, less fallible, responses are followed by more high-quality life events than those that followed their old habits. As people are helped to practise new habits that work towards high-quality lives in 'ordinary' environments for themselves and others, they will probably become less fallible in these and possibly other contexts. However, until new habits are in place, it is wise to develop and maintain reactive procedures aimed at limiting damage from predictable, destructive old habits such as severe challenging behaviours.

A key challenge is to create and maintain safe, interesting environments which facilitate participation in the activities of high-quality lives by all humans. The escalating costs of excluding increasing proportions of the population from participating in 'ordinary' high-quality environments or congregating people in inauspicious, expensive and extra-ordinary settings makes this an urgent and worthy challenge to applied research and service provision.

References

Beck, A.T., Rush, A.J. Shaw, B.F. and Emery, G. (1979) *Cognitive Therapy of Depression*, New York: Guilford Press.

Carr, E.G. (1988) 'Functional equivalence as a mechanism of response generalisation' in R.H. Homer, G. Dunlap and R.L. Koegel (eds) *Generalization and Maintenance: Lifestyle Changes in Applied Settings*, Baltimore, MD: Paul H. Brookes.

Carr, E.G. and Durand, V.M. (1985) 'Reducing behavior problems through functional communication training', *Journal of Applied Behavior Analysis*, 18, pp.111–26.

Dagnan, D.J., Look, R., Ruddick, L. and Jones, J. (1995) 'Changes in the quality of life of people with learning disabilities who moved from hospital to live in community-based homes', *International Journal of Rehabilitation Research*, 18, pp.115–22.

Dagnan, D., Trower, P. and Smith, R. (1998) 'Care staff responses to people with learning disabilities and challenging behaviour: A cognitive emotional analysis', *British Journal of Clinical Psychology*, 37, pp.59–68.

Dryden, W. (1987) *Counselling Individuals: The Rational-Emotive Approach*, London: Taylor and Francis.

Ellis, A. (1979) *Reason and Emotion in Psychotherapy*, Secaucus, NJ: Citadel Press.

Ellis, A. and Harper, R.A. (1975) *A New Guide to Rational Living*, Hollywood, CA: Willshire.

Emerson, E. (1992) 'Self-injurious behaviour: An overview of recent trends in epidemiological and behavioural research', *Mental Handicap Research*, 5, pp.49–77.

Emerson, E., Barret, S., Cummings, R., Hughes, H., McCool, C., Toogood, A. and Mansell, J. (1987) *The Special Development Team: Developing Services for People with Severe Learning Disabilities and Challenging Behaviours*, Canterbury: Institute of Social and Applied Psychology, University of Kent at Canterbury.

Felce, D. (1996) 'Ways of measuring quality of outcome: An essential ingredient in quality assurance', *Tizard Learning Disability Review*, 1, pp.38–44.

Felce, D. and Perry, J. (1995) 'Quality of life: Its definition and measurement', *Research in Developmental Disabilities*, 16, pp.51–74.

Goldiamond, I. (1974) 'Toward a constructional approach to social problems'. *Behaviorism*, 2, pp.1–84.

Hall, S. and Oliver, C. (1992) 'Differential effects of severe self-injurious behaviour on the behaviour of others', *Behavioural Psychotherapy*, 20, pp.355–66.

Hastings, R. and Remington, B. (1994a) 'Staff behaviour and its implications for people with learning disabilities and challenging behaviours', *British Journal of Clinical Psychology*, 33, pp.4,423–38.

Hastings, R. and Remington, B. (1994b) 'Rules of engagement: Towards an analysis of staff responses to challenging behaviour', *Research in Developmental Disabilities*, 15, pp.279–98.

Hastings, R. and Remington, B. (1995) 'The emotional dimension of working with challenging behaviour', *Clinical Psychology Forum*, 79, pp.11–16.

Homer, R.H., Dunlap, G., Koegel, R.L., Carr, E.G., Sailor, W., Anderson, L., Albin, R.W. and O'Neill, R.E. (1990) 'Towards a technology of "non-aversive" behavioral support', *Journal of the Association for People with Severe Handicaps*, 15, pp.125–32.

Kushlick, A. (1975) 'Some ways of setting, monitoring and attaining objectives for services for disabled people', *British Journal of Mental Subnormality*, 21, pp.84–102.

Kushlick, A., Felce, D. and Lunt, B. (1983) 'Monitoring the effectiveness of services for severely handicapped people: Implications for managerial and professional accountability' in R. Jackson (ed.) *Wessex Studies in Special Education*, Vol. 3. Winchester: King Alfred's College, pp.51–92.

Kushlick, A., Trower, P. and Dagnan, D. (1997) 'Applying cognitive behavioural approaches to the carers of people with learning disabilities who display challenging behaviour' in B. Kroese, D. Dagnan and K. Loumides (eds) *Cognitive Therapy with People with Learning Disabilities*, London: Routledge.

LaVigna, G. and Donnelan, A. (1986) *Alternatives to Punishment: Solving Behaviour Problems with Non-aversive Strategies*, New York: Irvington.

Remington, B. (1991) 'Behaviour analysis and severe mental handicap: The dialogue between research and application' in B. Remington (ed.) *The Challenge of Severe Mental Handicap: A Behavioural Analytic Approach*, Chichester: John Wiley.

Skinner, B.F. (1972) 'The analysis and management of neurotic, psychotic and retarded behaviour' in B.F. Skinner, *Cumulative Record: A Selection of Papers*, New York: Appleton-Century-Crofts.

Wessler, R.A. and Wessler, R.L. (1980) *The Principles of Rational-emotive Therapy*, San Francisco, CA: Josey-Bass.

10 Learning theory, addict and counselling

Gillian Tober

Whether or not one subscribes to the view that addiction behaviours are maintained by underlying causes as opposed to the reinforcement potential of the behaviour itself, it is widely, though not universally, held that control of the behaviour in the first instance is imperative for the purposes of improving health and social functioning and for future work on underlying causes where there is a need for it. The application of learning theory and cognitive psychology to the understanding and treatment of addictive behaviours has enabled practitioners from a variety of backgrounds to make significant progress in their ability to assist clients in the control of the behaviour in the short term in order to establish stable control and abstinence in the long term and thus to develop competence in dealing with a notoriously challenging client group. Hope, blind faith, persuasion and coercion have been replaced, or at least added to, by systematic, disciplined and highly structured interventions based in an understanding of the behaviour and applied to the initiation and maintenance of its change.

The addictive behaviours referred to in this chapter are those where the behaviour involves the use of a substance, either alcohol or other drugs. Learning theories have been applied equally to the non-substance-based addictive behaviours, but these will not be described specifically here.

Developmental milestones in the understanding of addictive behaviours

The belief that alcoholism and drug addiction were diseases gained currency throughout the nineteenth century and into the twentieth century. A combination of observation, liberalism, philanthropy and political expedience had provided the background for the development of this view; the idea that alcoholics or drug addicts could not help themselves, that they needed professional help in the form of treatment rather than punishment, was progress which paralleled developments in other areas of human behaviour. Until early in the second half of the twentieth century, the various substance dependencies were seen to be characterised by inevitable loss of control over consumption of the substance, an invariable inability to abstain, and inevitable deterioration if consumption was not halted.

The application of psychological principles of learning shifted the understanding of addictive behaviour out of the realms of these quasi-scientific explanations (Kalb and Propper 1976). Laboratory experiments with severely dependent 'alcoholics' carried out in the 1960s refuted the inevitability of the key concepts of 'alcoholism', namely 'loss of control' and 'craving'. In a series of experiments carried out in the United States, Mello and Mendelson (1965) demonstrated that subjects diagnosed with alcoholism were able to control their intake of alcohol and did so in response to certain outcome expectations and valued rewards. This work established the principle that people with alcohol dependence were able to make choices in the way that 'normal' people were able to do, albeit that their choices may be constricted by particular learning histories with regard to alcohol.

Serious practical considerations stood in the way of the wholesale adoption of these findings and their implications. The battle to establish alcoholism as a disease had been a hard-fought one, the benefits of which were to shift some of the prejudices in public opinion and health service provision away from the idea that alcoholics were badly behaved drinkers, or sinners who deserved to be punished. The case for treatment was making headway. Furthermore, it was not only in the North American private healthcare system that physical illnesses were more readily seen to be the legitimate target of healthcare resources than were behavioural disorders; these latter are still struggling for recognition in the British healthcare system to this day. In addition, the disease concept, based on the assumption of a biological state and beyond the ability of the individual to vary, had conceptual simplicity to recommend it. Readily understandable to the public, it served to take away individual responsibility for the condition, leaving only the need for the individual to acquiesce in treatment.

One of the problems with disease approaches was that their explanatory framework was circular: if there was loss of control and craving, there was disease; and the disease was defined by the presence of loss of control and craving. Moreover, this approach did not account for the phenomena observed: people did and do report loss of control and craving, but they do not invariably do so. Furthermore, the axiom of inevitable deterioration was refuted in numerous follow-up studies, most notoriously that of Polich and his colleagues in a major four-year follow-up of 84 per cent of an original cohort of 922 male patients drawn from eight alcoholism treatment centres around the United States (Polich et al. 1980). These researchers found that some subjects with severe alcohol dependence at intake were drinking in a controlled manner at the first and second follow-up assessments.

Differences in opinion on the question of loss of control might better be seen as differences in definition. In some societies, very high levels of consumption may be tolerated where the accompanying behaviour is none the less required to conform to strict codes of conduct. Loss of control might be defined by the behavioural outcome, rather than by the quantity consumed. In other societies, the quantity consumed and the pattern of consumption may in themselves be definitive of loss of control. The important point is that were the condition a disease state, it would be likely to have similar manifestations across cultures and time.

This perceived loss of control and the experience of inability to abstain in the face of drinking or drug-taking cues, far from being mysterious properties of an equally mysterious condition, are readily explainable in behavioural learning terms, and what is more, in terms that are equally capable of explaining the whole spectrum of substance use behaviours, from normal to excessive consumption.

A full exploration of this approach is beyond the scope of this chapter, and has been amply covered elsewhere (Orford 1985; Heather and Robertson 1988). However, a number of elements of learning and cognition need to be considered in order to elucidate the theoretical basis of the interventions to be examined.

Initiating factors in drug and alcohol use may be availability and social pressure to experiment; they may be internal biological factors such as the need to relieve pain or anxiety, the need to feel confident in social situations, the need or desire to escape from the routine. Whether these initiating factors are internal, external, biological or psychological or a mixture of several of these, drug use will be accompanied by an expectation of the outcome, an expectation that the need or desire will be fulfilled. The consequence of use, or the outcome of the behaviour, will itself to some extent be determined by these expectations. In other words, the way the user experiences the effects of the substance will to some degree be a function of what it was they expected to happen. With some drugs, the variation in effect is greater than it is with others. What has been referred to as the 'pathoplasticity' of the drug (Edwards 1974) – the extent to which the effect that is experienced is shaped by the internal and external environment of the user – will influence the subjective experience of taking the drug. Furthermore, the subjective experience of the effect (as opposed to the physiological reaction which occurs) will be affected by the values and beliefs of the user regarding what is important. Thus, the first dose of tobacco or heroin might make the user vomit, but it might also enhance feelings of belonging to a particular user group, which might be more important. In this way, the outcomes of use, as well as the circumstances of use, will be determined by the individual's past learning, which shapes his or her expectations, which in turn shape the experience of use.

Some researchers (for example, Russell 1974) claim that social learning factors such as environmental pressures of peer group and availability are the most common in the initiation into substance use, especially cigarette smoking, and that the next stage of use is more strongly determined by the pharmacological properties of the drug, namely the reinforcement potential of the drug effect. As dependence develops, so the physiological consequences of use, notably the neuro-adapted state, will become the most influential in shaping the pattern of use.

The neuro-adapted state refers to the consequences of continual presence of the drug in body tissue, and to the way the nervous system accommodates itself to this presence. One of the consequences of neuro-adaptation is that the individual is likely to need more of the drug to get the original effect. Another consequence is that when the drug is abruptly withdrawn by stopping its use, the individual is likely to experience withdrawal symptoms. Neuro-adaptation, or tolerance, with its attendant withdrawal syndrome, usually opposite to the drug effect and therefore opposite to the effect the user is keen to pursue, is a condition which has considerable negative reinforcement potential. Because of its opposite nature to the effect being pursued, the user is motivated to avoid it. In heavy users of alcohol and other drugs to which tolerance develops, the state of neuro-adaptation is one which so powerfully drives the repeated use of the drug that it has come to be seen as the essence of dependence.

However, some addiction scientists have looked beyond the physiological state to the psychological state which develops alongside the prolonged and heavy use of drugs. The reason for doing this is that the neuro-adapted state is insufficient to explain why relapse into use after a period of abstinence is such a common phenomenon. It can occur months after the experience of withdrawal symptoms has abated.

It is perhaps more illuminating to think of the mechanisms of drug use, dependence and change as a question of motivation which may partially be driven by physiological events, by the pharmacological effects of the drugs, by the immediate or the broader social milieu, or indeed by a combination or a sequence of all these.

Motivation and decision-making

A vast psychological literature debates the nature of motivation, entire modules of undergraduate study are devoted to the term and yet in the addiction field its exclusive application to the sense of 'readiness to change' has been promoted and preserved up to recent times. In one of the more popular textbooks of the 1990s two psychologists have reproduced a definition of motivation as being associated with readiness to change in exactly the same way as was initially so closely aligned with the disease perspective on the subject (Miller and Rollnick 1991).

However, many practitioners and researchers have found that this narrow use of the term is at the core of the difficulties in moving forward with clients with addiction problems. Rather than assuming that motivation necessarily has anything to do with change, it is more helpful to return to the proper understanding of it as a predisposition to behave in a particular way, a sum of the factors militating against a specific behaviour. Thus, the same explanatory framework enables us to understand why people carry on, why they change, and why they give up.

Motivation, whether in the biological, the cognitive or the behavioural sense, is best understood as the sum of drives and incentives surrounding a specific behaviour: the 'pushes and pulls' (Logan 1993) that determine whether the behaviour will occur or not. The drive to use emanates from the availability of drugs or alcohol, the pharmacological and social effects of the drug and its use, and the value placed on these by the user. The incentives are the experience of past rewards turned into expectations of future rewards, or the belief that these will follow use. Disincentives will emanate from fear of possible negative consequences. The balance of motivation will be the sum of drives and incentives determined by their value, immediacy and perceived need for the user.

Motivational change and motivational therapy

One of the debates in the addiction field has been the question of whether motivation can be changed therapeutically, or whether it only changes in response to naturally occurring life events. Edwards (1984) introduced the idea of an 'addiction career', compared with the more medically based concept of a 'natural history', and Raistrick (1991) has presented evidence which reveals the variety of patterns of substance use careers that may or may not be affected by treatment. The suggestion that the course of a substance use career cannot be changed therapeutically has resulted in some heroic harm-reduction interventions that have not gained great popularity over recent years. Rather, it has been the case that interventions accurately matched to stage of change have been adopted with some enthusiasm. For example, Tober (1990) has described the way in which harm-reduction strategies can be consistent with an attempt to initiate change. There is also a growing body of evidence that points to the effectiveness of interventions which target client motivational stage of change to give up problem drinking (Hester and Miller 1989) and problem drug use (Saunders et al. 1995).

Motivational change occurs when the perceived costs of continuing in the behaviour outweigh the perceived benefits. The authors of the model of change, Prochaska and DiClemente, have shown that this shift in the balance of perceptions occurs as a result of life events, maturation or coercion (Prochaska and DiClemente 1984). At particular points, which may be unexpected events or gradually developing lifestyle changes, drug or alcohol use ceases to be functional in the way that it once was. It may suddenly threaten continued life or liberty – for example, in the event of an arrest or an injecting accident – or it may simply be inconsistent with new values or new activities – for example, in the event of a pregnancy.

The question of whether these motivational changes materialise into behavioural changes depends upon another set of perceptions, the question of whether the knowledge and skills to change are there, whether the person believes in their ability to change (self-efficacy: see Annis and Davis 1989), and whether the person believes that change will make a difference, will make things better (positive outcome expectancy: Rollnick et al. 1996).

The counselling style known as 'motivational interviewing' was developed in the early 1980s with the specific aim of targeting that motivation which had hitherto been deemed so resistant to therapeutic endeavours. The original author of this newly conceived approach demonstrated the way in which the traditional approaches to counselling problem drinkers themselves elicited resistance in many people (Miller 1983). This was proposed to be the case most particularly in the 'contemplation' stage of change (Prochaska and DiClemente 1984) when people are experiencing the highest levels of ambivalence about the behaviour. So common is this ambivalence that Orford has described it as part of the condition of addiction or 'excessive appetitive behaviour' (Orford 1985).

Miller showed, both theoretically (Miller 1983) and in a series of outcome evaluation studies (Miller et al. 1993), that when people experience ambivalence about their behaviour, then a confrontational approach, rather than getting people to accept and admit there is something wrong which they must change, elicits a defence of their position. The rationale for this is that if one feels under attack, one defends oneself by saying 'It is not as bad as that', 'There is nothing I can do about it anyway', 'I am no worse than anyone else' and so on. Defence is a normal and healthy response to feeling attacked. In the process of so defending a behaviour, one becomes more committed to the behaviour, one talks oneself into it: another common and normal phenomenon. Eliciting resistance by the practice of challenging the ambivalent client is counter-productive; it results in the very opposite of the counselling intention. The principles and practice of motivational interviewing are therefore constructed on the premise that eliciting resistance is to be avoided. Motivational interviewing was developed as a therapeutic style which was designed to avoid confrontation with ambivalent clients, to heighten rather than tear down their ambivalence about the behaviour and to assist them in reaching a definition of the problem and a definition of the solution that is their own.

The principles underpinning motivational interviewing as a therapeutic style

Based on the finding that people who are ambivalent about their substance use are unlikely to respond well to a confrontational approach, Miller and his colleagues combined the components of different, effective therapeutic styles into one that aimed to use ambivalence as a first step towards change, rather than something which signalled resistance to change (Miller et al. 1993).

The literature on effective therapeutic styles has long supported the therapist attributes identified by Carl Rogers, namely empathy, a non-judgemental approach and positive regard (Rogers 1957); these are incorporated into the approach. Principles of reinforcement are used to encourage the client to speak about their substance use, to identify its problems in their own terms and to express the desire to change. The method is directive in the sense that the therapist guides the session by selectively reinforcing the client's verbal behaviour. The counsellor has a rigorously followed agenda: enhancing the motivation to change problem drinking or drug use.

Rather than eliciting defensiveness by confronting the client with the severity of the problem and its consequences, the counsellor aims to elicit from the client statements that are associated with problem recognition, problem definition, an intention to change, and optimism about change. The counsellor actively avoids stating there is a problem or offering a definition of it unless directly requested by the client. It is an entirely common phenomenon that people do not act on problems unless they have themselves identified the problem and decided on the preferred course of action. The art of motivational interviewing is one where the counsellor can get the client to describe their concerns and their own reasons for behaviour change.

Components of the motivational interviewing style

Motivational interviewing is a complex style of counselling, not least because elements of it are in complete contrast to those which have been associated with the commonly taught 'non-directive' style of counselling. In addition, the counsellor has to remember a lot of dos and don'ts simultaneously. For this reason, it is advisable to practise the separate components, the micro-skills and the tactics of motivational interviewing (Rollnick et al. 1992) as repeatedly as is possible. It is not a style that comes easily or naturally. It requires considerable concentration and discipline on the part of the counsellor practising it, so, rather like learning to drive a car, it is a good idea to relegate as much of it to the realms of semi-automatic or well-learned behaviour as possible.

Taking the driving analogy further, the tactics of motivational interviewing have been likened to knowledge of the road map which keeps the driver on course, and the micro-skills to the driving of the car. Changing gear, applying the brakes and signalling become semi-automatic responses to conditioned stimuli like traffic lights, stop signs and so on. In order to perform a complex behaviour efficiently, some of its elements need to become automatic responses.

The following steps constitute the tactics in motivational interviewing:

1 *Bringing up the subject*. By using carefully selected opening questions, the counsellor gets the client to mention the drinking or the drug use. Where the counsellor is the first to mention this, a difficulty can arise: the client has not given permission to talk about the subject unless they themselves have brought it up. This step is designed to elicit a description of the behaviour that is sufficient to alert the counsellor to the areas that are likely to be perceived by the client as problematic. Thus, if heavy drinking is taking place regularly in the evening, then the client is likely to feel uncomfortable in the morning in an aversive way. If there are chores to perform, like getting children ready for school or driving first thing, it is likely that the feelings of discomfort (note: *not* the drinking itself at this stage) will be perceived as a problem.

2 *Description of the good things about the drinking or drug use*. Once a sufficient description has been gained, the counsellor asks the client to report what it is they like about the drinking or drug-taking: 'Tell me the good things about …' The aim of this strategy is to get the client talking about the subject in a way that offers the counsellor the opportunity to reinforce certain statements and to develop rapport. The question itself suggests that the counsellor thinks the client is a rational human being

who does things for a reason, albeit that those things may not always be 'good for them'.

3 *Description of the less good things*. Once this rapport has been established, the counsellor can move on to the request to 'Tell me the less good things' or 'Tell me what you least like about your drinking [or drug use].' The counsellor can then build on the picture that was starting to take shape in the earlier discussion and can use points the client previously made as prompts. The counsellor can use the practice of selective reinforcement to encourage the client to explore the less good things, and then move on to the question of which particular less good things the client is most concerned about.

4 *Description of client concerns about the behaviour*. The expression of these concerns forms the basis of the 'self-motivational statements' alluded to in the previous section. While people can often give a long list of the negative consequences of something they do, this list is not necessarily consistent with motivational factors for change. A belief that negative consequences will happen to *me* as a result of *my* drinking or drug use have been shown to predict change in the addictive behaviours (McMahon and Jones 1993), the emphasis being on one's own experience and expectations, rather than what other people say about the problems of use.

5 *Eliciting statement of an intention to change*. This is a particularly important but difficult step. Many people will express an intention to change because they know how much the counsellor wants to hear it. Judging the quality of the statement can be assisted by applying the following criteria: Has the client demonstrated sufficient knowledge of what to do and do they have the skills to do it? Does the client have a belief in his or her ability to do it? Does the client believe that the problems caused by the drinking or drug use will stop or be made better if they change the behaviour? Does the client have a level of self-esteem that can be associated with a likelihood of behaviour change? (Prochaska and DiClemente 1986).

These criteria could be used by the counsellor in the form of a checklist to assess the readiness of the client to proceed to the next step: making behavioural plans to change the substance use. This is not the subject of motivational interviewing and can be dealt with in a more didactic style of counselling. Skills training and cue exposure will be indicated where the client requires further assistance to change the behaviour (Monti et al. 1989; Drummond et al. 1995).

This sequence of steps can be varied to some extent by the progress being made in the specific situation. Some practitioners will enquire about concerns in the course of eliciting the good things and the less good things, rather than doing this later. What then are the micro-skills which enable the counsellor to follow these steps?

1 *Asking open-ended questions*: these are questions which do not predetermine the reply and encourage the client to expand on a subject.
2 *Reflective listening* is active listening when the counsellor reflects back either simply, with changed emphasis or with exaggerated emphasis in order to reinforce what the client is saying, change direction or avoid arguments resulting from client resistance. Reinforcement is used selectively by the withholding of a response by the counsellor when the client makes statements associated with, for example, denial of problems, perceived helplessness or hopelessness.
3 *Summarising* is used to take stock, clarify what has been said, acknowledge things that have not been reinforced or to change direction.
4 *Affirmation* is the skill of acknowledging the client's difficult situation, the willingness to disclose those difficulties, efforts to change or even to consider change.

Case study illustrations

The following case studies are illustrative of opportunities to use motivational interviewing practice. The sessions are not reported in detail, but the reader is given a flavour of the direction the intervention takes.

Marie

Marie is 38, and she has five children. She came to England from Ireland in her late teens to work as a chambermaid. She met and married Fred in her early twenties, and gave up working to look after the five children they then had. Fred was a labourer who would drink heavily at the weekends, but according to Marie's account, always provided for her and the children and ensured that the rent and the bills were paid.

One day, he left her and disappeared with a woman who lived nearby. Marie felt devastated, and that she could not cope with the family without Fred. A neighbour offered consolation with large supplies of cider, which made Marie feel temporary relief. She began to drink on a daily basis, and gradually to commence drinking earlier in the day. Eventually, she was drinking from the morning, and the children were not getting to school, had no clean clothes and were not being fed regularly.

Marie approached the social services department for help. After a short period, the children were, one after the other, removed from her care. Marie continued to believe that she could not cope with the children by herself without considerable support. She had no family in the town where she lived. She felt that she would be able to cope with some sort of regular support from the local services. Primarily, she had come to believe that she could not cope with her life without the use of alcohol.

Counselling sessions focused upon an attempt to build up her belief in her ability to cope with her life, and feedback on the way in which alcohol impaired her ability to do so. However, her experience seemed to tell her the opposite. She continued to drink in the same daily, dependent manner. Eventually, she met a man with whom she became pregnant. The social worker who was involved with her five children told her she would not be able to keep her baby if she continued to drink.

She conveyed this to the alcohol counselling agency which she attended. Tober (1991) has described the way in which coercive gestures, such as the threat of a possible but unacceptable course of action, can be used in motivational interviewing where the client perceives that she has the ability to vary the outcome by her own actions. Marie was offered sessions of motivational therapy based on an understanding of her present condition, namely that her drinking had been reinforced to date by the ability of the alcohol to make her feel relaxed about what had happened and to enhance her belief that she could not cope with her five children. Furthermore, she had developed a dependence on alcohol that had resulted in daily drinking from the morning. The alcohol had taken on a life of its own which Marie felt unable to control.

The first task of the counsellor was to get Marie to describe the benefits of her drinking as she saw them. Very quickly, it became apparent that the description of each of these benefits was now qualified by a more important disadvantage to her drinking. Marie was herself arguing that the costs of her drinking outweighed the benefits. She thought she might be harming the foetus; the counsellor gave her objective, impersonal information (in the sense that it was not offered as 'If you ... then ...') on damage to the foetus at different levels of consumption of alcohol.

It was apparent that the balance of Marie's motivation regarding her drinking was shifting; the perceived costs of continuing were coming to outweigh the perceived benefits. When asked what concerned Marie most about her drinking, she responded that the potential harm to the foetus and the likelihood of the baby being removed from her at birth were her greatest concerns. She believed that if she were given the chance now, she could start again. This is something of an expression of the belief that her life could be better if she stopped drinking, that stopping drinking would make a difference. When asked what she thought would assist her in stopping, she said that if she could be taken into hospital for detoxification and be followed up with a prescription of disulfiram (a drug which reacts with alcohol to make the user feel very ill) which could be supervised on a daily basis, then she felt that she would be able to achieve and maintain abstinence.

Her motivation to abstain appeared high, in that she wanted to do it and to do it right away, she believed she could do it and that things would be better if she did. The usefulness of disulfiram is that it changes the expectations of the consequences of drinking. When faced with a high-risk situation – one in which overwhelming cues for drinking are presented – the fact of having taken the disulfiram enables the person to stick to their resolve in the short term.

What then was the role of the counsellor? Marie's growing ambivalence about her drinking was approached with careful exploration as to why she, Marie, thought it was a problem. She was given information on damage to the foetus when she sought it: that is, when she wanted to know it. The help that she requested was made available to her, and this enhanced her self-efficacy – her belief in her ability to do it. She had reached the point of making up her mind. It is possible that she would have got there by herself, but the specific motivational intervention which she received increased the likelihood.

Neil

Neil is 25. He has been using cannabis and amphetamine for the past five or six years. Recently, he has started to use Ecstasy as well and has become a dealer in order to support his use. He consumes alcohol daily, and the amount varies between three pints of lager every week day to fifteen to twenty pints at the weekend, or alternatively a bottle of vodka over a 24 hour period.

His drinking is sustained by his belief that he is more confident to conduct his dealing business if he is drinking, though not too much. His amphetamine and Ecstasy use are sustained by his belief that the use of these drugs is essential in order to have a nice time. When told that people enjoy themselves without the use of drugs, he says that this option is no longer available to him, and would not be in the future. Having tried drugs, he says, going to parties is never the same without them.

One day, following a weekend of drinking and drug use, he did not feel well and decided to stay in bed, abstaining from drugs and alcohol. The next morning he had a fit and his girlfriend arranged for him to go to the casualty department. After being detoxified from alcohol, he was sent home with an appointment to attend the addiction counselling agency.

With the benefit of the drug and alcohol history which had been taken in casualty (given in a very candid fashion by Neil), the motivational interview proceeded in the following way:

Counsellor: Can you tell me what made you come to this appointment?
Neil: Well, I was worried about what happened when I ended up in casualty.
Counsellor: What was it that particularly worried you?
Neil: I don't understand what happened. I had not done anything unusual, anything I had not done before.

He was ignoring the fact that he had been abstinent from alcohol for a day, which was unusual, and referring only to the usual drug and alcohol use which had occurred over the weekend.

The counsellor's agenda was to make a connection between the drinking, the day's abstinence and the fit, then to explore possible concerns about the drug and alcohol use. Thus the counsellor asked for a detailed account of Neil's drinking and drug use over the past two weeks. The drinking history was the most difficult to obtain: drugs are taken at intervals, whereas heavy drinking tends to be continuous; eventually, the only way to get any idea is to calculate on the basis of money spent and types of beverages purchased.

Having obtained the account of recent drug and alcohol use, the counsellor was alerted to possible areas of concern. She noted for example, that the Ecstasy use had escalated from an original dose of one or two tablets to twelve tablets per weekend. She asked Neil to tell her what he liked about his drug and alcohol use:

Neil: I enjoy it; it makes me feel good; it makes me have a nice time, it makes me feel good about myself. If I don't take drugs, I have nothing to say.
Counsellor: Is there anything that you don't like about it?
Neil: Some people comment on how much I take. That used to make me feel big. Now I wonder.
Counsellor: What do you wonder about?
Neil: I saw this programme recently on Ecstasy. They were saying that they didn't know what happened to people who used a lot of Ecstasy in the end. And anyway, I think my days are numbered. A guy I know was killed last week, and then there was this major raid in a club. You know, wherever I go people ask me for drugs. Everyone knows I'm a dealer. That means that the police must know it too. I reckon that if I don't get out, I'll either die – people are getting very territorial – or else I'll end up doing a long time in prison.

Neil has not yet been caught for any offence. It is not something he sees as an occupational hazard; he does not see it in any way as an acceptable price to pay. The idea of going to prison is quite unacceptable to him.

As Neil recounted his experiences under the influence of drugs and after taking them, the counsellor periodically interjected with information from research evidence to support his account. She only supplied this information to confirm a point that Neil had made with reference to himself. Having reinforced the negative account that Neil had given about the consequences of his use, she moved on to develop discrepancy between where Neil sees himself at the moment and where he would like to be:

Counsellor: Tell me how you see yourself in the future. Tell me where you would like to be five years from now.
Neil: Alive and not in prison.

There has been some debate in the addiction field about whether negative outcome expectancies of continued use or positive outcome expectancies of quitting are more influential in motivational change (McMahon and Jones 1996). For practical purposes, it is important to ensure that the client is pessimistic about the outcome of continued use and optimistic about the outcome of stopping or controlling the addictive behaviour.

The counsellor took the view that negative thoughts about continued use would be the basis of Neil's ambivalence about his drug and alcohol use, and she decided to focus on these. In order to move him closer to the possibility of change, he would have to believe that his life will be better if he does change. He believed that it might save him from going to prison, indeed save his very life, but are these things immediate and concrete enough? He wanted to change, but was not at all sure about the other factors, whether he was able to do it, and whether he might simply have to give up his social life, which he valued very highly, if he did.

The counsellor proposed, just for one week, that he attempt to abstain from just one drug. Neil returned the following week, having decided to go further than suggested, and had not taken any drug, only alcohol. He had met someone who thinks that there is something wrong with people who need to take drugs to have a good time, and he was surprised to find that he liked her. Previously, he had said that he could not get on with his girlfriend because she did not approve of his drug use. This experience shifted his belief that his drug use was the basis of his attraction and of his social life. He started to think about things he might enjoy doing where he would not be expected to take drugs and nor would the drug-taking cues be present. In this way, his expectation of the outcome of not using drugs was enhanced. His belief in his ability to abstain from drug and alcohol use looked more likely to result from the avoidance of drug-taking and drinking situations.

Neil might now be ready to embark upon some lifestyle changes that would be inconsistent with his continued use of drugs. To this end, the counsellor switched to setting behavioural goals for avoiding drug-taking situations. At each feedback point, the counsellor would examine Neil's motivation for abstinence by eliciting statements about the positive outcomes of change, and the potential negative outcomes of reverting to the previous behaviour. Kent (1991) has described the importance of addressing continuing motivation to change through all stages of the change cycle.

Applications of motivational interviewing

Motivational interviewing has been developed as a counselling style which is applied to specific interventions. One of these was the Drinker's Check-up (Miller et al. 1988), an intervention consisting of a battery of psychological tests and monitoring procedures followed by a counselling session designed to elicit client concerns about the objective findings of the tests.

More recently, an intervention named Motivational Enhancement Therapy (MET) was designed as part of Project MATCH in the United States (Project MATCH Research Group 1993). The components of motivational interviewing included in this intervention were a battery of tests for which the client received factual feedback, the elicitation of client concerns about the drinking, the expression of a desire to change, and optimism about the possibility of change. The therapist style used was an empathic, non-confrontational one, in which resistance was seen as a product of the interaction between the counsellor and the client, and treated as a sign to change course. Preliminary findings of the study suggest that this intervention, when offered on a one-to-one basis in four sessions over a period of 12 weeks, performed as well as 12 sessions of a Cognitive Behavioural Coping Skills intervention or a Twelve Step facilitation intervention when drinking outcomes were compared at twelve-month follow-up (Project MATCH Research Group 1997).

Following the conclusion of the trial, and with mountains of data yet to analyse, Miller has posed the question: what is it about motivational interviewing that works?

> Foremost in my own mind is the fundamental question of why this approach works at all. The individuals with whom it has been tested have often suffered a substantial volume of adverse consequences from their addictive behavior and usually have been well aware of that fact. Persistence of response despite

> clear negative consequences is, in fact, one of the classic defining aspects of addictive behavior. Often a variety of efforts from the individual and others have failed to evoke lasting change. How could it possibly be, then, that a session or two of asking clients to verbalise their own suffering and reasons for change would unstick a behavior pattern that has been so persistent? (Miller 1996, p.840).

He does not offer an answer to the question, but rather states that the now consistent finding that brief interventions can be as effective as extended ones (Heather 1996) guides us to look at the processes of changing motivation rather than to the processes of unlearning old and learning new behaviours. Skills training and counter-conditioning, in themselves found to be effective in the treatment of addictive behaviours, may simply not be necessary if we can accurately target the conditions for motivational change. The suggestion may be that 'making up one's mind' to do it may, in itself, be enough.

References

Annis, H.M. and Davis, C.S. (1989) 'Relapse prevention' in R.K. Hester and W.R. Miller (eds) *Handbook of Alcoholism Treatment Approaches*, New York: Pergamon Press.

Drummond, D.C., Tiffany, S.T., Glautier, S. and Remington, B. (1995) *Addictive Behaviour Cue Exposure Theory and Practice*, Chichester: John Wiley.

Edwards, G. (1974) 'Drugs, drug dependence and the concept of plasticity', *Quarterly Journal of Studies on Alcohol*, 35, pp.176–95.

Edwards, G. (1984) 'Drinking in longitudinal perspective: Career and natural history', *British Journal of Addiction*, 79, pp.175–83.

Heather, N. (1996) 'The public health and brief interventions for excessive alcohol consumption: The British experience', *Addictive Behaviors*, 21, pp.857–68.

Heather, N. and Robertson, I. (1988) *Problem Drinking* (2nd edn) Oxford: Oxford University Press.

Hester, R. and Miller, W. (1989) *Handbook of Alcoholism Treatment Approaches*, New York: Plenum.

Kalb, M. and Propper, M.S. (1976) 'The future of alcohology: Craft or science?', *American Journal of Psychiatry*, 133, pp.641–5.

Kent, R. (1991) 'Motivational interviewing and the maintenance of change' in W.R. Miller and S. Rollnick (eds) *Motivational Interviewing: Preparing People to Change*, New York: Guilford Press.

Logan, F. (1993) 'Animal learning and motivation and addictive drugs', *Psychological Reports*, 73, pp.291–306.

McMahon, J. and Jones, B. (1993) 'Negative expectancy and motivation', *Addiction Research*, 1, pp.145–55.

McMahon, J. and Jones, B. (1996) 'Post-treatment abstinence survivorship and motivation for recovery: The predictive validity of the Readiness to Change (RCQ) and Negative Alcohol Expectancy (NAEQ) Questionnaires', *Addiction Research*, 4, pp.161–76.

Mello, N.K. and Mendelson, J.H. (1965) 'Operant analysis of drinking habits of chronic alcoholics', *Nature*, 206, pp.43–6.

Miller, W.R. (1983) 'Motivational interviewing with problem drinkers', *Behavioural Psychotherapy*, 11, 147–72.

Miller, W.R. (1992) 'Client/treatment matching in addictive behaviours', *The Behaviour Therapist*, 15, pp.7–8.

Miller, W.R. (1996) 'Motivational interviewing: Research, practice and puzzles', *Addictive Behaviors*, 21, pp.835–42.

Miller, W.R. and Rollnick, S. (1991) *Motivational Interviewing: Preparing People for Change*, New York: Guilford Press.

Miller, W.R., Benefield, R.G. and Tonigan, J.S. (1993) 'Enhancing motivation for change in problem drinking: A controlled comparison of two therapist styles', *Journal of Consulting and Clinical Psychology*, 61, pp.455–61.

Miller, W.R., Sovereign, R.G. and Krege, B. (1988) 'Motivational Interviewing with problem drinkers, Part II: The Drinker's Check-up as a preventive intervention', *Behavioural Psychotherapy*, 16, pp.251–68.

Monti, P.M., Abrams, D.B., Kadden, R.M. and Cooney, N.L. (1989) *Treating Alcohol Dependence: A Coping Skills Training Guide*, New York: Guilford Press.

Orford, J. (1985) *Excessive Appetites: A Psychological View of Addictions*, Chichester: John Wiley.

Polich, J.M., Armor D.J. and Braiker, H.B. (1980) *The Course of Alcoholism Four Years After Treatment*, New York: John Wiley.

Prochaska, J.O. and DiClemente, C.C. (1984) *The Transtheoretical Approach: Crossing Traditional Boundaries of Therapy*, Homewood, IL: Dow Jones-Irwin.

Prochaska, J.O. and DiClemente, C.C. (1986) 'Towards a comprehensive model of change' in W.R. Miller and N. Heather (eds) *Treating Addictive Behaviours: Processes of Change*, New York: Plenum Press.

Project MATCH Research Group (1993) 'Project MATCH: Rationale and methods for a multi-site clinical trial matching patients to alcoholism treatment', *Alcoholism: Clinical and Experimental Research*, 17, pp.1,130–45.

Project MATCH Research Group (1997) 'Matching alcoholism treatments to client heterogeneity: Project MATCH posttreatment drinking outcomes', *Journal of Studies on Alcohol*, 58, pp.7–29.

Raistrick, D. (1991) 'Career and natural history' in I.B. Glass (ed.) *The International Handbook of Addiction Behaviour*, London: Routledge.

Rogers, C. (1957) 'The necessary and sufficient conditions of therapeutic personality change', *Journal of Consulting Psychology*, 21, pp.95–113.

Rollnick, S., Heather, N. and Bell, A. (1992) 'Negotiating behaviour change in medical settings: The development of brief motivational interviewing', *Journal of Mental Health*, 1, pp.25–37.

Rollnick, S., Morgan, M. and Heather, N. (1996) 'Development of a brief scale to measure outcome expectations of reduced consumption among excessive drinkers', *Addictive Behaviours*, 21, pp.377–87.

Russell, M.A.H. (1974) 'The classification of smoking by factorial structure of motives', *Journal of the Royal Statistical Society*, 137, pp.313–33.

Saunders, B., Wilkinson, C. and Phillips, M. (1995) 'The impact of a brief motivational intervention with opiate users attending a methadone programme', *Addiction*, 90, pp.415–24.

Tober, G. (1990) 'Helping the precontemplator' in R. Davidson, S. Rollnick and I. MacEwan (eds) *Counselling Problem Drinkers*, London: Routledge.
Tober, G. (1991) 'Motivational interviewing with young people' in W.R. Miller and S. Rollnick (eds) *Motivational Interviewing: Preparing People for Change*, New York: Guilford Press.

11 Behavioural work, crisis intervention and the mental health call-out

J.P.J. Oliver and Barbara L. Hudson

Crisis intervention: An overview

In the United Kingdom, the Mental Health Act 1983 enjoins social workers to make a formal assessment before proceeding with an application for admission to hospital. It is anticipated that in 'taking account all of the circumstances of the case' (Mental Health Act 1983, Section 13) the social worker will select the course of action which is the least restrictive to the client's civil liberties while meeting the need for care and medical treatment. The Act seeks to promote community care where possible. This consideration of community care as a suitable alternative to hospital admission depends not only on the availability of resources such as residential or day care, but also on the personal skills of the worker. Where the designated patient is not suffering severe mental illness or psychosis requiring medical treatment in a secure environment, but is, for example, reacting to severe and acute relationship problems or loss or disaster, or has attempted to harm him/herself, often it is the social worker's ability to intervene effectively utilising casework, groupwork or family therapy skills which is a deciding factor in the prevention of admission. These skills are the foundation upon which community care ultimately rests.

The most frequently recommended approach is 'crisis intervention'. In a study of Mental Welfare Officers (the predecessors of Approved Social Workers), Clarke (1971) observed that when called out to make an assessment under the Mental Health Act 1983, the workers either arranged admission to hospital or did nothing: they failed to take advantage of the opportunity to undertake crisis intervention.

Subsequently, the British Association of Social Workers (BASW 1982) and Olsen (1984), among others, advocated the establishment of interdisciplinary crisis intervention teams. Again, Fisher et al. (1984) commented on the failure to use these methods, and reported social workers' calls for crisis intervention teams. These recurrent exhortations are based on a belief in the theory of crisis intervention (Caplan 1964), and for their empirical justification appear to rely almost exclusively on the evaluative research by Langsley and his colleagues in the USA (Langsley 1972; Langsley and Kaplan 1968; Langsley et al. 1968).

There has been little empirical research during all the years that crisis intervention ideas have been current. This may be due in part to difficulty in defining 'a crisis' to anybody's satisfaction. Most crisis theorists would admit that they have not yet formulated a holistic, systematic theory with validated propositions. The theory derives from the unsystematic observations of the psychoanalyst Lindemann on the reactions of survivors of the Coconut Grove Fire (Lindemann 1944) and the theoretical work of Caplan (1964). Caplan (1964) conceptualised the crisis reaction as an upset in a steady state (otherwise described as 'equilibrium' or 'homoeostasis'). 'Steady state' appears to mean, simply, coping successfully with one's problems. When overwhelmed by new problems (whether coming from outside or from within), tension rises, a psychological struggle ensues, and if renewed efforts fail, the individual becomes 'disturbed'. The crisis is said to have a 'peak'. After this passes, tension levels fall, but one may not successfully resolve the problems, and may remain depressed or go on behaving 'maladaptively'. The crisis period is said to last about six weeks. The theory emphasises the coping capacities of the 'ego', and de-emphasises the influence of unconscious conflicts and early life experiences.

There are several objections to this theoretical formulation. First, it has little basis other than the uncontrolled observations of its proponents; and as with many of the propositions current in this field, what you see is what you expect to see. Attempts to study its propositions systematically suggest that there is little evidence for any of the following: that people respond to crisis in predictable, specific ways; that people in crisis go through a set of specific stages; that crises are limited to a matter of weeks (see Silver and Wortman 1980 for a detailed review of the evidence).

Second, as Bancroft (1979) suggests, the theory is unnecessarily convoluted for its relatively circumscribed content. Bancroft emphasises the coping aspect: coping is behaviour used to deal with a difficulty, which can take the form of problem-solving, regression, denial or inertia. A person faced with a difficulty will experience a rise in arousal, and will make efforts to solve the problem; if these efforts fail, he or she will experience increased arousal and distress and disorganisation; he or she will then try a variety of alternative ways of coping; if these also fail, he or she will become exhausted, and may begin to behave abnormally.

A third objection is that traditional crisis theory does not lead to any very specific guidelines for intervention – a theme we shall return to in the later part of this chapter.

While these objections do not constitute a neat learning theory analysis of 'crisis', learning theory does appear to offer an alternative, albeit incomplete framework. Crises can be viewed as behaviours elicited by that combination of events called the 'crisis situation' (antecedent stimuli). The consequences following on these crisis behaviours – consequences that act as positive or negative reinforcers – are also significant. Often, the crisis situation involves loss of positive reinforcement or of familiar cues for behaviour, and this results in disintegration of habitual patterns of behaviour. Because previous patterns are no longer effective, new ones may be readily learned at this time (emotional accessibility). Alternatively, using a learning framework with greater cognitive content, the experience of uncontrollable trauma leads to a mental set best described by Seligman's (1975) term 'helplessness': a belief that one's responses cannot affect one's environment. The procedures derived from these theoretical formulations will be discussed later.

Moving now from crisis theory to crisis intervention, what empirical basis is there for claims that crisis intervention is a highly effective way of helping people? Rigorous evaluations of the crisis intervention approach are not easy to come by, although all writers in this field claim favourable results. We have located only three control group studies evaluating crisis intervention in the mental health field (literature searches back to 1974 using the terms 'crisis intervention' and 'evaluation'/'outcome'/'effectiveness' uncovered only three papers, only one of which could be considered a controlled outcome study: Greenfield et al. 1995).

Decker and Stubblebine (1972) compared outcomes of a traditional treatment and a crisis intervention programme for young psychiatric patients over two years. The crisis intervention programme involved an interdisciplinary team acting rapidly to intervene in crisis situations, avoiding hospitalisation as far as possible. The experimental group were less likely to be admitted; if admitted, they were in hospital for less time; they did not become more dependent on Social Security. Langsley et al. (1968) reported very favourable initial results with their crisis family therapy cases, who did at least as well on social functioning measures and were significantly less likely to be hospitalised than the control cases who received ordinary hospital treatments – individual and group therapy, drugs, therapeutic community. However, at their 18-month follow-up, they reported little effect on long-term patterns of individual and family behaviour, and suggested that

50 per cent of those who had received crisis intervention treatments in fact needed longer-term treatment, and that post-crisis work was extremely important. (This last report reminds us that one needs to treat early research reports with extreme caution.) The other, perhaps crucial, problem with this research is that it may be interpreted as a test of family therapy, rather than of crisis intervention.

Greenfield et al. (1995) report on the impact of a similar package on hospitalisation rates and suicide rates among adolescents before and after the introduction of a crisis intervention service. Over their three-year follow-up period, they found a reduction in hospitalisation rates and no increase in suicide rates among the crisis intervention clients.

With these studies, we are left with a major question: 'If there was a difference, what made the difference?' In each study, the clients received a *package* of treatment procedures, as did the 'control' clients. As the contents of the packages were not clearly reported in these papers, we have turned to the writing of Rapoport (1970), who provides one of the nearest approximations to an explicit therapeutic approach, to try to tease out the key elements of 'good practice' in crisis intervention.

The most obvious element is timing. It is considered crucial to reach clients at the height of their distress, before the possibly maladaptive crisis resolution has begun; this generally means at the point of application for help at an emergency centre, or within a day or so of referral.

But there are several other elements. One is the time-limited nature of the help given (a series of one to eight interviews is suggested by Rapoport). Then there is the type of assessment – very much briefer than traditional psychodynamic and psychiatric assessments, with its concentration on the current difficulties and on the 'ego strengths', rather than on negative factors and distant history. Problems are broken down into limited tasks and goals. The first interview concentrates on this brief assessment, on reducing disabling anxiety, on helping the client gain a cognitive grasp of the situation, on giving a feeling of trust in the helping agency, and a feeling of being understood and cared for. The worker is more active than in more traditional casework or psychotherapy. A common first step is to intervene swiftly in the environment of the client, for example providing homemaker services or financial help, or seeking to involve family members in the effort to change. Rapoport stresses the importance of a contract in which the clients take on tasks. Treatment very often involves family members, and clients remain in the community if at all possible. As we hope to show, these elements are all present in social learning approaches.

Despite rapid expansion in the use of behavioural techniques in psychiatric treatment, there are still large gaps in our knowledge. The psychiatric emergency is one area that has received scant attention. We know little

about the application of behavioural approaches under acute conditions, and there are few properly articulated frameworks for beginning to establish a basis for practice.

Behavioural approaches in crisis work: Some indications

On the more practical side, behaviourally oriented practitioners have various objections to working in crisis or emergency situations, in particular lack of time to collect baseline data against which to measure progress. However, they will admit that they themselves sometimes forgo careful baseline measurement in favour of speedy intervention. Of course, many behavioural workers are clinical psychologist colleagues, who are usually spared the involvement in urgent situations that social workers and psychiatrists have to address.

To date, neither general texts on crisis intervention nor texts on mental health social work have addressed the issue. Probably the closest are those by Aguilera and Messick (1982) and Bancroft (1979). Aguilera and Messick proposed a 'problem-solving' approach. They provide a broad-based model for assessment, planning and intervention, but rely on conventional/traditional crisis notions of psychological disturbance as a basic theory to inform it. Bancroft (1979) writes in an eclectic spirit, but with a 'behavioural bias' (p.85). In addition, Rapoport (1970) mentions the possible role of modelling, operant conditioning and behaviour rehearsal in crisis work. Also, Auerbach and Kilmann (1977), in their systematic review of crisis intervention studies conducted in psychiatric settings, conclude that the term 'crisis intervention' simply refers to a variegated group of ideas which are loosely organised and cover a wide range of procedures. If this is true, then there would probably be no reason why behavioural techniques could not be applied. Indeed, it may well be that they already are, and that the active ingredients in conventional crisis intervention are in fact behavioural techniques not identified as such.

What few accounts there are of the employment of behavioural techniques in 'crisis situations' generally take the form of single-case reports or small-scale uncontrolled projects.

Belson (1971) has reported the use of behavioural techniques in the case of a man who developed a severe speech impediment and free-floating anxiety following a road accident. Instead of hospitalisation, the man received five sessions of behaviour therapy over a ten-day period. Marked improvement was shown on a variety of pre/post measures over that

period, and the man was able to return to work, improvements being maintained at six-month follow-up. Belson observes that in crisis work, the emphasis is on rapid symptom relief and enabling the client to modify his or her behaviour sufficiently to handle situational stress. However, this single-case design study lacks external validity.

In an uncontrolled group outcome study, Kinney et al. (1977) reported on the US crisis intervention project Homebuilders, which employs behavioural techniques with the aim of preventing family breakdown during crisis and removal of family members to hospital or into care. The workers attempt to resolve the immediate crisis, and also to teach new skills to prevent future crises. The agency works only with cases for whom there is apparently no viable alternative to admission to a residential facility.

During the study period, 125 out of 134 family members identified as at risk of removal (90 per cent) avoided placement, and at follow-up 117 (93.6 per cent) of these were still at home. Although the presentation of the data makes it difficult to extract the purely psychiatric emergencies, it appears that while approximately 22 of the total cases were destined for psychiatric admission, only 2 of these (9 per cent) were admitted, both acutely psychotic. Indeed, client problems, including such features as high suicide risk, drug abuse, alcohol abuse, emotional exhaustion and psychoses, accounted for a total of 72 cases, which supports the view that there was a very high proportion of psychiatric symptomatology in the entire sample. This also suggests that the outcome for psychiatric cases was no worse than for non-psychiatric cases in this service. The Homebuilders team utilise a number of behavioural techniques, in particular a problem-definition phase which includes making problem lists and work on a behavioural definition of problems.

The only controlled trial we have found is that by Liberman and Eckman (1981). They evaluated outcome for people who had attempted suicide, who were treated with intensive behaviour therapy during a ten-day admission compared with a group who received short-term psychodynamic therapy in the same setting. While both groups improved, the behaviourally treated group improved significantly more on all their measures (anxiety, depression and assertiveness). Unfortunately, because of small numbers and lack of an untreated control group, it was not possible to evaluate the effects of the treatments on subsequent suicide attempts.

Perhaps the clearest theoretical formulation to date of the rationale for using behavioural techniques during crises is that of Eisler and Hersen (1973; Eisler 1976), who based their observations on three successful cases of behavioural family therapy. Again, although the data are insufficient to demonstrate conclusively the effectiveness of the techniques, some relevant points are raised. These authors suggest that the emphasis on treating people in their natural environment and on helping people deal with what they themselves see as real-life stresses is equally present in the work of behavioural practitioners. They suggest that of the many potentially useful techniques available to the behavioural worker, special attention should be given to modelling and role-play, instruction-giving, behavioural rehearsal, feedback and the use of contingency contracts to structure exchanges and ensure reciprocal reinforcement among family members. They found it useful to concentrate their efforts on restructuring dysfunctional family relationships and developing new, adaptive problem-solving behaviours by pursuing the following objectives: to generate co-operative behaviour through a programme of mutual reinforcement, to foster the expression of both negative and positive feelings in respect of precipitating problems and to assist the family in applying their newly developed coping skills to other conflict-ridden situations (generalisation, or positive transfer).

Overall, they propose a brief process of evaluation, training and generalisation which, while simple, includes several of the central components of behaviour therapy. However, their framework is not sufficiently comprehensive to offer guidelines for the wide range of problem situations that may confront the worker.

Bancroft (1979) proposes a more cognitive-behavioural model, with a strong emphasis on problem-solving, which is already present in the traditional models, but which, in Bancroft's formulation, is more systematic and more closely linked to the other behavioural techniques. He suggests a three-stage general intervention approach: restore arousal to normal or near normal level; assess problems and assets; provide help with problem-solving.

More recently, Dattilio and Freeman (1994) and Roberts (1995) have produced edited books entitled, respectively, *Cognitive-behavioral Strategies in Crisis Intervention* and *Crisis Intervention and Time-limited Cognitive Treatment*. These are mainly 'cognitive' in orientation. The methods described (but not yet evaluated in the crisis context) and the rationale for their use are compatible with the ideas and methods outlined in this chapter. We have kept more to the behavioural than the cognitive approach, but we recognise that for problems with a prominent cognitive component (such as the distress of a rape victim), the cognitive therapy literature should inform the worker's intervention plan.

Rationale for employing a behavioural approach

What indications are there for using a behavioural approach in the management of psychiatric emergencies? We shall briefly review some key

principles of learning theory, and the indications for practice derived from these principles:

1 Abnormal behaviour is generally viewed as learned, not as a symptom of some underlying morbid process.
2 Although many psychiatric emergencies result from true illnesses, many do not, emanating instead from family or social stresses acting on vulnerable individuals. Further, many of the behavioural characteristics of people suffering from true illnesses are environmentally or culturally determined, and thus contain a large element of learning.
3 Abnormal behaviour, like normal behaviour, can be changed by a process of learning.
4 As dysfunctional, maladaptive behaviour is behaviour which is at odds with the client's current environment, it reduces the chances that he or she will be able to function effectively.

As it is viewed as an acquired pattern, in many instances what has been learned can be unlearned or modified. This would include many features of behaviour which we call 'signs' or 'symptoms'.

There now exists a broad range of techniques derived from learning theory, amounting to a 'behavioural technology' that can be employed to this end. From our general knowledge of the nature of crisis intervention work and what has been said above, there are several features, generally preferred by behavioural workers, which suggest that even in the absence of firmer evidence, a behavioural orientation might prove to be the most appropriate when dealing with crises. This is the case in as much as several aspects of the work of behavioural therapists are consistent with what is generally considered to be 'good practice' in crisis work. These preferences are:

- active and directive, rather than passive, non-directive style
- time-limited work utilising techniques such as 'homework assignments' between sessions to ensure generalisation and increase efficiency
- clear goals with a focus on explicit agenda
- and structured contracts, where possible.

All of these are recognised as desirable characteristics of crisis intervention work. In addition, behavioural workers prefer close, direct observation of behaviour; structured and regular recording, which of itself can be beneficial; monitoring; and evaluating outcome. These latter characteristics are particularly useful under conditions of risk where there is threat of destructive behaviour to self or others. Often the deciding factor between hospital admission or some other management plan is the degree to which a worker can ensure a safe outcome. That such work practices are an integral part of an approach, rather than grafted on as an afterthought, argues strongly for the validity of its usage.

Further, behavioural workers focus on current environmental determinants of behaviour, and not on historical antecedents. This means that the approach is closely associated with the sort of service most social workers are best equipped to deliver. In turn, this is unlikely to create unrealistic expectations on the part of the client, family or other professionals and lead to a tragic cycle of expectations and disappointments.

Finally, behavioural workers prefer to focus on public events and overt behaviour. The most frequent subjects of complaint in psychiatric emergencies stem from what people are actually doing. Behavioural practice specialises in addressing such aspects, rather than private phenomena and latent motivation, which, no matter how disturbing they may be, are less often the actual matters with which the client, the family or the general public require the social services and health professionals to deal.

Certain generally accepted characteristics of behavioural techniques seem to be positive indicators for their use in crisis work. They include the following:

When they work, behavioural techniques tend to work quickly. This is important because there is a very limited period during which the community can contain a crisis before conventional coping will break down. Hence, time is usually a critical factor in the management of psychiatric emergencies. The production of rapid (at least) short-term gains is usually indispensable to any realistic alternative to hospital admission.

The approach emphasises good data-gathering. Any work in a crisis (or at other times, for that matter) should demand this. This behaviour assessment and monitoring approach is generally helpful in clarifying the exact nature of the problem, especially in respect of its severity, and in serving as a guide to intervention. It establishes a clear baseline against which to evaluate subsequent intervention, and hence aids evaluation and research. It helps in establishing the exact circumstances under which a particular action is taken, and thus helps to clarify the status of one's professional activities under mental health legislation. In the UK, these would include potential departmental and Mental Health Act Commission reviews, Mental Health Review Tribunal hearings, or civil or criminal actions.

The emphasis on objective and reliable data-gathering in the behavioural approach is consistent with what is coming to be defined as the social worker's professional role in the management of psychiatric emergencies. This point relates to the various tasks and responsibilities outlined by the Mental Health Act

1983 for Approved Social Workers performing statutory functions. For example, the British Association of Social Workers' objectives, as elaborated in their recommendations to Parliament during the framing of this legislation, were outlined in their publication *Mental Health Crisis Services: A New Philosophy* (BASW 1977, p.7) which stressed the need to 'investigate a client's social situation and to help to determine the extent to which it and other environmental pressures have contributed to the client's observed behaviour', and then to 'apply professional skill to help modify any contributory personal relationship and environmental factors'. These basic premises have been recognised and elaborated upon by the UK Central Council for Education and Training in Social Work, and have formed an essential part of the recommended core curricula for Approved Social Worker training (training required prior to performance of specific statutory mental health social work duties such as making an application for hospital admission in respect of a mentally disordered client).

Behavioural approaches emphasise the need to treat the individual as part of an ongoing social scenario. Crises are experienced by individuals, but affect a much wider social network, and social work help must take into account not only the needs of the individual, but those of the wider social environment. Behavioural techniques, particularly but not exclusively those based on operant and social learning theory, involve others in the patient's natural environment. In the case of a family crisis, this is especially valuable. Family members may, often without knowing it, be behaving in such a fashion as to contribute to the client's crisis; they will almost certainly be affected by the client's behaviour. Involving them in assessment and treatment from the earliest stage is often advisable. At the very least, there is the possibility of alleviating pressure by reintroducing some element of control in the crisis-ridden home, and there is potential for promoting feelings of mastery in families who feel helpless in the face of the client's symptomatology.

Behavioural interventions lend themselves well to co-operative working with professional colleagues and others. In psychiatric emergencies, one should seldom be working in isolation.

Therefore, the following points are particularly important:

Explaining one's plan to non-behaviourally trained colleagues is easier than in the case of, say, psychodynamically based therapies. This approach should make it easier to enlist their aid. Psychiatric community nurses or clinical psychologists who may be most helpful allies are usually already well versed in behavioural procedures. Likewise, much is said about the importance of involving users and carers in treatment, but strategies for accomplishing this under such circumstances are still underdeveloped in the literature. It appears reasonable to assume that untrained people such as the client's family may feel more able to co-operate if they understand what is being requested of them.

Behavioural treatments can be used in conjunction with other forms of psychiatric help. It is important to remember that for some psychiatric conditions, especially in their acute phase, drugs are the only efficacious form of treatment available, and that in other cases they may be a necessary prerequisite to an effective behavioural treatment.

Finally, we would maintain that the very features which opponents of the behavioural approach see as weaknesses might in fact prove to be strengths in a crisis. These are discussed below:

Avoidance of dependency

This is sometimes viewed critically because it is said that discouraging dependency prevents the client from 'transferring' past conflicts onto the worker–client relationship and developing a proper relationship as a basis for working through these conflicts. However, the tendency during a crisis is often towards 'regression', and this needs to be guarded against. Behavioural approaches tend to promote positive, here-and-now problem-solving, and reinforce realistic thinking. Certainly, in a crisis, the restoration of the person's capacity to function independently at the earliest possible moment is critical if the goal is to avoid hospital admission.

Lack of emphasis on achieving 'insight'

This lack of emphasis is sometimes said to prevent a 'real cure'. This is truly debatable, not only because it is difficult to define what is meant by 'insight' or to recognise when this state is really achieved, but especially because achieving 'insight' has never been established as either a sufficient or a necessary condition of positive behavioural change. In any event, such a treatment goal is often unrealistic given the time and other constraints in operation during a crisis. By focusing on behaviour change, the worker has the distinct advantage of being able to work with many individuals (for example, those with 'personality disorders' or 'highly defended neurotics') who would not be considered suitable for insight-oriented therapy even under the most advantageous conditions.

More suitable for less intelligent and articulate clients

It is often maintained that, unlike the 'talking treatments', behavioural approaches favour less intelligent and less articulate clients. This is not necessarily so, and there is plenty of evidence of behavioural approaches being used with intelligent, articulate adults. But even if it were so, children and people with learning difficulties also experience psychiatric crises, and it can be very difficult to help them remain in the community. Certainly, the ability to work with clients at various stages of intellectual development is a great asset. Likewise, the lack of a common language, as in the case of a deaf client or a client from a non-English-speaking culture, can be a crucial factor leading to unnecessary hospitalisation. The capacity of an approach to be applied successfully in spite of intellectual handicap or language differences is an advantage.

Difficulty in generalising behavioural change from one setting to another

This oft-cited weakness of behavioural interventions is a valid criticism, and one which needs to be taken into account when assessing any case. Where the work is undertaken *in situ*, however, this is not a problem. In such instances, behavioural assessments and treatments can be designed for the 'natural environment', working directly with the actual conditions which affect dysfunctional behaviour, and there are now strategies for doing this (as highlighted in the Homebuilders approach mentioned above). Recognising the potential disadvantages of removing a person to hospital for treatment that might not retain its effect after discharge is an inducement to provide community-based work.

Case study: Mrs Linda Mason

We offer the following fictionalised case study to illustrate the behavioural assessment of a mental health emergency.

Referral

Following a visit by the family general practitioner, Mrs Mason, aged 28, was referred to the local Social Services Department for assessment for an admission to hospital under the Mental Health Act 1983. The reason for the referral was the extremely aggressive behaviour which Mrs Mason was showing towards her parents, Mr and Mrs Finlay, with whom she lived. Upon examination by the GP, Mrs Mason was observed to be agitated and restless. Her sleep had been disturbed for several days previously. Despite efforts 'to calm her down', for the previous three days she had been reported as not sleeping, but pacing the floor and using provocative and threatening language, particularly in reference to her ex-common law husband. The police had been contacted by annoyed neighbours. Mrs Mason was known previously to both the police and the social services department.

Personal history

Mrs Mason is the second of three children of working-class parents. Her father is a ticket collector on the railway, and her mother a housewife. Her older brother, Andrew, is a shop manager, and her younger sister, Carole, is a secretary. Both are married and live away from their parents.

Mrs Mason was born in April 1968, and weighed 7lb 4oz at birth. Although three weeks premature, the delivery was uneventful, and she reached all of her developmental milestones as an infant at a normal pace. She had been described as an active child, occasionally temperamental. As a child, she had contracted normal childhood illnesses, from which she recovered with no apparent after-effects.

She performed in the average range at school, and though her behaviour was sometimes overactive and teachers sometimes found her difficult to manage, she had many friends. At age 14 she was arrested with other children from school for stealing cosmetics in a local shop, and received a police caution. Following an episode of fighting later the same year, she and her family were visited by a social worker, but were not deemed to be 'at risk'.

Linda Mason left school, aged 17, having obtained three GCSE passes. After a brief period working in a local shop, she left following an argument with the owner. A series of different jobs ensued. Mrs Mason often left these because she was fed up, or was dismissed because of poor time-keeping, especially being late in the morning. At age 18 she married Trevor Mason, who was then 26 years old, and left home. The marriage lasted for only one year, with Mr Mason divorcing her because of her 'unreasonable behaviour'. She continued to work at a local supermarket, and returned to live with her parents.

While still living at home, she met Martin Ervine, a polite and quiet man, aged 30, who worked for a bank. She was very fond of him, but refused to marry him because of the failure of her previous marriage. Instead, they took a flat together, and she continued working until their daughter, Lily, was born. Mrs Mason and Mr Ervine separated early in 1996, following a hospital admission. The child is presently in Mr Ervine's custody.

Previous admissions

Mrs Mason is said to be fond of her common law husband and daughter, but experiences periods of upset during which she shouts angrily, and this frightens both Mr Ervine and Lily. During these periods, Mrs Mason complains about being fatigued. Normal work and childcare 'get her down', and go undone. Prior to this referral, she has experienced eight mental health admissions, the first of which was at age 20. Two of her admissions have been formal, and all have been brief. Among the reasons given for admission have been overdose (twice), depression (twice), anxiety and morbid jealousy.

During the past decade, she has been diagnosed variously as suffering from 'reactive depression', 'anxiety state', and 'deliberate self-harm in an immature personality'. At the time of referral, Mrs Mason has had no recent contact with either her GP or the consultant psychiatrist, whose out-patient clinic she refuses to attend. Mrs Mason has refused to be subject to the Care Programme Approach, and has no key worker.

Approved Social Worker assessment

A social worker approved by the Local Authority as having responsibilities and powers under the Mental Health Act 1983 arranged to visit the family. As witnessed by the GP, when the Approved Social Worker arrived the house was in a state of turmoil. Mrs Mason was discovered to be angry and agitated, threatening to harm Mr Ervine if she met him. She had smashed some of the crockery in the kitchen. She was verbally abusive to her mother, who was in tears. Her father was found sitting stoically in a chair watching the television. Both parents were requesting that 'somebody do something'.

In accord with her responsibilities to consider all of the alternatives to an admission, the Approved Social Worker discussed the possibilities of a behavioural intervention with the consultant psychiatrist, with whom she made a joint assessment. They identified two key conditions surrounding the presentation of Mrs Mason's behavioural problems: her aggressive outbursts, and the lack of reinforcement, seen as co-operation, from her parents. The professionals agreed that as an alternative to compulsory hospitalisation, a behavioural programme should be instituted. If successful, and if the crisis was contained, admission might then be avoided. Failing that, Mrs Mason might require admission for a period of assessment and treatment. A plan to treat Mrs Mason at home was discussed and agreed with the family, and a behavioural contract was formulated. The completed assessment form in Box 11.1 outlines a behavioural treatment regime, designed to contain the emergency, which the Approved Social Worker was to moderate and monitor progress on behalf of the specialist mental health team.

Box 11.1 Behavioural social work assessment form

1 Case name: MASON, Mrs Linda

Address: 333 Garden Terrace, Willow Grove Estate

Telephone: Ex-directory

2 Case details:

Age: 28
Gender: Female
Marital status: Separated from common law husband
Family composition: 1 child, Lily, resident with father. Currently resident with parents, Mr and Mrs Finlay.

3 Referral source: Referral was from the family GP, Dr Thomas, following complaints by Mr and Mrs Finlay that their daughter was 'going off'. Request is for assessment of Mrs Mason by an Approved Social Worker. Family demand that social worker 'do something'.

4 State the presenting problem in general terms: Mrs Mason is displaying extreme verbal and physical aggression towards Mr and Mrs Finlay, who reciprocate. She is also distressed over the loss of her child, showing anger towards the child's father and threatening him. Parents 'unable to cope'.

5 State the issues which must be taken into consideration (e.g. legal, clinical, organisational, professional/ethical):

Organisational: Worker's time; other resources
Legal: Protection of client and others; need for assessment
Clinical: Present mood is agitated; history of hospital admissions and deliberate self-harm; constitution; treatability
Social: Present residential needs; relationship with parents, husband and child; past relationship with social services
Psychological: Stress/vulnerability factors; conditioning

6 Is a behavioural approach justified in this case? (State reasons why/ what alternative approaches might be considered)

A Need for accurate assessment and monitoring
B Need for rapid improvement

C Strong learned component in client's maladaptive actions
D Behaviour controlled by pattern of reinforcement
E Need for positive, consistent structured response

7 State potential target behaviours and establish priorities:

A Mrs Mason's aggressive outbursts
B Lack of co-operative behaviour within the family
C Mrs Mason's feelings and thoughts concerning her loss of child and husband, and her adjustment to these

8 Who else will need to be involved?

A Mr and Mrs Finlay
B GP and consultant psychiatrist and team

9 Under what conditions should the intervention take place? (e.g. in conjunction with other help, location, etc.)

The intervention should take place in the client's residence.

10 Existing baseline data:

1 Outbursts
2 Co-operation

Variable	**Behaviour 1**	**Behaviour 2**
a **Frequency**	Nearly continuous	Infrequent
b **Intensity**	Severe	Weak
c **Duration**	Brief	Short lived
d **Resistance to extinction**	Stubborn	Easily extinguished

10.1 The reliability of this data is (good/average/poor):

The reliability is good. The behaviour has been independently recorded by three professional observers.

11 Controlling Events:

Mrs Mason's outbursts are related to lack of impulse control, poor models and inconsistent reinforcement.

Poor family co-operation is due to lack of understanding of more affiliative behaviour in their repertoire.

12 Intervention plan (i.e. treatment techniques to be tried):
Mrs Mason: 'Time Out'; active listening; shaping through reinforcement (contingency management); modelling; response prevention
Family co-operation: Contract; feedback; role-play; rehearsal and guided practice

13 Evaluation:

a Measurement:

Type of data needed: Direct observation while the Approved Social Worker is present
Method for gathering data: Behavioural recording when absent (i.e. check-list of frequency; diary to monitor contract); risk assessment by standardised instrument (e.g. depression scales; suicide intent scales)

b Method of control proposed:

Multiple-baseline design (controlling improvement of one behaviour against non-treated behaviours).

c Type/amount of change which would suggest success or failure:

1 *Short term*: Immediate reduction in frequency of outbursts and increase in positive overtures on part of the family.
2 *Long term*: Increased ability to plan and execute plans for realistic behavioural goal attainment with support from her family.

14 Any other conditions under which the approach is to be tried (e.g. the limits; consent; liaison; follow-up/'topping up'):
A time limit of five sessions to be tried in the first instance. No members of the family environment should absolutely reject the idea. Close liaison with the health service. Both behaviours will probably need 'topping up' sessions for some time.

Discussion: A proposed format for behavioural crisis practice

Given our rationale for the use of a behavioural approach in crisis situations, and the lack of guidelines in the literature, we feel it appropriate to suggest a format for assessment and intervention planning. Our format, as exemplified in the preceding case example, is not exhaustive, but contains a sufficient structure to enable the social worker to encompass the key elements of a behavioural approach outlined above.

In general, this format follows similar formats to be found in behavioural texts. The differences, which stem from the fact that we are here assessing a person with a psychiatric label in the context of a psychiatric emergency, include the following.

First, it is necessary to collect such basic information as is required to set the context of the referral. This should include previous admissions and current medication. Then, the descriptive statement of the presenting problem may include comments by other family members, members of the social network and professionals.

Because this is a psychiatric emergency, the range of factors to be taken into account before any action can even be considered, let alone initiated, include items of a clinical, organisational, legal and professional and ethical nature. These cannot be ignored or oversimplified, as they may either restrict or negate any type of psychological intervention.

There should always be some justification for any type of intervention. Sometimes, sadly, none exists. In such instances, the indications for hospitalisation, such as degree and type of disorder or extent of risk, are overwhelming, and the worker must proceed on that basis. However, if it appears that a psychosocial intervention could proceed, then the worker must give consideration to the type of approach to be used. When a behavioural approach is decided upon, a range of potential target behaviours usually exist. Experience suggests that crises tend, as often as not, to be overdetermined. It is important to establish who will be involved. This is not only for purposes of inclusion, but also for exclusion. Firm decisions regarding the roles of different professionals need to be made in order to avoid confusion and uncontrollable events confounding treatment outcome.

Some estimation of the veracity of the data must be arrived at, no matter how imperfectly done. While working under the less than ideal conditions of a psychiatric emergency, practitioners can console themselves with the fact that under such circumstances error is usually more a matter of degree than an absolute.

Concluding comment

In this chapter, we have sought to introduce the notion of using behavioural methods in psychiatric emergency situations. Although there is as yet little scientific evidence directly supporting this approach in such situations, there is adequate reason to justify its being tried in cases where psychosocial intervention is considered appropriate. We believe that the use of behavioural techniques in this field fits well with contemporary notions of 'good practice', and hope this contribution might serve to stimulate further debate and experimentation.

References

Aguilera, D.G. and Messick, J.M. (1982) *Crisis Intervention: Theory and Methodology* (4th edn), St Louis, MO: Mosby.

Auerbach, S.M. and Kilmann, P.R. (1977) 'Crisis intervention: A review of outcome research', *Psychological Bulletin*, 84, pp.1,189–217.

Bancroft, J. (1979) 'Crisis intervention' in S. Bloch (ed.) *An Introduction to the Psychotherapies*, Oxford: Oxford University Press.

BASW (1977) *Mental Health Crisis Services: A New Philosophy*, Birmingham: British Association of Social Workers.

Belson, P.M. (1971) 'The use of behavior therapy techniques in crisis intervention: A case report', *Journal of Behavior Therapy and Experimental Psychiatry*, 2, pp.297–300.

Caplan, G. (1964) *Principles of Preventive Psychiatry*, New York: Basic Books.

Clarke, J. (1971) 'An analysis of crisis management by Mental Welfare Officers', *British Journal of Social Work*, 1, pp.27–39.

Dattilio, F. and Freeman, A. (eds) (1994) *Cognitive-behavioral Strategies in Crisis Intervention*, New York: Guilford Press.

Decker, J.B. and Stubblebine, J.M. (1972) 'Crisis intervention and prevention of psychiatric disability: A follow-up study', *American Journal of Psychiatry*, 129, pp.725–9.

Eisler, R.M. (1976) 'Behavioral techniques in family crises', *Current Psychiatric Therapies*, 16, pp.255–62.

Eisler, R.M. and Hersen, M. (1973) 'Behavioral techniques in family-oriented crisis intervention', *Archives of General Psychiatry*, 28, pp.111–16.

Fisher, M., Newton, C. and Sainsbury, E. (1984) *Mental Health Social Work Observed*, National Institute of Social Services Library No. 5, London: George Allen and Unwin.

Greenfield, B., Hechtman, L. and Tremblay, C. (1995) 'Short-term efficacy of interventions by a youth crisis team', *Canadian Journal of Psychiatry*, 40, pp.320–4.

Kinney, J.M., Madsen, B., Fleming, T. and Haapala, D.A. (1977) 'Homebuilders: Keeping families together', *Journal of Consulting and Clinical Psychology*, 45, pp.667–73.

Langsley, D.G. (1972) 'Crisis intervention', *American Journal of Psychiatry*, 129, pp.734–6.

Langsley, D.G. and Kaplan, D. (1968) *The Treatment of Families in Crisis*, New York: Grune and Stratton.

Langsley, D.G., Pittman, F.S., Machotka, P. and Flomenhaft, K. (1968) 'Family crisis therapy: Results and implications', *Family Process*, 7, pp.145–58.

Liberman, R.P. and Eckman, T. (1981) 'Behaviour therapy vs insight-oriented therapy for repeated suicide attempters', *Archives of General Psychiatry*, 36, pp.1,126–30.

Lindemann, E. (1944) 'Symptomatology and management of acute grief', *American Journal of Psychiatry*, 101, pp.141–8.
Olsen, M.R. (ed). (1984) *Social Work and Mental Health: A Guide for the Approved Social Worker*, London: Tavistock.
Rapoport, L. (1970) 'Crisis intervention as a mode of brief treatment' in R.W. Roberts and R.H. Nee (eds) *Theories of Social Casework*, Chicago, IL: University of Chicago Press.
Roberts, A.R. (ed.) (1995) *Crisis Intervention and Time-limited Cognitive Treatment*, Thousand Oaks, CA: Sage.
Seligman, M.E.P. (1975) *Helplessness: On Depression, Development and Death*, San Francisco, CA: W.H. Freeman.
Silver, R.L. and Wortman, C.B. (1980) 'Coping with undesirable life events' in J. Garber and M.E.P. Seligman (eds) *Human Helplessness: Theory and Applications*, New York: Academic Press.

12 Intervention in group care for older people

Katy Cigno

Residential and daycare settings for older people do not generate case studies of systematic social work intervention to the same extent as establishments for children and young people. The impression given is that such a setting, combined with an older client group, is either not suitable for providing help of a psychosocial nature to the individual, or that the care workers are professionally ill-prepared to offer this kind of help, or at least diffident about their attempts to do so (Smith 1987). In spite of these difficulties, instances of therapeutic intervention directed at the person in group care exist. They can be used in evaluative research and, in case study form, have the advantage that they 'allow an investigation to retain the holistic and meaningful characteristics of real-life events – such as individual life cycles, organizational and managerial processes' (Yin 1994, p.3).

This chapter reports a study of the use of behavioural social work with Miss 'B', a 70-year-old woman in a home for older people mainly with a history of learning difficulties, many of them formerly housed in 'subnormality' hospitals. The emptying of the asylums was given impetus in the 1970s after the findings of researchers such as Morris (1969). Further impetus came through the impact of newspaper articles and reports during the same decade (see, for example, Departmental of Health and Social Security/Welsh Office 1971; Jones 1975). Later, the Wagner Report (National Institute for Social Work 1988a and 1988b) required the residential sector to 'respond effectively to changing social needs' (1988a, p.1), and made a case for community-based residential care. The National Health Service and Community Care Act 1990, following the Griffiths Report (Griffiths 1988), accelerated the need for local government and health services policies to put in place co-ordinated community care arrangements for vulnerable people such as older people and those with learning difficulties.

To an extent, then, the case described here can be seen in the wider context of the aftermath of movements of parts of the population of large, often isolated institutions to small, local residential care homes. It illustrates, too, the change from a more punitive approach to dealing with an aggressive and exasperating client to a programme combining positive reinforcement with the teaching of self-control and social skills. Staff involved in such a programme have to bear in mind the clear distinction between the person – who always has an intrinsic value, and must always be respected – and the behaviour, which is undesirable and needs to be eliminated in order to improve the quality of life not just of the client in question, but also of the other residents. These notions are not new, but are worth repeating to both client and staff by the worker in charge of the programme. The key features of the intervention are as follows:

- the appropriate training of all workers, including domestic staff, in daily contact with the client
- the formulation of a contract (an agreement on how to proceed) between the client and the key worker
- the use of symbolic and real rewards, accompanied by social reinforcement.

Older people, quality of life and residential settings

Is social casework right for older people? Is there a danger that the 'interfering', task-centred social worker, whether residential or field, will fail to see the person as a whole being, directing attention instead at getting the older person to be more sociable by jollying him or her into various activities? Wilkes (1978 and 1981) has directed our attention to some consequences of positive social work. Or, on the other hand, does the danger lie in accepting too readily older clients' status quo, and in not considering that they may have goals that they might like to achieve? Gambrill (1986), Cigno (1993a) and Manthorpe (1996) all consider these issues for social workers. Even when older people live at home with their families, we may think of them as having no will of their own (Randall 1990), or no useful role, as Harrison pointed out in 1978. Careful consideration of these matters, and an ecological approach as advocated by Gambrill (1986), should guide workers in helping their older clients improve the quality of their lives.

Booth et al. (1990), in their survey of staff attitudes and caring practices in residential homes for older people, found institutional inertia a major obstacle to the development of good practice in residential care: 'People often balk at the effort involved in bringing about change' (p.128). Another finding was that there was often no agreement as to what constituted good practice, a point highlighted by the content and orientation of the present chapter. The situation should be starting to change, for the late 1980s and the 1990s have seen almost yearly reports by the Department of Health (for example, Department of Health 1992) and the Social Services Inspectorate on standards in care and on what residential homes should be like from the point of view of the residents. One jointly published report gives clear messages to staff on how they should create an atmosphere of 'homeliness' while responding to the needs of those in their care (Department of Health, Social Services Inspectorate 1989), while a more recent one emphasises the importance of equity for older people (Department of Health, Social Services Inspectorate 1995).

In residential settings, as Goffman (1968) eloquently demonstrated in a seminal work, the institutional regime, consciously or unconsciously, can aim at maintaining residents as an inactive group. Moreover, it may not encourage staff efforts to get to know residents as individuals with separate needs. Some residents seem to encourage the staff to aim above all for a quiet life, giving up their independence too easily, even to the extent of not having to decide when to eat (Personal Social Services Council 1977). In this tranquil atmosphere, success may come to be defined as a day without incidents. Some residents and staff members show hostility towards anyone who tries to alter the routine, even if in a helpful and positive way, as students on placement in such settings have often pointed out. The Wagner Report also brought these difficulties to our notice (National Institute for Social Work 1988a).

Often, though, the resident may see that the only way to get attention is by making a scene and therefore becoming unpopular. Unpopularity may be the price to pay for retaining a strong sense of self and some control over daily events.

The concept of group living

One problem for people forced to live with those they have not chosen is compatibility. It may not be realistic to expect that members of a residential group become integrated (Booth and Phillips 1987). Once former daily routines like shopping, dusting, cooking and washing-up are lost, the common characteristics of residential life are apathy, withdrawal or disorientation. The majority of residents become dependent on the home's routine. Any form of independence may appear to be discouraged.

In a residential group of vulnerable persons like older people, some forms of deviation on the part of one of their members may be not only undesirable but potentially harmful for the physical and mental health of the others. Seaton (1993) discusses what constitutes a 'major incident' (for example, an assault on a resident by another resident, or serious damage to property) and procedures which staff should follow to record and deal with it, but does not go on to suggest how behaviour change may be effected. Workers may therefore perceive a conflict between quality of life and safety for the group on the one hand, and the right of individuals to express themselves differently from the rest on the other (Lawton and Namehow 1973). A vicious circle may be created when a resident, feeling isolated, behaves aggressively in order to be noticed. At first, the resident may well succeed, but in the long term, he or she will become more isolated.

Another factor contributing to feelings of isolation and frustration in older residents is the lack of contact with significant relatives (Cigno 1979). Long-term hospital patients and residents of homes for older people are especially affected. The absence of relatives and of unpaid carers, or stress on carers, may also have been reasons for a person's admission into care in the first place (National Institute for Social Work 1988a and 1988b). The Carers National Association (Pitkeathley 1995) has worked successfully for recognition of the role of unpaid carers (largely female relatives) in the community in recent years (see the resulting legislation: Department of Health 1996), and is in part responsible for the attention now given to the family in outcomes for vulnerable people needing care (see, for example, Tooth 1987; Barritt 1990; Manthorpe 1994).

Miss B's story

Miss B is 70. Physically, she looks like many other healthy and robust women of that age. She is sociable. She was admitted to a subnormality hospital at the age of 26, but it is not clear, because of lack of relevant documentation from that time, to what extent she had learning difficulties. Little is known of her family. Miss B says of herself 'I was a nuisance' and 'I was naughty.' We know that in the past many people were admitted to institutions not because of a mental impairment, but because they were orphans or because their different or 'immoral' behaviour, together with other personal circumstances such as social and educational disadvantages, combined to make them unwelcome in their neighbourhoods (Morris 1969).

During the long years in hospital, according to information still available, Miss B got the reputation of being argumentative. She often quarrelled with other patients and with the nurses. She was also accused of stealing. These behaviours were cyclical. After a period of calm, she would begin to pick quarrels. These episodes ended in an angry scene where she banged doors, shouted, knocked chairs over. Then she would pretend to be ill or she would present herself to the nurse with a small wound which was apparently the result of a minor accident.

A consequence of this behaviour was that Miss B became unpopular, both with patients and with nursing staff. Other negative consequences followed for her: she was often the scapegoat for other patients, who exploited her unpopularity by blaming her for incidents involving theft and fights. This situation caused her behaviour to deteriorate further. When the ward staff could no longer tolerate her behaviour, she was transferred to another ward. After a while, the cycle repeated itself.

In the wake of the closure of large psychiatric and subnormality hospitals and the placing of ex-patients in the community, Miss B, together with 15 other older women, was transferred to a new local authority residential home. Other residents came either from different hospitals or were admitted from the community because they could no longer cope at home. The home houses 40 residents altogether.

Miss B's problems in the home

Although Miss B's 'anti-social' history was known to staff and, of course, to other residents who knew her in hospital, she made efforts to render herself acceptable in her new home. She was friendly, respected the feelings of others, and offered to help less able residents. She showed a sense of humour, and participated enthusiastically in meetings.

Unfortunately, her reputation in hospital was talked about by some of the residents. Partly in response to this and partly through one or two trigger incidents which were reminders of the past, her relationships with residents and staff deteriorated and began to resemble those she had previously shown during her institutional life. She began to be disruptive, arousing negative feelings in staff and residents. She shouted, upset and sometimes frightened other residents, and behaved badly at table – just as she had in hospital. Soon these episodes were occurring daily.

One result was that the care workers were spending a lot of time with her, reproving her and threatening to remove certain 'privileges', such as going on trips. Miss B responded by increasing the disruptive behaviours. The staff increased the amount of time they spent in 'punishing' Miss B by scolding her.

Although she was getting attention, her self-image became less positive. At mealtimes, no one wanted to sit at her table because sometimes she protested loudly that she did not want to eat or that she wanted to be served first, or she threw something on the floor. She complained to the staff that no one liked her. In her behaviour, she appeared to be living up to others' expectations of her. The 'vicious circle' of the behaviours noted in hospital began to repeat itself.

The time arrived when staff did not want to take her on trips or to the shops because they dreaded a scene. Sometimes she had to be led away from social events taking place in the home, and was therefore excluded from entertainment. Her residential key worker and other staff became worried about her. After an increase in 'rows' involving Miss B and others, the staff body decided to review her behaviour with a view to drawing up a plan which would enable them to cope more successfully with her problems.

Review of Miss B's problem behaviours

Six months had passed since Miss B was transferred to the home. There had therefore been enough time for the staff to observe her behaviour, the reactions of others to the behaviour, and the consequences. In a special staff meeting, three important elements of interaction with Miss B were noted:

1 In order to effect some control, and for the sake of the well-being of the group, at times Miss B was excluded from trips and other social events. But this form of control rarely immediately followed the undesirable behaviour, and it was therefore depressing to and poorly understood by Miss B. In short, members of staff were in danger of re-creating a punitive environment for this client, who nevertheless persisted in her anti-social behaviour.
2 Such a punitive regime is not ethically justifiable. It was also ineffective in its attempts to improve matters with regard to this resident. Moreover, staff realised that in their wish to avoid a possible escalation of problem behaviour, they sometimes reproached Miss B for minor incidents tolerated in other residents.
3 There were times when Miss B did well – for instance, she might assist another resident in some way, or tidy up her own room – but these actions were largely ignored because they were considered 'normal'.

The conclusion was that staff and residents had helped shape up aggressive and disruptive behaviour in Miss B. The staff group decided that it was not necessary to teach her new, desirable behaviours because these were present, though presently at a low level. They decided that they did need to help her to understand the negative effect of her actions on others, to encourage the existing desirable behaviours, and to extinguish the undesirable.

A simple ABC analysis

An analysis of the relevant antecedents, behaviour and consequences gives more precise information on problem behaviours, enabling the care staff, led by the key worker, to formulate a plan of intervention to help the client. The behaviours that caused the most trouble for Miss B and for those around her were those involving *aggression* and *argumentativeness*. The questions to ask are:

A Where does the behaviour take place? What are the circumstances? Who is present?
B How can the behaviour be best described? What does the person actually do?
C What happens immediately afterwards?

In Miss B's case, the following analysis emerged.

Antecedents

These are almost any situation where others are present: the dining-room, the lounge, the corridor. Sometimes Miss B reacts to a look or a word she perceives as hostile, although no such hostility was intended. Sometimes it is the mere presence of others that acts as a stimulus.

Behaviour

Miss B insults someone. She swears. She raises her voice. She becomes excited and shouts. If in the dining-room, she throws a cup on the floor. She goes into the kitchen to argue with the cook.

Consequences (immediate)

Residents near her start to murmur, then complain. They accuse her, or show fear. A member of staff tries to calm her down, does not succeed, so scolds her; the incident often ends with a heated discussion between Miss B and the staff member. In many cases, the scene changes and a similar incident is repeated more noisily.

An important point to note is that Miss B is robust, while many residents are frail. Staff naturally fear that she may hurt someone. Her attempts at making friends are heavy-handed and clumsy, causing others to draw back. This discourages Miss B. In hospital, she had found that one sure way of getting attention was to make a scene. The subsequent fuss and attention of the nurses largely compensated for her lack of success in making friends with other patients and enjoying a social life. In the long run, though, her inability to make herself liked by fellow patients or residents has saddened her, and she has expressed this feeling of sadness to her key worker.

The role of the residential key worker

Each key worker is responsible for getting to know a small group of residents, and takes a special interest in the welfare of this group. Miss B's key worker decided that the best way to help her was through a behavioural programme. Given the environment, the client's characteristics and the need to involve all care and domestic staff, she decided that simple and easily explainable methods were best. The first task was to discuss a possible programme with Miss B, and obtain her consent. The next was to ensure the support of all staff, to explain the principles of the behavioural approach to them and brief them on how to approach Miss B from now on, especially when the key worker is absent and cannot intervene herself (see Chapter 1 for an account of operant conditioning and the importance of the reliability of reinforcement schedules).

The view held here is that it would not be ethical to proceed without fully involving the client. Neither would it be possible to carry out an intervention without the understanding and support of colleagues. Many interventions fail because the objectives of the client are different from those of the worker, or because other mediators, either openly or covertly, sabotage the programme. This may be because they do not properly understand it (in this case, the worker must ask herself 'Did I explain procedures clearly and thoroughly, and did I check that everyone had understood?') or because they do not agree with the methodology, or lack the skills and control to act coherently at all times in interaction with the client (Gambrill 1983).

Many writers (for example, Hudson and Macdonald 1986; see also Chapter 9) pinpoint the necessity of teaching skills of reinforcement to the client's significant others. Booth et al. (1990) stress the importance of staff meetings to discuss aspects of care: they go on to mention staff supervision and training as factors necessary for working towards shared, coherent, good practices. These 'messages for staff' are also repeated by Social Services Inspectors (Department of Health, Social Services Inspectorate 1995).

Miss B's programme

The programme developed for use with Miss B avoided controlling undesirable behaviour by threatening to remove or removing resources normally available for all residents – a common but punitive reaction to challenging behaviour. Instead, it aimed to recognise and increase Miss B's efforts to behave in a sociable, acceptable and less dangerous way by rewarding them. It was also structured in such a way that she could earn special treats of her choosing through her own efforts.

Once a possible strategy was outlined, the first thing to do was talk to Miss B about it. Using examples from past experiences, the key worker rehearsed with her what is a desirable and what is an undesirable behaviour. She explained that others did not like her argumentative and aggressive way of behaving, stressing that it was the behaviour that was not liked and not Miss B. (This is a difficult concept to get across. Many of us remember from childhood being called 'bad boy' or 'bad girl' when we had committed some misdemeanour.) For example, it is not a popular way of going about things to go into the kitchen at mealtimes and insist on being served first, nor does a resident like being insulted for picking up Miss B's plate by mistake.

Together, the key worker and Miss B discussed how to avoid such situations. Miss B said she behaved aggressively because she felt people scapegoated her: 'They pick on me.' Using other examples of her behaviour, the worker discussed with her how this had come about, what Miss B herself could do to change her image, and how to cope with a situation she saw as trying. For example, if she found herself in a situation where she knew she was going to lose her temper, she could walk away, or call (not shout) for the help of a member of staff. The key worker explained that all the staff understood her difficulties and wanted to help her. They would all be aware of her new programme.

The key worker suggested the use of a simple chart to monitor progress. Miss B liked the idea, deciding that she would pin it on the inside of her cupboard door so that she could show it only when and to whom she chose. The chart was, for this client, an incentive in itself to change her behaviour.

It was important to plan the programme in such a way that Miss B could quickly experience success. For this reason, Miss B and the key worker decided together that Miss B could earn a star to stick on the chart after half a day of what was defined as 'reasonable behaviour' – half a day without swearing or behaving in such a way as to frighten or endanger others.

It was agreed that unless serious, an episode of 'undesirable behaviour' would be ignored. As most people in a position of carer, paid or unpaid, are aware, this is very difficult to do; first, because the carer feels provoked, as we have seen in Miss B's case, into a reaction of scolding, and second, because ignoring a behaviour feels like 'doing nothing', or even condoning it. It was therefore important from the outset for all staff members to understand how behaviours are maintained. At the end of each half-day session (therefore twice a day), one of the staff would review how things had gone.

Miss B would be invited to add her comments. Then she would either stick a star on her chart or it would be explained to her why she was not to have one. Five stars (two-and-a-half days of 'reasonable behaviour') would give Miss B the right to choose a reward.

Next, Miss B made a list of her favourite activities. These were: visits to the library, the social centre and the shops, and special group outings organised by staff. She would choose from this list when she had accumulated five stars.

The importance to the programme of the co-operation of colleagues is worth repeating. It was very important that Miss B should quickly experience success and that she was not discouraged by some form of punishment. To this end, the care staff must understand the behavioural principles underlying the programme. In a special meeting, the key worker made the following points:

1. Miss B's behaviour is maintained by the attention she receives.
2. No attention should be paid to aggressive or capricious behaviour, wherever possible (that is, where there is no immediate danger to others or herself), in order to facilitate its extinction.
3. It is necessary to practise restructuring one's own thoughts so as not to expect incidents of 'bad behaviour' from Miss B.
4. Attention should be paid when Miss B is trying to present herself in a positive light; these attempts should be encouraged immediately.
5. The charts must be completed after each session.
6. Coherence in staff relationships with Miss B is the aim.
7. Negative comments ('Oh, it's you again!') are to be avoided.

Results

Miss B soon earned five stars. She chose for her reward a visit to the library with a member of staff. During the first week, she 'lost' only half a day. She was very pleased with herself, and became more conscious of her behaviour and the effect it had on others. She was now capable of explaining why a particular behaviour was acceptable or unacceptable.

After only one week, it was decided that Miss B could realistically aim to maintain her behaviour at the agreed reasonable level for a whole day before being given a star. Miss B felt ready for this, and succeeded in maintaining her progress without lapses. She used her next five stars for a theatre trip.

Four weeks later, the key worker extended the period needed to earn a star to two days. This time, Miss B did not earn any stars at all. The key worker discussed with her what had happened. Miss B said that two days were too long: she was afraid of failing. They agreed to go back to the initial stage: one star for half a day of 'reasonable behaviour'. It is clear here that the client's self-confidence had to be rebuilt.

There were no further lapses of this kind. The programme lasted about six weeks. During the last phase, Miss B had to maintain her behaviour at the agreed level for two-and-a-half days before receiving a star, after which the charts were withdrawn. The whole programme sequence is shown in Table 12.1.

Table 12.1 Miss 'B': Periods of 'reasonable behaviour' required to earn one star

Duration	Chart No.	Period Required
6 days	1	½ day
5 days	2	1 day
5 days	3	2 days
5 days	4	½ day
5 days	5	1 day
10 days	6	2 days
10 days	7	2½ days

At this point, Miss B no longer needed the charts because, at the end of the six-week period, she found her new situation pleasing and therefore self-reinforcing, and she was also obtaining just as much attention as before, but of an image-enhancing, 'feel-good' kind: smiles and praise, company and conversation, instead of frowns, scolding and arguments. Both residents and staff were showing themselves more willing to spend time in her company.

Reviewing the situation six months later, it was noted that now and again, some of Miss B's problem behaviours recur. When this happens, a star chart is reinstated for a specific period. This method redefines for the client which behaviours are acceptable and which are unacceptable. She responds well to this approach, going through her old programme in an abbreviated form, and therefore quickly reaching the desired level of social behaviour.

Some reflections

The key values underpinning residential care, according to the Department of Health, Social Services Inspectorate (1989), are privacy, dignity, rights, independence, choice and fulfilment. Any approach to change should consider whether it allows these values to be upheld. Staff working in group care, especially residential institutions, have to know how to combine compassion with skills and professional competencies, among which is the ability to find an equilibrium between individual and group needs. When working with a third-age population in particular, there is the risk of losing sight of the importance of giving individuals a positive image of themselves as well as helping them to improve this image by changing their behaviour. Being able to do this also influences the quality of life of the whole group. It is therefore essential to remind ourselves that older people do still have goals, but that they may need help in formulating these and discovering how to work towards them, as Sutton (1994), drawing on the earlier work of Barrowclough and Fleming (1985), also points out.

The use of star charts in a home for older people may seem mechanistic and inappropriate, but they have been widely accepted, sometimes in slightly modified forms, by people with learning difficulties, especially those with a history of institutionalisation, and are often popular and successful with children in schools and in the home setting (see, for example, the case studies by Bunyan 1987 and Bourn 1993). This study shows that in certain cases, the methodology is justified and effective as part of an integrated programme of positive reinforcement aimed at encouraging social behaviour, discouraging anti-social behaviour and increasing self-esteem. It has already been pointed out that the client herself liked the idea, finding the charts and the activities surrounding them rewarding in themselves. It is also useful to reiterate the point that the client's approval of, and involvement in, the methods employed is important. The charts are withdrawn once the desired behaviour is established, so that they do not become a fixed element of a regime which has as its aim the creation of an informal and homely environment.

In this case study, the key worker had to overcome an initial aversion to this kind of intervention on the part of the staff, but not from the client in question, who readily agreed to the change, enjoyed using the charts, and benefited, as described above, from the results. She was a conscious participator in a programme designed in consultation with her. For many workers, the systematic use of cognitive-behavioural methods is a novelty and, moreover, poorly understood and poorly applied, if at all. These obstacles need to be overcome in order for the programme to work; the co-operation of all staff is necessary. Reference has been made to the importance of the training and control of mediators. Swann, a social work practitioner writing on why some programmes fail, says: 'Even in more structured situations, problems are encountered in ensuring that all members of staff are involved, otherwise the behaviour to be changed could be intermittently reinforced' (Swann 1982, p.18).

The method of intervention itself need not be complicated, as the work with Miss B shows, and indeed, can be simple to administer – an important point for busy practitioners, who find some methodologies too time-consuming for the reality of everyday life. (In fact, no systematic baseline of Miss B's behaviour was taken prior to initiating her programme, and an opportunity to assess and monitor her progress was therefore missed. As the residential key worker commented: 'It happens'.)

Miss B's progress was not linear. The mistake was made of forcing the pace in passing from 'one day – one star' to 'two days – one star'. The client was not able to reach this new target. In such cases, it is necessary to return to a stage in the programme where the client can feel sure of success. To put her in a position where she is likely to fail again is demoralising and unnecessary, as well as being poor practice, and would lead to abandoning the intervention, probably with the judgement that a behavioural approach 'doesn't work'.

The key worker realised at the beginning the importance of not getting involved in long arguments with Miss B after incidents where she behaved aggressively towards other residents. This had been the old way of handling Miss B's behaviour: all it did was reinforce the problem behaviour. It is therefore essential in an intervention of this kind that the behaviour to be extinguished is not involuntarily reinforced.

Another point to consider is the attitude of the other residents towards someone who is receiving an extra reward. Will they become envious? Here, it must be noted that the others had something to gain from Miss B's programme in the form of a more pleasant and harmonious environment. Nevertheless, there is still the possibility of feelings of resentment if one resident appears to be unjustly rewarded or receives more attention from staff. Again, Miss B was already receiving considerable time and attention from staff, so the question of increased resentment did not arise. The key worker system is also crucial to the intervention, in that each resident can consult and request explanations from his or her assigned worker, and therefore does not feel neglected.

Finally, it must be remembered that rewards chosen by an individual are not necessarily seen as rewarding by another. Various systems of reinforcement exist in any case in institutions large and small; some of them can be quite complex. It is worth studying them carefully before undertaking programmes involving change, whether at the group or individual level.

Acknowledgement

This material first appeared in *The British Journal of Social Work* by Katy Cigno (1993).

References

Barritt, A. (1990) *New Directions in Care: A Review of County Council Strategies for Elderly People and Family Carers*, London: Family Policies Studies Centre.

Barrowclough, C. and Fleming, I. (1985) *Goal Planning with Elderly People*, Manchester: Manchester University Press.

Booth, T. and Phillips, D. (1987) 'Group living in homes for the elderly: A comparative study of the outcomes of care', *British Journal of Social Work*, 17, pp.1–20.

Booth, T., Bilson, A. and Powell, I. (1990) 'Staff attitudes and caring practices in homes for the elderly', *British Journal of Social Work*, 20, pp.117–31.

Bourn, D.F. (1993) 'Over-chastisement, child non-compliance and parenting skills: A behavioural intervention by a family centre social worker', *British Journal of Social Work*, 23, pp.481–99.

Bunyan, A. (1987) 'Help, I can't cope with my child: A behavioural approach to the treatment of a conduct disordered child within the natural home setting', *British Journal of Social Work*, 17, pp.237–56.

Cigno, K. (1979) 'Where do they all come from?', *Community Care*, 1 December, pp.26–7.

Cigno, K. (1993a) 'Social work and old age: Two cultures?', *Elders: The Journal of Care and Practice*, 2, pp.57–64.

Cigno, K. (1993b) 'Changing behaviour in a residential group setting for elderly people with learning difficulties', *British Journal of Social Work*, 23, pp.629–42.

Department of Health (1992) *Long-term Care for Elderly People: Purchasing, Providing and Quality*, London: HMSO.

Department of Health (1996) *Carers (Recognition and Services) Act: Policy Guidance and Practice Guide*, London: Department of Health.

Department of Health and Social Security/Welsh Office (1971) *Better Services for the Mentally Handicapped*, London: HMSO.

Department of Health, Social Services Inspectorate (1989) *Homes are for Living in*, London: HMSO.

Department of Health, Social Services Inspectorate (1995) *Responding to Residents*, London: HMSO.

Gambrill, E. (1983) *Casework: A Competency-based Approach*, New Jersey: Prentice-Hall.

Gambrill, E. (1986) 'Social skills training with the elderly' in C.R. Hollin and P. Trower (eds) *Handbook of Social Skills Training*, Vol. 1, Oxford and New York: Pergamon Press.

Goffman, E. (1968) *Asylums*, Harmondsworth: Pelican Books.

Griffiths, Sir R. (1988) *Community Care: Agenda for Action*, London: HMSO.

Harrison, P. (1978) 'Living with old age' in V. Carver and P. Liddiard (eds) *An Ageing Population*, Sevenoaks: Hodder and Stoughton/Open University Press.

Hudson, B.L. and Macdonald, G.M. (1986) *Behavioural Social Work: An Introduction*, Basingstoke and London: Macmillan.
Jones, K. (1975) *Opening the Door: A Study of New Policies for the Mentally Handicapped*, London: Routledge.
Lawton, M.P. and Namehow, L. (1973) 'Ecology and the aging process' in C. Eisdorfer and N.P. Lawton (eds) *The Psychology of Adult Development and Aging*, Washington, DC: American Psychological Association.
Manthorpe, J. (1994) 'The family and informal care' in N. Malin (ed.) *Implementing Community Care*, Buckingham: Open University Press.
Manthorpe, J. (1996) 'The potential of social work in the rehabilitation of older people' in A.J. Squires (ed.) *Rehabilitation of the Older Person*, London: Chapman and Hall.
Morris, P. (1969) *Put Away: A Sociological Study of Institutions for the Mentally Retarded*, London: Routledge and Kegan Paul.
National Institute for Social Work (1988a) *Residential Care: A Positive Choice: Report of the Independent Review of Residential Care*, London: HMSO.
National Institute for Social Work (1988b) *Residential Care: The Research Reviewed*, London: HMSO.
Penhale, B. (1993) 'The abuse of elderly people: Considerations for practice', *British Journal of Social Work*, 23, pp.95–122.
Personal Social Services Council (1977) *Residential Care Reviewed*, London: PSSC.
Pitkeathley, J. (1995) 'Pushed to the limits', *Community Care*, 25 May, p.11.
Randall, P. (1990) 'New skills or old?', *Community Care*, 9 November, pp.26–7.
Seaton, (1993) 'Effective procedures: Critical or major incidents', *Elders: The Journal of Research and Practice*, 2, pp.33–9.
Smith, J. (1987) 'What makes a home homely?', *Health Service Journal*, 19 March, p.336.
Sutton, C. (1994) *Social Work, Community Work and Psychology*, Leicester: British Psychological Society.
Swann, P. (1982) 'Why some programmes fail', *Behavioural Social Work Review*, **3**, 2, pp.17–19.
Tooth, J. (1987) *Partnership in Caring: A Strategy for the Support of Frail Elderly People*, London: Age Concern, Greater London.
Wilkes, R. (1978) 'General philosophy and attitudes to aging', *Social Work Today*, **9**, 45, pp.14–16.
Wilkes, R. (1981) *Social Work with Undervalued Groups*, London and New York: Tavistock Publications. .
Yin, R.K. (1994) *Case Study Research: Design and Methods*, Applied Social Research Methods Series Vol. 5 (2nd edn), Thousand Oaks, CA and London: Sage Publications.

13 The prevention and management of elder abuse

Jonathan Parker

The acceptance of elder abuse as a social phenomenon has had a long history of development. The first professional interest in Britain is credited to Baker (1975) and Burston (1975 and 1977). Almost a decade later, Eastman (1984) raised the profile again by publishing his case studies of elder abuse. This activity had little impact. Phillipson and Biggs (1995) suggest this resulted from three factors:

1 society was still adjusting and responding to the realities of child abuse and domestic violence
2 the status of older people and those who worked with them was low
3 the lack of a precise definition of elder abuse.

The influence of North American research led to a resurgence of interest in the 1990s, culminating in the passing of such legislation as the National Health Service and Community Care Act 1990 and the Carers' (Recognition and Services) Act 1995.

This chapter will review some of the major definitions of abuse of older people, and debate some of the issues and problems arising from these. Theories concerning this abuse will then be debated. This will be followed by locating the case study in theoretical and conceptual approaches to abuse. While cognitive-behavioural approaches are deemed to be beneficial in working with elder abuse, this is not meant to imply a privileging of either psychopathological or socio-environmental aetiologies of abuse. Rather, it is presented as a micro-level response within the repertoire of the social work practitioner to issues that operate on numerous levels and across many dimensions within care management practice.

Definitions

Matters of definition are complex and subject to disagreement (McCreadie 1996). The many definitions proposed often lack clarity and precision (Glendenning 1993). Thus, there are difficulties in reading and drawing conclusions from the research. While the definitional debate remains unresolved, a general consensus has been reached on the types of abuse. Pillemer and Finkelhor (1988), Wolf and Pillemer (1989), Tomlin (1989), Penhale (1992) and Glendenning (1993) include variations of the following:

- physical violence
- involuntary isolation or imprisonment
- psychological, mental and verbal abuse
- neglect and wilful deprivation of necessary items
- material abuse.

Vernon and Bennett (1995) suggest that the problem of clarity in definition leads to a pragmatic response based on 'the principles of individual choice, autonomy and empowerment wherever possible' (p.178). This approach is adopted by Pritchard (1992), who recognises that a dangerous responsibility has been left with individual practitioners. The development of practice guidelines in many local authority social services departments throughout the early 1990s was underpinned by a value base promoting choice, privacy, independence, quality of life and protection where necessary. This approach was given further credence by the Social Services Inspectorate's (1993) report on older people in domestic settings.

McCreadie's first exploratory study into elder abuse identified the focus of concern as influential to those making definitions (McCreadie 1991). Pillemer and Finkelhor (1988) are influenced by their research purpose; Eastman (1984) was motivated by raising the issue of hard-pressed carers; Bennett (1990) wrote from the perspective of a medical practitioner. To ensure that a contextual approach was adopted that took into account personal, behavioural and taxonomic factors, McCreadie suggested there were seven aspects to a clear definition:

1. chronological age
2. setting of the abuse
3. abuser
4. direction of abuse – age and dependency of actors
5. intention
6. what constitutes abuse
7. categories of abuse.

She returned to this search for clarity later (McCreadie 1996). The importance of clarity lies in finding solutions. If, for instance, abuse only affects vulnerable persons, the policy response must be one of protection. The type of abuse, effects and setting determine the response.

The context of abuse is important. Contexts and settings are important to a cognitive-behavioural understanding of elder abuse. The context may provide the trigger or cue for a particular behaviour, or may provide the setting in which the behaviour is rewarded. Perceptions and associations based on past experiences may evoke certain responses in certain contemporary situations.

An approach that allows for the identification of abuse and can suggest possible strategies is promoted by Johns et al. (1991). An axial framework that considers and relates the violation of personal boundaries and the legitimacy of that violation helps to locate the abuse (see Figure 13.1).

This model also accords well with cognitive-behavioural approaches. It elicits questions about the severity and effects of the abuse which can be operationalised in cognitive and behavioural terms, and about observable

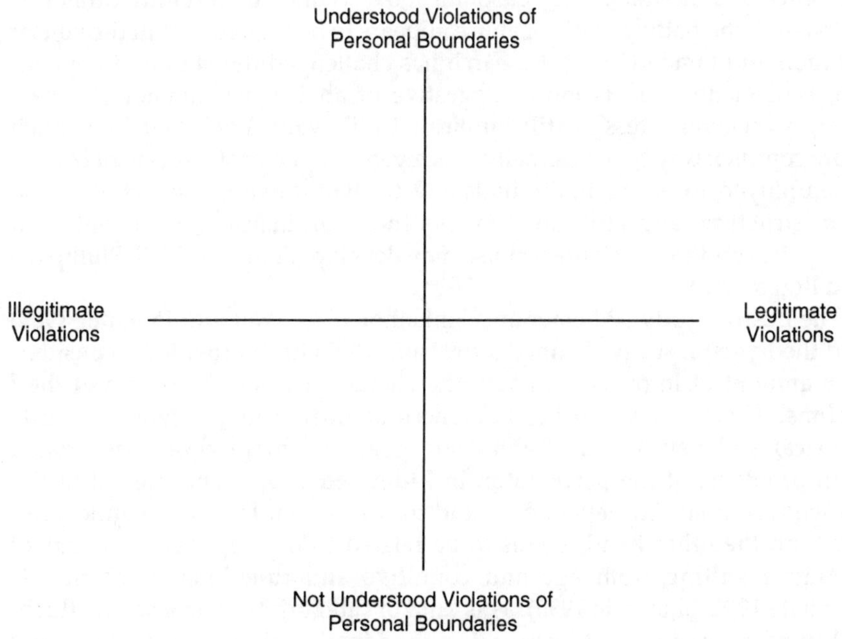

Figure 13.1 The violation of boundaries and identification of abuse

Source: Johns et al. (1991)

temporal factors such as persistence and frequency. It provides a framework to locate and respond to abuse, and from which to measure change. Too great an emphasis on general precision may prescribe a rigidity which fails to take account of individual factors and the socio-cultural context of the abuse. This model allows precision at the level of the individual, and thus appears more responsive and sensitive to each situation, while preserving a sense of clarity.

Different definitions were employed in the studies, and it is difficult to draw any conclusions from this comparison. It is important to note, however, that abuse of all types occurs, and that the search for understanding continues in order to identify the most appropriate and effective interventive strategy.

Characteristics and risk factors

Caregiver stress was identified as a common cause of abuse in early studies (Skolnick and Skolnick 1977; Eastman 1984). While this certainly cannot be dismissed, the pathogenesis of abuse appears to be located within the abuser (Vernon and Bennett 1995). Research has challenged the notion of dependent, frail victim, and is more suggestive of abuser dependency (Penhale 1992). Caregiver stress is still implicated (Sijuwade 1995), but in a much more complex way than originally conceived. Caregiver stress can, of course, be employed to blame individuals and to play down or deflect attention from structural and attitudinal factors that marginalise older people and create the conditions in which abuse may develop (Sijuwade 1995; Phillipson and Biggs 1995).

The Boston study (Pillemer and Finkelhor 1988; Wolf and Pillemer 1989) and the Ryerson study (Podnieks 1990 and 1992) have provided a considerable amount of information about the characteristics of abusers and their victims. There appear to be differences according to the type of abuse. Physical and psychological abuse are generally more closely associated with problems of the perpetrator, including emotional and mental health difficulties, financial dependence and dysfunctional family dynamics. Neglect, on the other hand, seems to be related to the dependency needs of victims resulting from age and cognitive and functional impairments (Penhale 1992; Sijuwade 1995). This kind of categorisation has been influential in more recent work concerning the identification of risk, abuse and intervention (Kosberg and Nahmiash 1996).

Researchers are attempting to identify a range of characteristics that acknowledges the interconnections and complex interplay of factors concerning abusers and victims. According to Booth et al. (1996), victims are, *inter alia*, more likely to be white, female, over 75, dependent on the abuser and suffering from memory loss. Abusers are typically relatives, financially dependent on the victim and with poor self-control. While Booth et al. (1996) rely, to a large extent, on North American research for these profiles, these are useful for a general understanding of possible interplays among factors and, therefore, are of fundamental importance for designing and implementing effective interventions.

As these characteristics are wide and varied, so are the causal factors identified. Booth et al. (1996) suggest that society and environment act as a backdrop against which abuse is possible. Society and the wider environment interact with the local culture, family history of violence and the caregiver stress and individual psychopathology. Ansello (1996) agrees that unicausal theories are simplistic. By adopting an 'interactive perspective', first proposed by Steinmetz (1988), Ansello (1996) identifies five risk factors:

1 a history of either substance abuse or mental ill-health in either the caregiver or recipient of care
2 a previous history of elder abuse in a caregiving context
3 the financial dependence of the caregiver on the older person
4 chronic illness or impairment affecting the older person, who also lacks informal supports
5 chronic illness or impairment affecting the older person which exceeds the capacity of the caregiver.

Glendenning (1993) and Homer and Gilleard (1990) concur with this multicausal or interactive approach. While caregiver stress is not the sole causal factor in abuse, and large numbers of caregivers under considerable stress do not abuse the person they care for (McCreadie 1996), it is not a factor that can be easily dismissed. Steinmetz (1988) proposed that it was the *perception* of stress that was correlated with the abuse, rather than the stress itself. The individual's perception of events is, of course, based upon multiple factors, including past experiences of coping with stress (Kelly 1955; Dattilio 1994), perceived outcomes (Lefcourt 1976), beliefs in self-efficacy (Bandura 1977), belief systems (Ellis 1962 and 1979; Beck 1976) and social support. The perceptions are further affected by socio-environmental and health factors. These interconnect to form the conditions in which possible abuse can occur.

An understanding of the risk factors discussed above leads us to a consideration of the theoretical conceptions derived to help understand elder abuse. It is clear, however, that individual differences, experiences and beliefs are important factors. This suggests the potential benefits of an approach which deals with the interaction of person and environment, of beliefs, perceptions and subsequent action. Cognitive-behavioural approaches acknowledge the individual response to situations and environments.

Theoretical frameworks

A number of models have been developed for intervention in cases of elder abuse. Authors provide between three and five distinct but interconnected models developed from Phillips's earlier three-model framework (Phillips 1986). Glendenning (1993) describes the first model as being situational, the second as based on social exchange theory, and the third on symbolic interactionism. Phillipson and Biggs (1995) add a pathological model, and along with Biggs et al. (1995), a social construction/political economy model. Ansello (1996) takes a slightly modified approach, subsuming symbolic interactionism within exchange theories, reintroducing transgenerational violence theories, and including a vulnerability hypothesis. In this section, we shall briefly review the four models. (Social constructionist approaches have been integrated with symbolic interactionism, since the two converge in many respects):

- psychopathological models and theories of transgenerational violence
- social exchange theories
- symbolic interactionist approaches, and social construction and political economy models
- the vulnerability hypothesis, and excessive situational demands.

Following this review, a multi-factor model that links the theories and the perceptions, beliefs and constructions of key individuals will be proposed which links these models with a cognitive-behavioural approach. While cognitive and behavioural approaches have been used to treat and manage elder abuse, there has been no development of a cognitive-behavioural model to explain some of the abusive situations which occur.

Psychopathological models link the abuse to the social and mental health status of the abuser (Phillipson and Biggs 1995). Characteristics and risk factors indicate an association between the mental and emotional well-being of the abuser and the occurrence of abuse. Ansello (1996) points out that this model only fits in a small number of cases. The family dynamics, belief and interaction systems, however, may have such an effect on family members as to develop and pass on patterns of violent interaction. Past violence is seen as the best predictor of future abuse. This model is limited, since it relates only to physical violence. Having said this, it does offer potential for positive and effective intervention in these cases. Violent behaviour patterns are seen as learned responses, they can therefore be unlearned, and more adaptive behaviours learned to replace them.

Social exchange theories also include a cognitive-behavioural element. Interactions between people involve rewards or benefits, and punishments or costs (Nye 1982; Thibault and Kelley 1959; Klein and White 1996). People seek to maximise rewards and to minimise costs to self and others in their interactions (Glendenning 1993). When this distributive justice or 'norm of reciprocity' (Finch 1989; Frude 1990) fails, then anger, resentment and potential for abuse may occur (Ansello 1996). Societal assumptions about older people and changed relationships over time may contribute to changed perceptions of the costs and benefits of interactions and create the conditions necessary for abuse to occur.

There are difficulties in testing this theory empirically, and it does not allow us to predict abuse (Glendenning 1993). However, it is useful in planning interventions that will maximise the rewards for the individuals involved. The importance of individual assessment and identification of positive reinforcements is indicated.

In *symbolic interactionist approaches*, there is a constant renegotiation over time of the meanings assigned to interactions in order to achieve a workable and valid consensus. Where there are mismatches in assigned meanings, either termination of the sequences of interaction or conflict may result. Elder abuse is therefore conceptualised as inappropriate or inadequate role-enactment. Examples may be found in the association between past and present perceptions of the capabilities of the person suffering from dementia (Glendenning 1993), or the shift from quantification to qualification of the sense of burden (Ansello 1996).

Social construction and political economy models take symbolic interactionism further, and see a wider political influence creating and maintaining many of the social inequalities faced by older people.

The *vulnerability hypothesis* may derive much of its power from social constructions about older people internalised by individuals. It is suggested that incapacities and impairments render a person frail, and therefore at risk of exploitation. If dependency causes vulnerability and stress in caregivers, then intervention must seek to reduce dependency and increase benefits in exchanges with caregivers. There are clear links here with *situational models*. While situational stress (Skolnick and Skolnick 1977) has been challenged as a complete explanation for abuse (Phillips 1986), the interactions within contexts and perceptions of events and situations affect future actions (Clipp and George 1993; Ansello 1996).

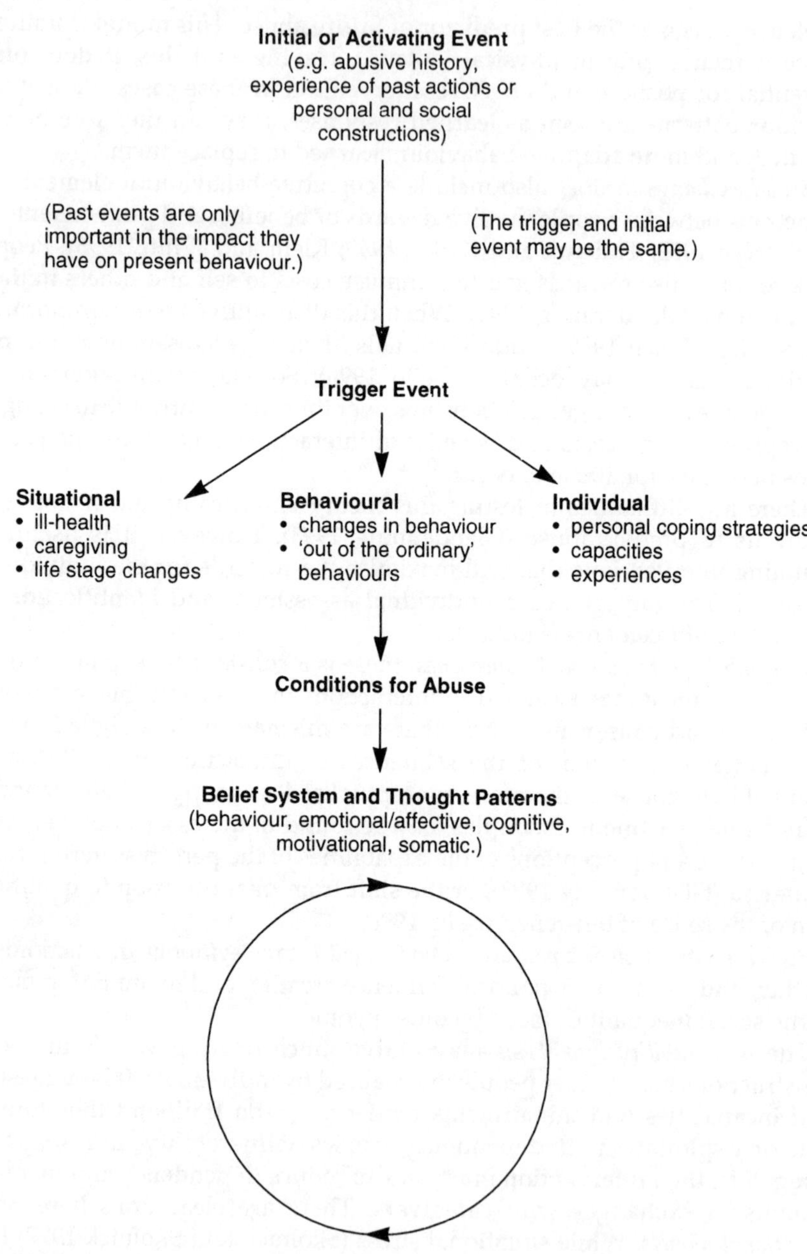

Figure 13.2 A cognitive-behavioural model of elder abuse

The models are distinguished for heuristic purposes. It is clear that they all interconnect and overlap (Glendenning 1993; Penhale and Kingston 1995). The importance of theoretical models for the practitioner lies not only in explanatory and predictive values, but in planning an effective response. By utilising present theoretical conceptions, we can see in the following cognitive-behavioural model a useful framework from which to approach elder abuse and plan interventions.

Cognitive-behavioural thinking links a person's behaviour with the thoughts and beliefs he or she has about outcomes and consequences in certain situations (Hawton et al. 1989; Trower et al. 1988; Sheldon 1995). It is not necessarily the event or situation that leads to consequences, but one's beliefs about and evaluations of these events. Trigger events or antecedents may activate beliefs and distort thinking patterns. When the association is made between event and thought, the conditions for abuse to occur may be satisfied. An event may be assuming a caregiving role, or changed relationships and roles resulting from physical or mental impairment. In themselves, these will not inevitably cause abuse. Potential abuse is more likely to be actualised when beliefs about the event lead to harmful responses to the initial conditions. A framework for a cognitive-behavioural model is shown in Figure 13.2. Two case examples demonstrate the model in practice.

Case example: The Jacksons

Mrs Jackson has been married for 46 years to Jim, an ex-soldier and truck driver. Jim drank heavily throughout his life, often spending the housekeeping on drink and returning home late at night in an argumentative and aggressive mood. His continued heavy drinking led to increased impairment of his memory and problem-solving skills. After a fall resulting in a broken hip and a bout of bronchitis, he became very dependent on Mrs Jackson. The changed relationship triggered memories of past problems, resentment and anger, and feelings of low self-worth. She took on new responsibilities in line with her sense of duty and feelings of 'just desserts'. She felt she *must, ought* and *should* care for him, and that this would never have happened if she had been 'a good wife'. Her low self-esteem was reinforced by his constant criticism of her 'inability to do things properly', and his anger towards her. She also suffered from high blood pressure, which led to even greater feelings of inadequacy. This in turn increased her stress levels and her husband's criticism of her. The changed relationship exacerbated the abuse experienced by Mrs Jackson, and reconfirmed her beliefs in her own low self-worth.

The model helps to understand matters from the perspective of the abused person. It may be argued that this leads to blame and pathologising the victim. This is not the case. As can be seen by reference to Mrs Jackson's case, the situation developed from experiences, interactions and perceptions over time, and in response to abusive actions by another. The model also suggests possibilities for empowerment, utilising alternatives and retaking control. The model may also be used in respect of the abuser, as the following case study demonstrates.

Case example: The Hunts

Mr Hunt married a former girlfriend after his first wife committed suicide in the early years of the Second World War. He worked as a long-distance lorry driver, and was away from home for long periods. After retiring, he aimed to spend his time travelling with his wife. On a trip to visit a daughter, Mrs Hunt was taken ill. She suffered a small stroke, from which she recovered physically within a short space of time. Unfortunately, her memory did not recover, and proceeded to deteriorate. Mr Hunt became frustrated with her continual forgetting of everyday things, and especially her constant requests to go to the toilet. He believed she was doing this on purpose, and could, if she tried, change this behaviour and remember things. His frustration led him to take over domestic roles, personal hygiene and responsibility for dressing – although with prompting and time, she was still able to manage these tasks – and to telling her and others in her presence that she was 'useless' and 'like a vegetable'.

Mr Hunt's belief in the deliberateness of her actions and her incapacity led to actions that outpaced her, treated her like a child, and reinforced his thinking as she internalised a lack of capacity and low self-worth. This led to further frustration on his part.

There are, of course, limitations to the cognitive-behavioural model. It does not, for instance, directly acknowledge elder abuse as a distinct category of abuse. This is important, as many of the recent developments in understanding and managing elder abuse have stemmed from a recognition of the specific needs of older people and the fact that abuse is situated within a particular social and political context. The emphasis on small environments may be used to deflect attention from socio-economic factors that influence and maintain the conditions that make abuse more likely. The cognitive-behavioural approach does, however, propose a multi-causal hypothesis that sees each case in individual terms and provides a specific framework for intervention.

The model has relevance across the major theoretical frameworks designed to explain elder abuse. Situational triggers may lead to certain behaviours or events after mediation via the cognitions of those involved. The personal experiences and characteristics of individuals – including maladaptive coping strategies – affect and influence events and outcomes, but the emphasis is not on simplistic and linear cause-and-effect relationships, such as 'stress or pathology result in abuse', but on a more complex interplay of factors that are contingent on the perception and actions of significant people involved.

Such a model lends itself to empirical validation, because behavioural change can be rigorously evaluated, and change in belief systems can be correlated with this. Assessment is fundamental in cognitive-behavioural approaches (Kirk 1989; Parker and Randall 1997). Objective, quantifiable measures can be employed alongside self-report and qualitative reports of change from those concerned. Hawton et al. (1989) emphasise the importance of expressing concepts in operational terms, the empirical validation of treatment and replicability. This allows for definitions that take account of individual and case-specific factors which do not demand a global definition of elder abuse.

Interventions

The search for effective interventions is still in its early stages in the UK (Penhale 1992). There is continuing debate between the need for increased protective services and to develop therapeutic and support services (Bulmer et al. 1994). Penhale (1993) and Pritchard (1992) have commented on what they see as a lack of protective legislation, but also indicate the rich and flexible responses possible under existing legislation.

Intervention undertaken from the perspective of social work values is important. Phillipson (1994) suggests that an empowerment approach can operate with carers and older people. Support groups, sensitivity and flexibility in services can assist caregivers, while advocacy, self-help and collective action can assist the older person. Approaches must be transparent however, and this is one advantage of cognitive-behavioural approaches. The values underpinning any action will influence that action and its conceptualisation (Vernon and Bennett 1995). A co-ordinated and multidisciplinary approach (Pritchard 1992), the need for training (Penhale 1993; Phillipson 1994) and clear procedural guidelines (Penhale 1993; McCreadie 1996) are of paramount importance in establishing a basis for effective action.

Homer and Gilleard (1990 and 1994) suggest that behavioural approaches may be more effective than increased care services and practical support (see also Reay 1994). This was taken up by Manthorpe (1993) but she does not debate the point further. However, McCreadie (1996) argues that services are important, but depend on the type of abuse, the reasons for it, and the decision-making capacities of those involved (see also Sadler 1994).

There is evidence that cognitive-behavioural approaches are useful in responding to situations of abuse. Keller (1996) reports favourably on an anger management training programme for care staff in institutional settings. It was found to lessen stress, promote relaxation and self-control, assist in the identification of triggers, and promote the adoption of more adaptive behavioural and cognitive responses. This echoes work on crisis intervention and cognitive-behavioural strategies where violence and aggression are issues (Hamberger and Holtzworth-Munroe 1994; Wistedt and Freeman 1994).

One of the most developed approaches is the staircase model (Breckman and Adelman 1988). Intervention proceeds through three stages – reluctance, recognition and rebuilding – with mentally competent victims of elder abuse. The limitations are that the model does not suggest intervention for the abuser, which may be more warranted (McCreadie 1991), and incompetent victims are excluded. Despite this, the model lends itself to cognitive-behavioural strategies that may be transferred across settings, as explained below.

At the first stage, *reluctance*, the practitioner works to identify feelings of isolation, guilt and self-blame with the intention of increasing self-acceptance and identifying appropriate alternatives. As well as practical support and information, an approach akin to rational-emotive-behavioural therapy is suggested. Irrational and distorted thinking and imperative statements are identified and matched against reality (Ellis 1962 and 1979). Throughout the second stage, *recognition*, the person is encouraged to seek more adaptive and rational thought patterns, and to increase self-acceptance and lessen their social isolation. In the final stage, *rebuilding*, older people pursue active strategies for leading their lives free from mistreatment with the experience of self-efficacy and knowledge of appropriate responses in given situations (Bandura 1977).

Intervention is indicative of the practitioner's or agency's theoretical and conceptual base. Thus, the service-delivery perspective implies a stress perspective, and the legal model implies a vulnerability/dependency conceptualisation. While cognitive-behavioural intervention certainly has clear theoretical implications, it does not privilege one conception above another. Rather, it acknowledges a multi-model approach to conceptualisation. One advantage of the approach lies in acknowledgement of its limitations. Cognitive-behavioural approaches transcend barriers and present options in certain given situations under certain circumstances. The clarity in identifying behaviours, interactions and interacting factors and situations leads to well-formulated and measurable actions for change. Such an approach takes into account individual case factors, and acknowledges the fundamental importance of user participation in the process (Sadler 1994). It is situation-specific. The cognitive-behavioural approach offers a return of control to the stressed and out-of-control individual. It provides effective and non-stigmatising coping strategies for dealing with abuse.

Case study: The Walkers

Mr and Mrs Walker married over fifty years ago. They met in a park before the outbreak of the Second World War. Mrs Walker had asked for a light for her cigarette and Mr Walker had been so impressed by her 'bravery' that he asked her out. During the war years, Mr Walker served in the army, while Mrs Walker stayed with his mother. After a bombing raid in which their house was ruined, Mrs Walker moved nearer to her husband, who was posted to a barracks near Devon. They have been together ever since, spending no time apart, and undertaking the same hobbies and pastimes – walking, ballroom dancing and going to the cinema. They have two children, now grown up with families of their own.

Five years ago, they moved to their present bungalow because it was easier to heat, clean and manage. Mr Walker had developed Padget's disease, and suffered from arthritis. This affected his ballroom dancing, walking and gardening. The painkillers he was prescribed helped ease the pain. He also took a large whisky each night to help him sleep.

About two years ago, Mrs Walker had a fall, resulting in a severe bump to the head. She was said to have recovered her physical health quite quickly. From that time onwards, however, Mr Walker described an increasing tearfulness, depression, confusion and worry in Mrs Walker. This now resulted in her not leaving him alone, following him from room to room, and continually packing and unpacking clothes into a suitcase. Mr Walker was also experiencing increased pain resulting from his arthritis and Padget's disease. Their daughter, a legal secretary, rang the local social services department for assistance.

The initial assessment focused on the concerns expressed by the Walkers' daughter, the descriptions of Mrs Walker's changed behaviour and Mr Walker's experience of stress, changed relationship and roles, and his ill-health. It was during these initial exploratory discussions that concerns were highlighted. When Mr Walker described his wife's behaviour, he became distressed and animated. He expressed how angry he felt about the unfairness of the situation, how he could not help shouting at and 'belittling' his wife, and how he had grabbed the suitcase from her, thrown it across the room, pushed her onto the bed and slapped her. He was visibly upset when describing these incidents. These concerns became the focus of the assessment.

After talking through the problems arising from the interview, and after consultation with the team manager, health visitor and general practitioner, it was decided with Mr and Mrs Walker to work with them towards reducing Mr Walker's stress, reducing his anger and seeking ways of distracting and adapting some of the more frustrating of Mrs Walker's behaviours. As an adjunct to this, a package of services aimed at motivating Mrs Walker, providing Mr Walker with a break from the strains of caring and providing direct help in the home was devised. Mr Walker was reluctant to agree to help in the home, and initially felt that he ought to be the one who cared for his wife. He therefore refused respite care at this stage.

In order to assist in meeting the three agreed aims, further assessment work was carried out. This comprised undertaking a functional analysis of his anger. His anger was operationalised as shouting and swearing at Mrs Walker and calling her names. These were chosen because of the frequency with which they happened. Slapping was not included, although it had occurred, since this appeared to be a single incident. Alongside this, a social history was taken to find out about past relationships and significant events, coping strategies and possible alternatives and/or reinforcements. It was felt that Mr Walker's stress and anxiety were related to his anger, and that at this point it would be better to concentrate on his anger. At the same time, however, and in an attempt to begin to increase his feelings of self-control, ability to cope and care, Mr Walker was asked to record a functional analysis of Mrs Walker's packing/unpacking behaviour. This comprised an ABC assessment, where A represented the antecedents (what happened prior to the behaviour), B was the behaviour itself, and C referred to the consequences occurring immediately after the behaviour. Samples of the records are shown in Boxes 13.1 and 13.2.

The results of these initial analyses showed a fairly consistent pattern, in which Mr Walker became angry, shouted and swore, felt guilty, and gave Mrs Walker extra and special attention. It also seemed to be the case that her packing/unpacking behaviour led to their spending time together, and occurred when she had little else to distract or occupy her. It was interesting to note, from the social history, that Mrs Walker worked as a food packer for many years.

Following this baseline assessment period, further exploration of Mr Walker's anger was undertaken. A cognitive-behavioural analysis was

Box 13.1 Sample of ABC recording sheets (Mr Walker)

A Antecedent	B Behaviour	C Consequence
Jean kept mumbling something about her mother. I was trying to get the washing-up done after lunch, but she wouldn't leave me alone.	I told her she was a stupid old cow and that she'd better go away and let me get on before I put her in a home.	She burst into tears. I had to calm her down, and so sat and cuddled her. I said sorry.
I couldn't find my shirts. After looking, I found them crumpled in a pile in a bag under the bed.	I threw the shirts at her and asked if she knew how long it took me to iron them. I stormed out.	She cried. I came in after about ten minutes, made sure she was all right and made a cup of tea.

Box 13.2 Sample of ABC recording sheets (Mrs Walker)

A Antecedent	B Behaviour	C Consequence
I was in the garden. It was early afternoon, I think.	I heard activity in the bedroom. She was putting the clean clothes from the wardrobe into a suitcase.	I took them out, told her not to do this, and led her into the living room. We had a cup of tea.
I must have nodded off in my chair. It was about 4 p.m. I don't really know what happened.	Jean came in with a carrier bag packed full of dirty and clean clothes. She took them out on the coffee table and put them back again. She did this several times.	I got fed up and cross and took them off her. We went for a stroll around the garden.

undertaken (see Box 13.3). When he became angry and frustrated, he felt he was letting down his wife, his family and his values. He believed he was bad, weak, and felt ashamed that he responded in this way. Mr Walker's beliefs about his anger led to him trying harder, and increased his physical stress and self-blame and loathing, thus increasing his mental stress.

Box 13.3 Cognitive-behavioural analysis (Mr Walker)

A Activating Event	B Beliefs (About A)	C Consequences
I told her she was useless and would be better off dead.	I do not think I am a good husband. I am a spiteful and vindictive person and should be more sympathetic.	I try to look after her. I give her extra special attention. I try harder.
I pushed her out of the way when she was following me around the home with a bag of clothes.	I try to ensure the house is clean, that she is looked after by me, and not to be so selfish. I feel I can't carry on, I'm tired and not able to do a good job.	When I think she's doing it deliberately to get at me, I feel I must have been a very bad husband.

As a result of these assessments, a meeting was held with Mr and Mrs Walker to determine ways of assisting them to take back control and learn alternative ways of coping with their present situation. Interventive strategies included anger management – comprising the recognition of anger, establishment of self-talk and replacement techniques – providing information and education about Mrs Walker's condition and about the understandability of his frustration and anger but the unacceptability of its outcome, and relaxation training for Mr Walker. They also included the development of a programme of differential reinforcement regarding Mrs Walker's behaviour. This included using distraction techniques in the antecedent phase.

The overall programme was quite intensive, and employed the services of a senior social work practitioner and care officer staff. It also used the Walkers' daughter, and Mr Walker, however, and offered the potential for generalisation to other areas in their lives, and thus genuine empowerment to take back control. The high costs of the initial input could be justified in the longer term by avoiding future abuse and lessening the need for a greater level of service input.

The programme ran over a two-week baseline period, followed by eight weeks' anger management and relaxation training and the concurrent programme of differential reinforcement. An outline of the two programmes follows.

Programme to assist with managing anger

1 *Introduction*

Topic What makes you angry?

Method Discussion and exploration

Summary and homework Monitoring anger, recognising triggers and situations

2 *Review of last week*

Topic What happens when you get angry?

Method Self-examination and recognition of specific situations, formal input concerning anger and arousal

Summary and homework Continued self-examination and report

3 *Review of previous week*

Topic How would you like to react?

Method Discussion and exploration; examination of personal coping styles; barriers to effective coping; setting feasible targets and goals

Summary and homework Self-report and examination throughout the week

4 *Review of previous week*

Topic How to keep calm

Method Relaxation techniques; breathing exercises; muscle relaxation

Summary and action plan for home practice

5 *Review of previous week*

Topic How not to let anger take control

Method Self-talk, instruction (such as talking through the situation as it happened, waiting and talking through an alternative way of acting) and positive reinforcement rehearsal and role-play

Summary and action plan for practising during the week

6 *Review of the previous week*

Topic Review of relaxation and self-talk exercises

Method Further rehearsal and practice

Summary and continuation at home

7 *Review*

Future plans and generalising the learning

8 *End and evaluation*

Agreement

The following is the agreement drawn up between Mr Walker, Mrs Walker and Exford Social Services Department:

1 Mr Walker will sit with Mrs Walker for one hour each afternoon and look through photograph albums, booklets and slides of places visited in the past.
2 Mr Walker will leave the washing-up until later.
3 If he goes into the garden, he will ask Mrs Walker to help clear leaves, weeds and sweet papers into a bag.
4 If she seems restless, Mrs Walker will be encouraged to pack newspapers in a pile or empty a drawer to tidy it. This will be undertaken in a matter-of-fact manner.

5 If she is found to be packing and unpacking clothes, Mr Walker will count to ten and ignore the behaviour.

Monitoring by Mr Walker of Mrs Walker's behaviour, self-report and monitoring of his anger and response, discussion with Mrs Walker, her daughter, the general practitioner and health visitor, and observational reports of the care officer allowed rigorous evaluation of the interventions. The evaluation relied to a large extent on the honesty of Mr Walker, but was taken in conjunction with these other sources.

It was not possible to determine which programme effected change, whether one was more effective than another or which parts worked best, as both the programme of differential reinforcement and the anger management programme ran alongside one another. However, it was possible to document change and use the visual displays to increase work and motivation with all parties involved who saw the positive benefits of the work. Parts of these are shown in Figures 13.3 and 13.4. The following short extract from the care officer's report also demonstrates the changes made:

> Mr Walker was very suspicious of me at first. He followed me about the house and checked everything I did. He seemed to think I wanted to take over and he is a very proud man. Since Mrs Walker has stopped packing and unpacking her clothes as often he appears calmer and more relaxed. In fact, he has stopped shouting at things being out of place and is much more patient with Jean. He has now asked me to help with the housework so he can spend more time with Jean.

In this case, the parties were willing to engage in work, and acknowledged the difficulties and potential for abuse. Mr Walker's actions could be categorised as 'understood but illegitimate violations of personal boundaries' (Johns et al. 1991). Mr Walker believed he was a bad husband who was not fulfilling what was expected of him by himself, his family and society. This in turn led to affective distress and maladaptive behavioural responses. His shouting, swearing and belittling of his wife reinforced his belief in his inadequacies, which led to greater frustration and greater possibility for maladaptive response. By altering the contingencies and adapting his thinking processes, change was possible.

Service users often do not acknowledge difficulties and the need to change. When the risks involved are not acknowledged, matters are much more difficult, and questions of ethics arise in implementing programmes without the participation or consent of other people involved. However, it is possible to work with someone who does not agree they have a problem. The author worked with a man in a residential setting who targeted cognitively impaired women for inappropriate touching. Although seen on

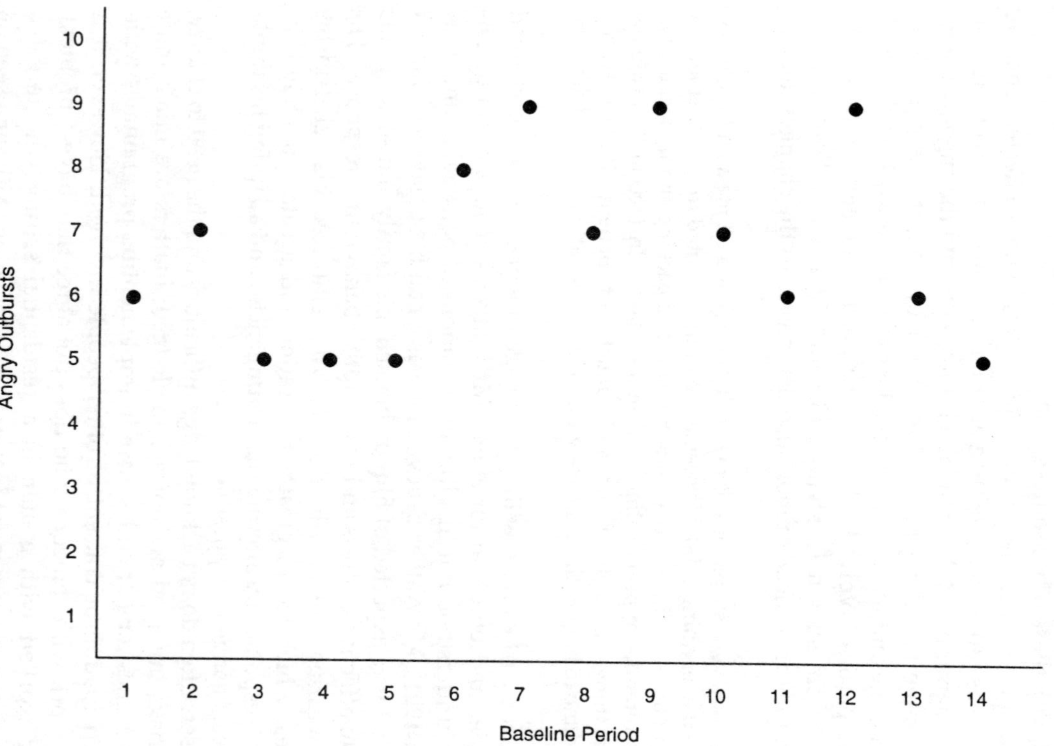

Figure 13.3 Mr Walker: Outbursts of anger during the baseline period

Note: Anger was operationalised as shouting, swearing and verbal insults directed at Mrs Walker.

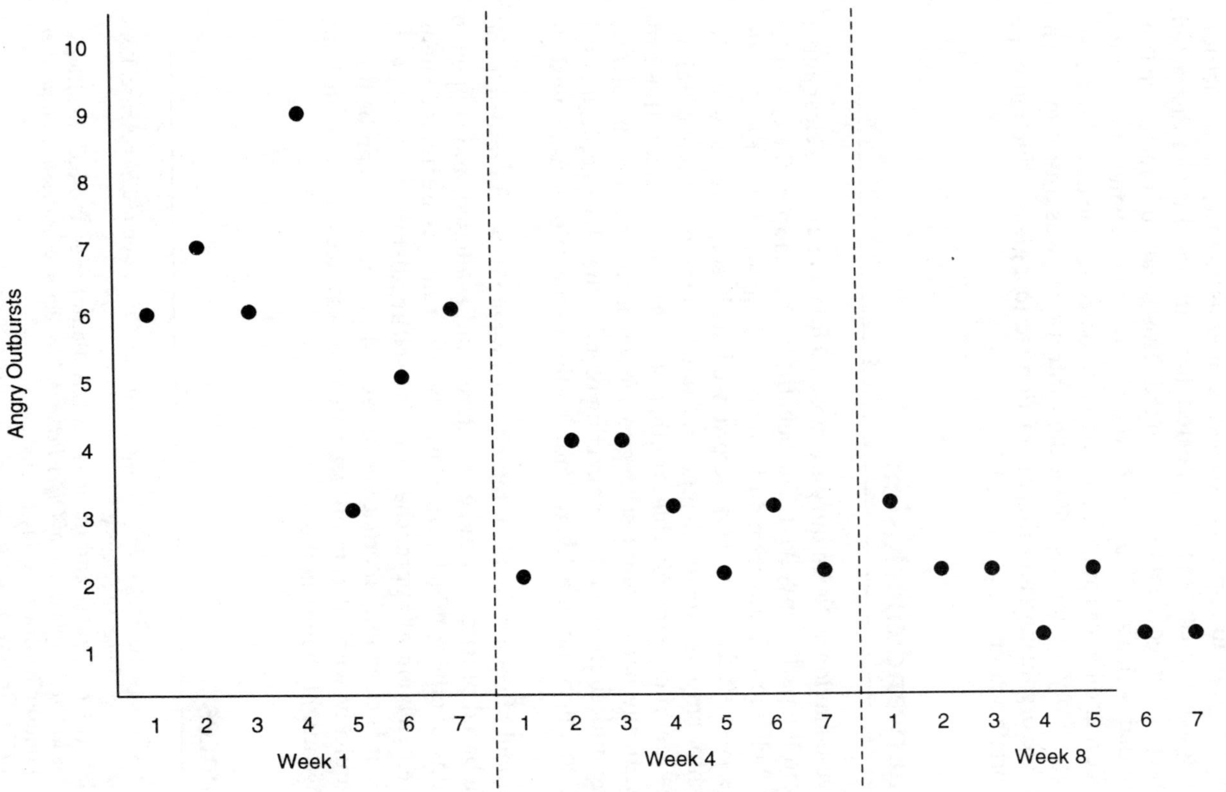

Figure 13.4 Mr Walker: Outbursts of anger at selected points during the intervention

many occasions, he offered plausible excuses for his behaviour, and denied any attempt to fondle or touch these women. It was explained to him that his actions would be monitored to check the stories. On a number of occasions, he was seen to approach women to offer assistance, but in fact fondled and touched them when it appeared that staff were busy or distracted. The triggers or antecedents were changed. This meant in practice that he was provided with a small task immediately after lunch, when staff were at their busiest and he was most likely to touch someone. The task chosen was collecting, emptying and replacing the ashtrays. He was a tidy man who was used to organising, and this distraction led to a great reduction in his inappropriate actions.

Summary and conclusion

Cognitive-behavioural techniques are most useful when there is clear agreement from the parties involved. The benefits of these approaches lie in the somatic, behavioural, affective and cognitive changes, as described in the Walker's case study. They also accord well with social work values of partnership, empowerment, change and hope. Cognitive-behavioural approaches are often generalisable to other settings, and provide those involved with alternative coping strategies. However, in certain circumstances involving undesirable behaviour affecting other vulnerable people, it is still possible to intervene effectively without the perpetrator's clear wish to change.

The model offers a valuable intervention strategy based on research and evidence-based practice. It can be monitored and evaluated, and is open to the scrutiny of others, which is increasingly important in care management. Cognitive-behavioural approaches are also self-regulatory. When they do not work, it is clear, and alternatives or revised programmes can be implemented quickly without committing valuable resources in the vain hope that things might change in the future.

References

Alzheimer's Disease Society (1993) *Position Paper on Prevention of Elder Abuse*, London: Alzheimer's Disease Society.

Ansello, E.F. (1996) 'Causes and theories' in L.A. Baumhover and S.C. Beall (eds) *Abuse, Neglect and Exploitation of Older Persons: Strategies for Assessment and Intervention*, London: Jessica Kingsley Publishers.

Baker, A. (1975) 'Granny bashing', *Modern Geriatrics*, 5, pp.20–4.

Bandura, A. (1977) *Social Learning Theory*, Englewood Cliffs, NJ: Prentice-Hall.
Beck, A.T. (1976) *Cognitive Theory and the Emotional Disorders*, New York: International University Press.
Bennett, G. (1990) 'Action on elder abuse in the '90s: New definition will help', *Geriatric Medicine*, April, pp.53–4.
Bennett, G. and Kingston, P. (1993) *Elder Abuse: Concepts, Theories and Interventions*, London: Chapman and Hall.
Biggs, S., Phillipson, C. and Kingston, P. (1995) *Elder Abuse in Perspective*, Milton Keynes: Open University Press.
Booth, B.K., Bruno, A.A. and Marin, R. (1996) 'Psychological therapy with abused and neglected patients' in L.A. Baumhover and S.C. Beall (eds) *Abuse, Neglect, and Exploitation of Older Persons: Strategies for Assessment and Intervention*, London: Jessica Kingsley Publishers.
Breckman, R.S. and Adelman, R.D. (1988) *Strategies for Helping Victims of Elder Mistreatment*, London: Sage Publications.
Bulmer, J., Craig, Y. and Wilkinson G. (1994) 'What can we do about elder abuse?' *Elders*, 3, pp.14–17.
Burston, G. (1975) 'Granny battering', *British Medical Journal*, 3, p.592.
Burston, G. (1977) 'Do your elderly patients live in fear of being battered?' *Modern Geriatrics*, 7, pp.54–5.
Clipp, E. and George, L. (1993) 'Dementia and cancer: A comparison of spouse caregivers', *Gerontologist*, 33, pp.534–41.
Dattilio, F.M. (1994) 'Families in crisis' in F.M. Dattilio and A. Freeman (eds) *Cognitive-behavioral Strategies in Crisis Intervention*, New York and London: Guilford Press.
Decalmer, P. (1993) 'Clinical presentation' in P. Decalmer and F. Glendenning (eds) *The Mistreatment of Elderly People*, London: Sage Publications.
Decalmer, P. and Glendenning, F. (eds) (1993) *The Mistreatment of Elderly People*, London: Sage Publications.
Eastman, M. (1984) *Old Age Abuse*, Mitcham: Age Concern.
Ellis, A. (1962) *Reason and Emotion in Psychotherapy*, New York: Lyle Stuart.
Ellis, A. (1979) 'The theory of rational-emotive therapy' in A. Ellis and J.M. Whitely (eds) *Theoretical and Empirical Foundations of Rational-emotive Therapy*, Monterey, CA: Brooks/Cole.
Finch, J. (1989) *Family Obligations and Social Change*, Cambridge: Polity Press.
Frude, N. (1990) *Understanding Family Problems: A Psychological Approach*, Chichester: John Wiley.
Glendenning, F. (1993) 'What is elder abuse and neglect?' in P. Decalmer and F. Glendenning (eds) *The Mistreatment of Elderly People*, London: Sage Publications.
Grafstrom,, M., Norberg, A. and Winblad, B. (1994) 'Abuse is in the eye of the beholder', *Scandinavian Journal of Social Medicine*, 21, pp.247–55.
Griffiths, A. and Roberts, G. (eds) (1995) *The Law and Elderly People* (2nd edn), London: Routledge.
Hamberger, L.K. and Holtzworth-Munroe, A. (1994) 'Partner violence' in F.M. Dattilio and A. Freeman (eds) *Cognitive-behavioral Strategies in Crisis Intervention*, New York and London: Guilford Press.
Hawton, K., Salkovskis, P., Kirk, J. and Clark, D. (eds) (1989) *Cognitive Behaviour Therapy for Psychiatric Problems*, Oxford: Oxford University Press.
Homer, A. and Gilleard, C. (1990) 'Abuse of elderly people by their carers', *British Medical Journal*, 301, pp.1,359–62.

Homer, A. and Gilleard, C. (1994) 'The effect of in-patient respite care on elderly patients and their carers', Age and Ageing, 23, pp.274–6.
Johns, S., Hydle, I. and Aschjem, O. (1991) 'The act of abuse: A two-headed monster of injury and offense', *Journal of Elder Abuse and Neglect*, 3, pp.53–64.
Keller, B.H. (1996) 'A model abuse prevention training program for long-term care staff' in L.A. Baumhover and S.C. Beall (eds) *Abuse, Neglect and Exploitation of Older Persons: Strategies for Assessment and Intervention*, London: Jessica Kingsley Publishers.
Kelly, G.A. (1955) *The Theory of Personal Constructs*, Vol. 1, New York: W.W. Norton.
Kingston, P. and Penhale, B. (1995) *Family Violence and the Caring Professions*, Basingstoke: Macmillan.
Kirk, J. (1989) 'Cognitive-behavioural assessment' in K. Hawton, P. Salkovskis, J. Kirk and D. Clark (eds) *Cognitive Behaviour Therapy for Psychiatric Problems*, Oxford: Oxford University Press.
Klein, D.M. and White, J.M. (1996) *Family Theories: An Introduction*, London: Sage.
Kosberg, J.I. and Nahmiash, D. (1996) 'Characteristics of victims and perpetrators and milieus of abuse and neglect' in L.A. Baumhover and S.C. Beall (eds) *Abuse, Neglect, and Exploitation of Older Persons: Strategies for Assessment and Intervention*, London: Jessica Kingsley Publishers.
Law Commission (1995) *Mental Incapacity*, Law Comm. No. 231, London: HMSO.
Lefcourt, H.M. (1976) *Locus of Control: Current Trends in Theory and Research*, Hillsdale, NJ: Lawrence Erlbaum.
Manthorpe, J. (1993) 'Elder abuse and key areas in social work' in P. Decalmer and F. Glendenning (eds) *The Mistreatment of Elderly People*, London: Sage.
McCreadie, C. (1991) *Elder Abuse: An Exploratory Study*, London: Age Concern Institute of Gerontology.
McCreadie, C. (1996) *Elder Abuse: Update on Research*, London: Age Concern Institute of Gerontology.
Nye, F.I. (ed.) (1982) *Family Relationships: Rewards and Costs*, Beverley Hills, CA: Sage.
Parker, J. and Randall, P. (1997) *Using Behavioural Theories*, London: Open Learning Foundation.
Penhale, B. (1992) 'Elder abuse: An overview', *Elders*, 1, pp.36–48.
Penhale, B. (1993) 'The abuse of elderly people: Considerations for practice', *British Journal of Social Work*, 23, pp.95–112.
Penhale, B. and Kingston, P. (1995) 'Social perspectives on elder abuse' in P. Kingston and B. Penhale (eds) *Family Violence and the Caring Professions*, Basingstoke: Macmillan.
Phillips, L.R. (1986) 'Theoretical explanations of elder abuse: Competing hypotheses and unresolved issues' in K.A. Pillemer and R.S. Wolf (eds) *Elder Abuse: Conflict in the Family*, Dover, MA: Auburn House.
Phillipson, C. (1994) 'Elder abuse and neglect: Social and policy issues' in Action on Elder Abuse Working Paper No. 1, *A Report on the Proceedings of the 1st International Symposium on Elder Abuse*, London: Action on Elder Abuse.
Phillipson, C. and Biggs, S. (1995) 'Elder abuse: A critical overview' in P. Kingston and B. Penhale (eds) *Family Violence and the Caring Professions*, Basingstoke: Macmillan.
Pillemer, K.A. and Finkelhor, D. (1988) 'The prevalence of elder abuse: A random sample survey', *The Gerontologist*, 28, pp.51–7.

Podnieks, E. (1990) *National Survey on Abuse of the Elderly in Canada*, (The Ryerson Study), Toronto: Ryerson Polytechnical Institute.

Podnieks, E. (1992) 'National survey on abuse of the elderly in Canada', *Journal of Elder Abuse and Neglect*, 4, pp.5–58.

Pollack, D. (1995) 'Elder abuse and neglect cases reviewed by the appellate courts', *Journal of Family Violence*, 10, pp.413–24.

Pritchard, J. (1992) *The Abuse of Elderly People: A Handbook for Professionals*, London: Jessica Kingsley Publishers.

Reay, A. (1994) 'Research update', *Action on Elder Abuse Bulletin*, 5, p.1.

Sadler, P. (1994) 'What helps? Elder abuse interventions and research', *Australian Social Work*, 47, pp.27–36.

Sheldon, B. (1995) *Cognitive-Behavioural Therapy: Research, Practice and Philosophy*, London: Routledge.

Sijuwade, P.O. (1995) 'Cross-cultural perspectives on elder abuse as a family dilemma', *Social Behaviour and Personality*, 23, pp.246–52.

Skolnick, A. and Skolnick, J.H. (eds) (1977) *The Family in Transition* (2nd edn), Boston: Little, Brown.

Slater, P. (1993) 'Elder abuse and legal reform', *Elders*, 2, pp.23–8.

Social Services Inspectorate (1992) *Confronting Elder Abuse*, London: HMSO.

Social Services Inspectorate (1993) *No Longer Afraid: The Safeguard of Older People in Domestic Settings*, London: HMSO.

Steinmetz, S.K. (1988) *Duty Bound: Elder Abuse and Family Care*, London: Sage.

Thibault, J.W. and Kelley, H.H. (1959) *The Social Psychology of Groups*, New York: John Wiley.

Tomita, S. (1982) 'Detection and treatment of elderly abuse and neglect: A protocol for health professionals', *Physical and Occupational Therapy in Geriatrics* 2, pp.37–51.

Tomlin, S. (1989) *Abuse of Elderly People: An Unnecessary and Preventable Problem*, London: British Geriatric Society.

Trower, P., Casey, A. and Dryden, W. (1988) *Cognitive-behavioural Counselling in Action*, London: Sage.

Vernon, M. and Bennett, G. (1995) 'Elder abuse: The case for greater involvement of geriatricians', *Age and Ageing*, 24, pp.177–9.

Wistedt, B. and Freeman, A. (1994) 'Aggressive patients' in F.M. Dattilio and A. Freeman (eds) *Cognitive-behavioral Strategies in Crisis Intervention*, New York and London: Guilford Press.

Wolf, R.S. and Pillemer, K.A. (1989) *Helping Elderly Victims: The Reality of Elder Abuse*, New York: Columbia University Press.

14 Epilogue: Education for effective practice

Katy Cigno

Theory and research

Every chapter written in this book is based on research, which was nicely described in the Seebohm Report of 1968 as 'an important insurance against complacency and stagnation' p.142, para. 458). Ironically, the Report heralded a large-scale social welfare experiment – the creation of social services departments from welfare agencies, defined by category – which was never systematically evaluated, so a golden opportunity was missed.

Yet, by contrast, social work students – and therefore, by implication, qualified practitioners – are required to relate theory to practice and evaluate their work. In addition, they must now also be able to assess the 'strengths, limitations and applications of methods of evaluation and research, including criteria for evaluating the effectiveness of social work intervention' (Central Council for Education and Training in Social Work 1995, p.23).

Theory matters – the pages here are a testimony to this – but not *all* theories matter, or should. A better way of proceeding, which has only recently come into favour and been included in CCETSW's guidelines for the assessment of student practice (see the quotation above), is for social workers, including practice teachers and other helping professionals, to think in terms of research for practice, the importance of which is clearly stated in the first chapter of this book. Basing practice on research evidence of what works for whom (the title, incidentally, of a recent, useful book by Roth et al. 1997) is a much sounder way forward.

Currently, practitioners as well as those yet to be qualified struggle with what is a theory, an approach or a model, and frequently use these terms interchangeably. In the findings of their research on the readiness of social workers and probation officers for practice, Marsh and Triseliotis (1996) disconcertingly report that the newly qualified staff and supervisors interviewed described over eighty theories for practice, although many said that theory and research were badly taught on their courses (probation officers fared slightly better), tutors were alleged to be out of touch with practice, and practice teachers out of touch with theory. Considering this state of confusion, should we be glad that, of these eighty 'practice theories', 'behavioural work' was only one of three cited regularly, the others being 'counselling' and 'task-centred', even though by only 1 in 10 students?

It is unclear what the respondents understand by these 'theories', and how they use them in their work. Task-centred social work, we know, is a favourite, tried-and-tested 'golden oldie', whereas unspecific 'counselling' as a method (surely not theory?) is the popular newcomer. With regard to counselling in particular, it is of concern that many social work and other students, as well as qualified practitioners, apparently do not read the research literature on effectiveness and client opinion, and are therefore ill-equipped to make decisions about useful theories for practice. Further, research by the National Health Service Centre for Reviews and Dissemination at the University of York into various aspects of mental health promotion found that the evidence so far is that generic counselling is not effective, but that specific sorts of counselling, in particular cognitive-behavioural therapy, can have good results in this and other areas (NHS Centre for Reviews and Dissemination 1997; see also Chapter 10). Substitute 'social work intervention' for 'counselling', and these results are very similar to those found by Reid and Hanrahan (1981) in their earlier effectiveness review.

Yet instead of saving money by avoiding unproven counselling courses, the number of counsellors continues to increase because, it seems, people like doing it, and may go on to make money out of it; it is the therapeutic earner of the 1990s (Cigno 1997). The British Association for Counselling now has over 15,000 members, while 'many counsellors have set themselves up with little or no qualifications and competence varies widely' (Hawkes 1997, p.7).

Effective and ethical practice

At the same time, over the years, research and assessment with a variety of client groups with diverse conditions and problems, as the preceding chapters demonstrate, indicate what we have known for a long time (see, for example, Sutton 1979): that those with whom we intervene (often they have little choice) value warmth, honesty and reliability in the practitioner, and find that help with behaviour problems, especially what is now usually called 'challenging behaviour', is hard to get (see Malek 1993; Grimshaw with Berridge 1994; Webster-Stratton and Herbert 1994; Department of Health 1995 and Sinclair et al. 1995 for discussion of these issues).

Infuriatingly, then, alongside careful studies which should increasingly make it difficult to do our own thing or follow fashion rather than heed research findings (if we take the latter course, we can always revise our practice in the light of new evidence), a certain amount of nonsense is being taught and practised (see Cigno 1998). Consider this example: a member of a team running a highly respected mental health centre recounted how one day he had to put out a chip pan fire, and discovered that some of the fire-fighting equipment was missing. On another occasion, when a client collapsed from an epileptic fit, no one knew how to help him. The writer goes on to say:

> Raising the issue of health and safety at a staff meeting some time later, I met with an unexpected response ... it was suggested that my concern for the physical well-being of whoever used the place was a disguise for my worries over funding. Unwilling to face up to cuts and closures, I was informed, I had unconsciously transferred my anxieties on to easily resolved problems surrounding physical safety (Javanaud 1994, p.11).

There is more:

> People would often arrive at the centre to ask for help with practical problems, only to be met with offers of help they had not requested like counselling (Javanaud 1994, p.11).

Disregard for safe and effective practice, together with a cavalier attitude towards clients' definitions of their problems, should be regarded as unethical. Equal access to ineffective services is a rather dubious ground for a profession. Among the thousands, probably millions, of words written about anti-oppressive practice and anti-discriminatory issues, few address the specific ethical question of the practitioners' duty to have regard to the effectiveness of their approach with clients. Those with a background in evidence-based practice, and consequently in cognitive-behavioural intervention, do so; it is built into its basic philosophy, as we have said in the Introduction. This principle has been reiterated by Macdonald and Macdonald (1995) in a piece on ethical issues in social work research.

Securing the future of social work

In a trenchant review of a book on the theme of the relevance of social work to social policy developments in recent times (Jackson and Preston-Shoot 1996), Pinker notes that 'nothing will change for the better until social workers stop talking to each other about their distinctive and superior values and start trying to find some common normative ground with ordinary citizens' (Pinker 1997, p.30). Such a weighty view detracts attention from what social workers *do* do well, but it is one which we ignore at our peril in the context of the future of social work. Values have to be grounded in competent practice.

A survey carried out in Spring 1997 of 265 social service staff in the public, voluntary and private sectors found that 92 per cent of respondents felt that forms of client contact would change over the next five years, while 86 per cent believed that employment structures would change, particularly in the growing area of temporary and contract work; 67 per cent thought that traditional social work roles would change a great deal. Many felt that social work would not exist in fifty years' time (Reed Social Care Personnel 1997). While it is true that we do not have as much control over our destiny as we would like, disagreements over social work's research base do not help its cause. As Philpott (1997) writes: 'despite the positive advances made in the research field, it still cannot be said that social work has established a tradition of research or that its culture has become research-based' (p.24). He links this with the crisis over social work's future.

Yet social workers still take sides over using the evidence of applied research to guide practice, as the debate over Neate's (1997) article in *Community Care* about evidence-based social work and the need for the dissemination of research findings showed. (It also showed that social workers do at least read *Community Care*!) The letters following her piece would appear to indicate that practitioners and managers are either strongly for or against systematic applied research. I can recall few articles which have aroused such fury on the one hand (for example, 'Social work and science don't mix', (Letters page, *Community Care,* 22–27 August 1997, p.10) and such patient reasoning on the other (for example, 'Research skills are key to practice' (letters page, *Community Care,* 4–10 September 1997, p.14).

And finally:

> If our basic training curricula do not reflect, or better still, actively model, rigorous attitudes to questions of evidence, then it is unreasonable to expect students to discover and apply these for themselves later on in the embattled conditions of field social work (Sheldon 1987, p.575).

The good news is that many students, practitioners and managers *are* interested in how theory and research relate to practice, as many of us know through the requests we receive from social work courses and professional groups in social services departments to talk about research into practice. The problem is that they are not always helped to do this routinely in the lecture hall or in the field (I include residential and day care settings in this context) as the Marsh and Triseliotis (1996) research revealed. More than teaching about pieces of research, it is crucial to get across critical ways of thinking, so that should the evidence about the usefulness of any particular approach change, then we are prepared to revise our practice.

Berger (1966) once wrote that the sociologist's role in society was to stand back, pause and ask, 'Says who?' Such an approach would not come amiss in social work, if we are determined to offer the best possible services to those who need them. Otherwise we may well comment, along with Horace: 'kings are mad and the people are punished for it.'

References

Berger, P.L. (1966) *Invitation to Sociology: A Humanistic Perspective*, Harmondsworth: Penguin.

Central Council for Education and Training in Social Work (1995) *Assuring Quality in the Diploma in Social Work-1: Rules and Requirements for the DipSW* (rev. edn), London: CCETSW.

Cigno, K. (1997) 'Downsizing, restructuring, purchasing and providing: Social work and social services in a value-for-money climate', *International Journal of Sociology and Social Policy*, 17, pp.87–96.

Cigno, K. (1998) 'Cognitive-behavioural practice' in R. Adams, L. Dominelli and M. Payne (eds) *Social Work: Themes, Issues and Critical Debates*, London: Macmillan.

Department of Health (1995) *Child Protection: Messages from Research* (prepared by Dartington Social Research Unit), London: HMSO.

Grimshaw, R. with Berridge, D. (1994) *Educating Disruptive Children: Placement and Progress in Residential Special Schools for Pupils with Emotional and Behavioural Difficulties*, London: National Children's Bureau.

Hawkes, N. (1997) 'Study counsels caution on a cure-all for life's ills', *The Times*, 19 August, p.7.

Jackson, S. and Preston-Shoot, M. (eds) (1996) *Educating Social Workers in a Changing Policy Context*, London: Whiting and Birch.

Javanaud, R. (1994) 'Shrinking credibility', *Care Weekly*, 3 February,

Macdonald, G. and Macdonald, K. (1997) 'Ethical issues in social work research' in R. Hugman and D. Smith (eds) *Ethical Issues in Social Work*, London: Routledge.

Malek, M. (1993) *Passing the Buck: Institutional Responses to Controlling Children with Difficult Behaviour*, London: The Children's Society.

Marsh, P. and Triseliotis, J. (1996) *Ready to Practise? Social Workers and Probation Officers: Their Training and First Year in Work*, Aldershot: Avebury.

NHS Centre for Reviews and Dissemination (1997) *Effective Health Care: Mental Health Promotion in High Risk Groups*, University of York.

Neate, P. (1997) 'Face facts', *Community Care*, 17 July, pp.18–19.

Philpott, T. (1997) 'Dedicated followers of fashion', *Community Care*, 31 July, pp.24–5.

Pinker, R. (1997) 'A matter of policy', *Community Care*, 20 March, p.30.

Reed Social Care Personnel (1997) *The Millenium Report: Predicting Changes in Social Work*, London: RSCP.

Reid, W.J. and Hanrahan, P. (1981) 'The effectiveness of social work: Recent evidence' in E.M. Goldberg and N. Connelly (eds) *Evaluative Research in Social Care*, London: Policy Studies Institute/Heinemann Educational Books.

Report of the Committee on Local Authority and Allied Personal Social Services (1968) (The Seebohm Report), Cm 3703, London: HMSO.

Roth, A. and Fonagy, P., Parry, G., Target, M. and Woods, R. (1996) *What Works for Whom? A Critical Review of Psychotherapy Research*, New York and London: Guilford Press.

Sheldon, B. (1987) 'Implementing findings from social work effectiveness research', *British Journal of Social Work*, 17, pp.573–86.

Sinclair, R., Garnett, L. and Berridge, D. (1995) *Social Work and Assessment with Adolescents*, London: National Children's Bureau.

Sutton, C. (1979) 'Research in psychology: Applications to social casework', *Social Work Today*, 10, pp.17–19.

Webster-Stratton, C. and Herbert, M. (1994) *Troubled Families – Problem Children*, Chichester: John Wiley.

Index